Primary Mathematics for Trainee Teachers

Primary Mathematics for Trainee Teachers

Edited by Marcus Witt

Series editor Alice Hansen

Los Angeles | London | New Delhi
Singapore | Washington DC

Learning Matters
An imprint of SAGE Publications Ltd
1 Oliver's Yard
55 City Road
London EC1Y 1SP

SAGE Publications Inc.
2455 Teller Road
Thousand Oaks, California 91320

SAGE Publications India Pvt Ltd
B 1/I 1 Mohan Cooperative Industrial Area
Mathura Road
New Delhi 110 044

SAGE Publications Asia-Pacific Pte Ltd
3 Church Street
#10-04 Samsung Hub
Singapore 049483

Editor: Amy Thornton
Development Editor: Jennifer Clark
Production Controller: Chris Marke
Project Management: Deer Park Productions, Tavistock
Marketing Manager: Catherine Slinn
Cover design: Wendy Scott
Typeset by: C&M Digitals (P) Ltd, Chennai, India
Printed by: Henry Ling Limited at The Dorset Press, Dorchester DT1 1HD

Library of Congress Control Number: 2014947111

British Library Cataloguing in Publication data

A catalogue record for this book is available from the British Library.

MIX
Paper from responsible sources
FSC
www.fsc.org   FSC™ C013985

ISBN 978 1 4739 0588 7 (pbk)
ISBN 978 1 4739 0587 0

At SAGE we take sustainability seriously. Most of our products are printed in the UK using FSC papers and boards. When we print overseas we ensure sustainable papers are used as measured by the Egmont grading system. We undertake an annual audit to monitor our sustainability.

Contents

Acknowledgements

The work for Chapter 6 has been partially possible thanks to the iTalk2Learn project that is co-funded by the European Union (EU) under the Information and Communication Technologies (ICT) theme of the 7th Framework Programme for Research and Development (RandD) (FP7) GA No 610467. The contents of the chapter do not represent the opinion of the EU, which is not responsible for any use that might be made of them.

Table 4.1 in Chapter 4 reproduced by kind permission of the authors, Alison Borthwick and Micky Harcourt-Heath, and the British Society for Research into Learning Mathematics.

Gapminder graph of income vs life expectancy in Chapter 12 – free material from www.gapminder.org included by kind permission of the authors.

About the editor, authors and series editor

Marcus Witt

Marcus began his teaching career in the hills of South India teaching foreign languages in an international school before teaching 'elementary' school children in rural Kentucky and then completing his PGCE. Since then he has spent many years teaching in primary schools in the UK. During that time he has been mathematics co-ordinator and was a local authority 'leading maths teacher' giving demonstration lessons in support of the implementation of the National Numeracy Strategy. He completed his PhD looking at the role of working memory in children's mathematical learning and has spent the past six years as senior lecturer in primary mathematics education, first at Bath Spa University and now at the University of the West of England, teaching mathematics to postgraduate and undergraduate trainee teachers.

Balbir Ahir

Balbir is a Senior Lecturer in Primary Mathematics at the Institution for Education, University of Wolverhampton. She joined Wolverhampton after being a primary school teacher and a leading mathematics teacher for a number of years and has supported Continued Professional Development (CPD) in mathematics of teachers in local authorities. She has been involved in a number of Primary National Strategy projects and initiatives and has research interests in supporting learners who have difficulty with learning mathematics, learners with English as an additional language (EAL) needs in mathematics as well as 'fit for purpose pedagogy'.

Ronit Bird

Ronit is a specialist teacher who has written several books of practical ideas for teaching numeracy to children who struggle with mathematics. With a background of teaching learners with specific learning difficulties (SpLD) in both primary and secondary schools, Ronit spent a number of years as a Special Educational Needs Co-ordinator (SENCO) before beginning to develop and deliver dyscalculia training for teachers. Alongside her continuing work as a teacher and a trainer, Ronit enjoys making short videos to demonstrate her teaching methods and numeracy games. Many of the videos are embedded in a new series of ebooks created for parents whose children need to develop a stronger feel for numbers.

Catherine Foley

Catherine was a primary school teacher in West Berkshire and Oxfordshire and subsequently became a leading mathematics teacher and local authority consultant.

After several years working for the Primary National Strategy as a senior adviser in the mathematics team she moved to her current role as mathematics tutor in initial teacher training at the University of Reading, working across a range of undergraduate and postgraduate programmes. Her research interests include the ethnographic study of children's perceptions of mathematics, and she continues to work closely with schools providing CPD for teachers and support for parents.

Alice Hansen

Alice is the Director of Children Count Ltd, an education consultancy company that provides CPD for teachers in primary mathematics education and primary schools in curriculum development in England and abroad. Prior to her current role she was a primary school teacher and senior lecturer in primary education before becoming a programme leader of a teacher training programme. Alice is an active researcher and her research interests include technology-enhanced learning. Her current research focuses on developing effective tasks for children to further their conceptual understanding of fractions.

Jonathan Leeming

Jonathan currently works as a senior leader and class teacher at Moorside Primary School in Lancaster where he leads mathematics. He is a Mathematics Specialist Teacher having completed the Mathematics Specialist Teacher course and is now working on the final part of his MA in primary mathematics pedagogy. Jonathan has more than fifteen years of classroom teaching experience, both in the UK and abroad, and is a National Centre for Excellence in the Teaching of Mathematics Professional Development Accredited Lead.

Jane McNeill

After many years as a primary teacher, Jane has worked in primary mathematics education in a number of roles. She has worked extensively as a mathematics consultant for Oxfordshire Local Authority, the National Strategies and the National Centre for Excellence in the Teaching of Mathematics. She has contributed to many publications and guidance documents on primary mathematics. Jane is currently a Senior Lecturer in Primary Education at Oxford Brookes.

Caroline Rickard

Caroline is a primary mathematics lecturer teaching on both undergraduate and Postgraduate Certificate in Education (PGCE) courses at the University of Chichester. She very much enjoys sharing her passion for mathematics and has recently published *Essential Primary Mathematics*. Prior to her lecturing role, Caroline was a classroom teacher for 12 years in local first schools (Year R to Year 3); for over half that time she co-ordinated mathematics. She has a Master's in Mathematics Education having explored students' beliefs about how mathematics should be taught, and is particularly interested in the use of open-ended mathematics tasks, believing that all children can become mathematicians.

John Smith

John was Mathematics Co-ordinator and a Leading Teacher of Mathematics in a large, urban primary school for 11 years before joining the Faculty of Education at Manchester Metropolitan University (MMU), as a Senior Lecturer in Primary Education, in 2000. Since then, he has taught Mathematics and Thinking Skills on initial teacher training courses and courses of CPD and he has also been involved in a range of school and curriculum development projects. As this book goes to print, John is in the process of moving on from his post at MMU in order to undertake a range of new projects (details available at www.talkandreason.com).

Diane Vaukins

Diane is currently the Director of London Programmes and Partnerships at the London campus of the University of Cumbria. Before becoming a university lecturer Diane was a primary school deputy head teacher. Her main subject area is mathematics for which she has a passion and she has delivered many school-based sessions working alongside teachers and trainees.

Introduction

A comedian was having a terrible time with his act. His audiences were becoming hostile and the heckling was getting worse. He found himself not being invited back to the clubs where he performed. In desperation, he went to one of the comedy club owners to get some advice about how to improve his act.

'It's simple', said the club owner.

'Yes', replied the comedian eagerly.

'Just be funnier!'

It sometimes feels that advice about developing your pedagogical skills as a primary mathematics teacher is a little like a comedian being told to 'be funnier'. There is a huge amount of advice about what to do (get the children to investigate, encourage reasoning, allow the children to ask questions, etc.), but less about how to do it. In some respects the Primary National Curriculum document might be seen as the curricular equivalent of being told to 'be funnier'. As a teacher of primary mathematics, you are expected to 'deliver' demanding mathematical content to children, as well as meet some of the exacting demands set out at the beginning of the document: to develop children's mathematical fluency; to engage them in solving problems; and to encourage them to reason mathematically. However, the Primary National Curriculum leaves it largely up to teachers and schools to determine precisely how this will happen. This is both challenging and hugely exciting at the same time.

This book aims to do more than exhort you to 'be funnier'. Using the Primary National Curriculum document as a guide, we will look closely at some of the key ideas set out in the first two pages of the document and consider how mathematical reasoning and problem solving can be woven into your teaching without compromising your coverage of the curriculum content, and how children can become fluent with calculations without losing conceptual understanding.

Throughout the book there are case studies from classrooms to illustrate the ideas being offered. They are intended to give you a sense of what the ideas 'look like' in practical situations and to help you to translate some of the ideas to your own classrooms. There are a number of teaching ideas, but they are intended to be illustrative rather than serve as an exhaustive list. A short hunt online, or in any one of a number of books, will yield plenty of ideas for teaching. This book aims to explain some of the underlying mathematical ideas and pedagogical principles, which will allow you to make a discerning choice about which teaching activities to use and how to adapt them to suit your learners. The book will also help you to adapt and modify teaching ideas so that they give your children opportunities to think and reason mathematically.

The chapters also contain a number of activities for you to engage in. We recommend that you take a few minutes as you read each chapter to complete these. Considering your own personal response to some of the ideas offered is the most powerful way to develop your own teaching practice.

We all have theories about mathematical learning. You have them too. You may not always be aware of them, but they are there and they have an impact on the kind of primary mathematics teacher you are. Each chapter contains a research focus, where we underpin classroom-based practice with theoretical understanding. The best primary mathematics teachers act in ways that are thoroughly underpinned by an understanding of theory.

Chapter 1 looks at mathematical reasoning and mathematical curiosity. Reasoning mathematically is one of the key priorities in the National Curriculum for mathematics. The chapter explores what is meant by mathematical reasoning and aims to offer some concrete suggestions about how you can encourage the children in your mathematics lessons to engage in reasoning. The chapter suggests that mathematical curiosity and reasoning work together; that curious children engage in reasoning and that the act of engaging in reasoning fosters curiosity.

In Chapter 2, Catherine Foley takes a detailed look at the Primary National Curriculum for mathematics. She explores particular curriculum content providing examples of problem-solving questions. She encourages you to read between the lines of the new curriculum and to consider some of the aspects of successful maths teaching that are implied rather than stated in the curriculum.

In Chapter 3, we turn our attention specifically to some of the content of the curriculum. John Smith explores early number, counting and place value. Specifically he offers practical suggestions about how to help children acquire these fundamental skills and conceptual understanding which will provide a firm foundation to enable fluency in calculation and sound mathematical reasoning later in the curriculum.

In Chapter 4, Jane McNeill takes a detailed look at addition and subtraction. She explores some fundamental ideas of what addition and subtraction involve mathematically and uses case studies to consider how you might encourage children to deepen their understanding of these operations. She outlines strategies to help children become fluent calculators, while preserving their understanding of the calculations they are performing.

In Chapter 5, Balbir Ahir looks closely at multiplication and division and particularly at the development of children's written calculations. She uses the examples from Appendix 1 of the National Curriculum for mathematics as a basis for exploring the development of calculation and suggests ways of helping children to make the connection between experiences of multiplication and division and written calculations.

In Chapter 6, Alice Hansen and Jonathan Leeming explore fractions, decimals, percentages, ratio and proportion. They provide a robust definition for fractions as well as teaching ideas to enhance your pedagogical subject knowledge of this traditionally challenging area to teach.

In Chapter 7, Diane Vaukins looks at geometry and measurement and suggests that this is a particularly rich area of the curriculum for developing children's mathematical reasoning skills. She also considers some of the key skills children need to develop in order to measure and make practical suggestions about the teaching of time.

In Chapter 8, Caroline Rickard examines the skills that children need to make sense of data and explores the 'data handling cycle', giving several suggestions of things to consider as you plan sequences of lessons on data handling. She explores the possibilities that data have for encouraging reasoning and for connecting mathematics to the children's lived experience.

In Chapter 9, Marcus Witt looks at ways of planning with discernment. In 2014, finding an overwhelming number of ideas for teaching anything is only a mouse click away. He discusses how you might make sense of all these ideas and look at them discerningly, matching teaching activities carefully with your own class. He also looks at a way of preparing for teaching a sequence of maths lessons to ensure that you can identify and therefore respond to misconceptions, can choose examples that will help your children avoid misconceptions and deepen their conceptual understanding.

In Chapter 10, Balbir Ahir looks at communicating mathematically. She considers the importance of mathematical vocabulary and ways of helping the children in your class to learn the language of mathematics. The chapter offers practical suggestions to develop your questioning of the children so as to lead to greater communication of mathematical ideas between the children and between the children and you.

In Chapter 11, Ronit Bird considers some of the reasons why certain children find learning mathematics difficult. She looks at issues such as mathematics anxiety and dyscalculia and offers you many highly practical suggestions to enable all the children in your class to become numerate.

Finally, in Chapter 12 Marcus Witt explores why we spend so much time teaching children mathematics and how mathematics lessons can be a place where children do a lot more than simply learn mathematics; they can be places where children are prompted and challenged to think about the world they are growing up in. He suggests that mathematics can be a force for social change, highlighting injustice and inequality. The chapter also explores how our values about mathematics and about the world can be conveyed in our mathematics teaching.

While we have tried to make connections between the chapters, and the National Curriculum runs through the whole book, each chapter stands alone. Some chapters (3–8) are more content focused, while the others look at general mathematical issues that sit outside specific areas of the curriculum. Wherever you are in your personal journey towards becoming an outstanding teacher of primary mathematics, we hope that there will be something in these chapters that will challenge your thinking and will offer ideas that you can take and apply to your own practice immediately. Above all, we hope that we have gone beyond telling you to 'be funnier' and have offered some thoughts about how you might do it.

1 Mathematical curiosity and reasoning

Marcus Witt

Learning outcomes

In this chapter, we will aim:

- to explore what we mean by mathematical curiosity and reasoning;
- to consider the kinds of teacher behaviours that are likely to foster mathematical curiosity and reasoning in children;
- to identify factors that might limit or hinder the development of mathematical curiosity and reasoning in children and therefore to consider ways that these factors might be overcome;
- to locate these mathematical skills in the curriculum and wider context of research on children's mathematical learning.

TEACHERS' STANDARDS

1. **Set high expectations which inspire, motivate and challenge pupils**

   establish a safe and stimulating environment for pupils, rooted in mutual respect

2. **Promote good progress and outcomes by pupils**

   be aware of pupils' capabilities and their prior knowledge, and plan teaching to build on these

   demonstrate knowledge and understanding of how pupils learn and how this impacts on teaching

3. **Demonstrate good subject and curriculum knowledge**

   if teaching early mathematics, demonstrate a clear understanding of appropriate teaching strategies

4. **Plan and teach well-structured lessons**

   promote a love of learning and children's intellectual curiosity

5. **Adapt teaching to respond to the strengths and needs of all pupils**

   have a secure understanding of how a range of factors can inhibit pupils' ability to learn, and how best to overcome these

---

Introduction

There is a difference between doing mathematics and thinking mathematically. Many adults and children are able to 'do mathematics', to perform mathematical calculations and arrive at correct answers. Far fewer really understand and question what they are doing. This opening chapter explores two essential elements in mathematical thinking: being curious about mathematics and reasoning mathematically.

Reasoning

I will begin with a consideration of mathematical reasoning. Before continuing, it might be worth considering what mathematical reasoning is and what it might look like in the classroom.

Activity: What does mathematical reasoning 'look like'?

Spend a couple of minutes considering what you think of as mathematical reasoning. All-encompassing definitions are often difficult, so maybe you would like to consider what mathematical reasoning would 'look like' if your children were engaged in it.

The Advisory Committee on Mathematics Education (ACME) response to the draft National Curriculum called for a clear definition of mathematical reasoning and suggested the following:

Mathematical reasoning requires analysing information presented in different forms, recognising given information, identifying what additional information is needed and what forms of reasoning can provide it; identifying and conjecturing patterns, relationships, and generalisations; testing, inducing, deducing, and proving; and communicating ideas in mathematical language.

(ACME, 2012, p.5)

The New Jersey Mathematics Curriculum describes reasoning as follows:

Mathematical reasoning is the critical skill that enables a student to make use of all other mathematical skills. With the development of mathematical reasoning, students recognise that mathematics makes sense and can be understood. They learn how to evaluate situations, select problem-solving strategies, draw logical conclusions, develop and describe solutions, and recognise how those solutions can be applied.

(New Jersey Mathematics Coalition, 1996, p.45)

A strong sense in both of these definitions is that being able to reason mathematically involves children actively engaging in and making sense of mathematics rather than simply following an apparently arbitrary set of rules or procedures. Reasoning also indicates an ability to apply mathematics thoughtfully. Mathematical reasoning therefore prompts and invites children to understand the mathematics more deeply, to make mathematical connections and to draw mathematical inferences. Nunes and Bryant (1996) suggest that exploring logical relations is one of the prerequisites for children engaging in mathematics and mathematical thinking. Logic is not possible without reasoning, so reasoning sits at the very heart of *every* child's mathematical learning; it is not something only for the highest attaining children.

To understand mathematical reasoning more clearly, it may be useful to consider a classroom example. In this example, we will look at two teachers in action. As you read about their practice, consider the extent to which the children in the two classrooms are engaging in mathematical reasoning and how the teachers are seeking to draw out and develop their reasoning.

Case Study: Reasoning in action

Edward is a newly qualified teacher. Joyce is a more experienced teacher in a parallel Year 3 class. They are working to develop their children's mental addition and subtraction skills. In Edward's lesson the children have been shown two different strategies for mental addition and two for subtraction. The children are then asked to complete a list of specific calculations, which are presented horizontally. At the end of the lesson, the children are going through their answers and making a note of how many they got right.

Edward: What did you get for the first question, 8 add 9? Joe?

Joe: 17.

Edward: Really good Joe. Well done. If you got 17 for that one, you can give yourself a tick.

Joe: It's a near double.

Edward: You're right. 8 and 8 is 16, so this needs to be 17. What about this next one, 34 take away 9? Clare, what do you think?

Clare: 23.

Edward: Really? How did you get 23?

Clare: Is that wrong?

⟶

Edward: Let's have a look at what you did.

Clare: Well, let's see. 34 take away 10 would be 24, but it's not 10, it's 9, so one more away makes 23. Is that wrong?

Edward: Do you remember what we said about these ones? If we take away, we have to give it back ... Can someone help her out?

Zoë: It's 25.

Edward: Fantastic Zoë, well done. Clare, can you see now that it's 25?

Clare: Nods slowly, but with brow still furrowed.

Zoë: If you take off 10, you've taken off too many, so you have to give one back. It's like money, if you have to give me 9p, but you give me 10p, I have to give one back to you.

The lesson moves on in this way, with some, often unsolicited, input from the children, and a lot of congratulations for questions that are 'right'. Now return to the initial question and consider what reasoning is going on and whether Edward is helping it to happen.

In Joyce's room, the children are solving a puzzle, which looks like the one below.

★	★	★	★	8
£	$	&	♣	17
★	♠	★	♠	16
$	★	€	♣	11
9	11	14	18	

Figure 1.1   Reasoning and problem solving (used with kind permission of Anitra Vickery)

The discussion centred on the ways in which the children had solved the puzzle:

Joyce: How did you start the puzzle?

Anish: I saw that the top row was all stars. There are four stars and together they come to 8, so I knew that the star must be worth 2.

Joyce: (Feigning not to understand fully) So, explain to me exactly how you knew each one was worth 2.

Anish: Well, there are four stars. The whole row comes to 8, so I knew that four stars equals 8, so each star must be worth 2. See 2 and 2 more is 4 and 2 more is 6 and 2 more makes 8.

Joyce: Fantastic, good strategy. Thank you for explaining that to me so clearly. Can someone else explain how they went on from there?

Sam: Once you know what the star is worth, you can find out the other symbols.

⟶

Joyce: Good thought. Can you give us an example of how you worked out one of the other symbols?

Sam: Well, it's hard to explain. In the bit where you have two stars and two spades, you can add the two stars together to get 4. As they all come to 16, you know that the spade must be worth 6.

Joyce: I'm not sure I followed what you said at the end. How did you know that the spade must be worth 6?

Sam: It's easy, miss. The two spades must be worth 12 altogether, because the two stars are worth 4 and the total is 16. If the two spades are worth 12, then each one must be worth 6.

Joyce: Fantastic, now I've got it. Does anybody want to ask Sam about how he got 6?

Kim: Now it's easy. Once you know a couple of the symbols, you can find out the others.

Joyce: Can you give us an example of another symbol that you found out?

Kim: Easy. In the column with two stars, a spade and a dollar, you only have to find out the dollar thing. You know all the others.

This discussion is less about the different calculation strategies and more about the problem-solving strategies that the children are using. However, the children are still using and applying a number of different mental mathematics strategies.

Curriculum Link

In the National Numeracy Strategy (DfE, 1999), mental mathematics was given a high profile, but problem solving and reasoning were not strongly represented. The Primary National Curriculum makes explicit mention of mental calculations, although specific strategies are not stipulated. Reasoning is expected and is highlighted explicitly on the first page of the new document. However, although there is a clear expectation that teachers will develop their children's reasoning, there is no further guidance about how to do this. It will be up to teachers to see and exploit opportunities for reasoning rather than expect direct curriculum guidance.

Research Focus: How important is mathematical reasoning?

The National Curriculum contains this strong injunction to engage children in mathematical reasoning and there is an assumption that reasoning is somehow 'important' in mathematics. However, there is a growing collection of research evidence to show

→

that children's mathematical reasoning is not only important, but is *the* key predictor of their future progress in mathematics. Nunes et al. (2009) measured the mathematical attainment of a very large group of children by looking at their mathematics scores when they were in Year 4. They also measured a number of other cognitive skills, including their working memory (their ability to hold information while they were carrying out other cognitive tasks) and their mathematical reasoning along with social and emotional measures. They then measured the children's mathematical attainment at age 11 and again at age 14. Using statistical techniques (structural equation modelling) they were able to identify the key predictors of future mathematical attainment.

The findings from the study were clear:

> *Children's ability to reason about mathematical relations was easily the most powerful predictor of children's mathematical achievement, out of all the relevant cognitive measures. It strongly predicted their mathematics achievement in Key Stage 2 and 3 even after controls for the effects of differences in intelligence and calculation ability.*

> (Nunes et al., 2009, p.3)

The children's initial level of arithmetic understanding made a clear and distinctive contribution to their future mathematical attainment, but this was less important than, and separate from, their ability to reason mathematically. The authors conclude that developing the ability to reason with numbers and about mathematical relations is the key component of a child's mathematical education at primary school.

This conclusion might come as a surprise if your own mathematical education consisted of repeated calculation practice in order to become proficient in arithmetic. While an understanding of and facility with calculation is certainly important (and will be addressed later in the book), solving mathematical problems requires more than arithmetic skill. Arithmetic competence is of little use if not accompanied by an insight into which calculation to perform, or how to check and make sense of the result. Understanding what to do with the numbers in the problem, how best to manipulate them and how to interpret the answer require children to engage in mathematical reasoning.

Haylock (2010) has written in some detail about the different key processes in mathematical reasoning, such as generalising, hypothesising and conjecturing. I do not intend to repeat that discussion here. Rather, I will focus on ways that you might develop this kind of thinking in your children.

Developing reasoning skills in children

In Edward's classroom, there was little encouragement towards mathematical reasoning. His lesson involved modelling calculation strategies, giving the children a number of examples through which to practise their calculation skills and then an opportunity to check their answers. While this approach to calculation might yield a number of 'correct answers' (and therefore be seen as a 'successful' lesson, with children making progress), there may be little mathematical thinking beyond the application of a set of rules and procedures and arguably no reasoning. The experiences of some of the children, who were struggling with the strategies that required them to adjust their answers, suggested that, for some children at least, the application of procedures was not enough to secure understanding.

Activity: Ways of developing children's reasoning

Spend a few minutes considering what Edward might have done to develop the reasoning skills of his children. Were there opportunities for developing reasoning, which he could have taken?

The discussion in Edward's classroom suggested that the children were trying to make sense of the task they had been given and were therefore engaging in mathematical reasoning without having been prompted. Zoë's explanation to Clare about making the correct adjustment in the subtraction strategy involved a substantial amount of reasoning. She tried to engage in reasoning in her attempt to help Clare understand the direction of the adjustment after having subtracted ten. Her appeal to and use of reasoning to aid Clare's understanding contrasts with the rote application of a process. Nunes et al.'s (2009) research suggests that teachers who can spot this kind of mathematical reasoning in their classrooms and encourage it will be preparing their children to make greater mathematical gains in the future.

There are several key words associated with mathematical reasoning, which might help teachers to identify it. Children's use of words such as 'because', 'so' or 'therefore' in their mathematical explanations are a clear indicator that they are engaging in reasoning. Questions, which naturally trigger the use of these words, are likely to lead to mathematical reasoning.

Activity: Questioning to lead to reasoning

What kinds of questions could you ask which naturally lead children to use words such as 'because', 'so' or 'therefore' in their answers?

Think back to a lesson you have taught recently, or forwards to one that you will teach shortly, and note opportunities to ask these kinds of questions as a prompt for the children to engage in more mathematical reasoning.

Composing these questions is not something that necessarily comes easily, particularly if you are at the beginning of your teaching career; we suggest that you plan some of these questions to give the children the chance to express their reasoning (see Chapter 9 for more detail on planning).

In Table 1.1 are some suggested key words or phrases that you might like to use in your teaching as a way of prompting the children to explain their reasoning. We have included some hypothetical answers to those questions, so that you can listen for words that might signal that a child is engaging in mathematical reasoning.

Table 1.1 Suggested key words and phrases to prompt children

Question (key words underlined)	Answer (reasoning words underlined)
How did you know that the answer was 45?	I knew *because* 20 and 20 is 40, *so* 20 and 25 must be 40 and 5 more.
Why do you think the answer will be an even number?	*I think* it will be even *because* an even number added to an even number *always* makes an even number.
What made you so sure that the shape couldn't be a square?	*If* the shape was a square, *then* it would have to have only right angles. As that corner isn't a right angle, the shape can't be a square.
Can you explain why you added one back?	*If* you are trying to take away 9, but you have actually taken away 10, *then* you've taken away too much, *so* you have to give one back.
Tell us how you knew it would be more than 10.	*Whenever* you add two numbers together, unless one's a minus number, they *will always* make a bigger number. *So* 10 and something *will always be* bigger than 10.
What do you think will happen when we add 10 to this number? *Why?*	*I think that* the digit in the middle column will go up by one, but the others won't change, *because* we are only adding a 10, *so* only the tens column will change.
Is it always true that adding 10 will only change the tens digit?	It's not always true, because sometimes, *if* the tens digit is already a 9, *then* the tens digit will go to zero and the hundreds digit will go up by one.
Is it possible for a fraction to have a bigger number on the top than the bottom? *How?*	*It is possible, because* sometimes a fraction is more than one, like 5 quarters, *so therefore* you would have to write the 5 first and then out of 4.
What makes you think these are a group?	All those are a group *because* they all end in a 5, or a 0. *But*, actually, those others could be a different group *because* they are all less than 12.

The language and vocabulary of reasoning is something that you could introduce to the children and you could draw their attention explicitly to its use. Along with technical mathematical vocabulary, it might be possible to have a display of words involved in reasoning in the classroom. This list of vocabulary could then act as a prompt for children as they try to explain their thinking. This could be as simple as a list of words, or some sentence prompts:

I think ... because ...

If ..., then ...

... will always happen because ...

... will never happen because ...

It can't be ... because ...

If ..., so ...

If ... and ... then ... because ...

Be mindful that the mere use of particular words does not cause mathematical reasoning to occur; rather giving children the language to express their mathematical reasoning encourages them to reason more and make their reasoning processes clearer to other children, which helps them develop their own reasoning skills. Vygotsky's (1978) work suggested that language is internalised and then becomes a psychological tool for thinking, i.e. developing children's reasoning vocabulary may do more than simply give them the tools to explain themselves more clearly. The increased use of this language will directly develop the children's reasoning skills.

Possible barriers to reasoning

Not allowing children the time to express their reasoning
If you know the answer, or the line of reasoning which the child has engaged in, there is a temptation to 'complete' the reasoning for the child, or 'join the dots' up without the process being clear to the other children in the class. If you do so, the interaction can become a dialogue between you and the child to the exclusion of the children in the class who have not yet fully understood the line of reasoning that led to an answer.

Underestimating a child's reasoning
You may unwittingly shut down a line of reasoning that the child has engaged in simply because it is not the same as your own. Askew (2012) cites an example of a child in a reception class who had sorted some objects (bears) in to two categories rather than just the one, which the teacher had envisaged. This led the teacher to assert that the child had sorted the bears incorrectly, whereas the child's reasoning had simply been more sophisticated than the teacher had imagined, or expected.

Learning objectives for reasoning

Along with your content-focused learning objective(s), consider having a learning objective that makes explicit to the children the fact that the lesson is also intended to develop their skills in mathematical reasoning. This not only draws the children's attention to reasoning, but helps to give reasoning a higher profile in your lessons and keeps you focused on it as you teach.

Here are some suggestions for learning objectives (written as 'I can' statements) that make reasoning explicit. You would, of course, develop your own to fit with the particular tasks and children you were teaching.

Key Stage 1:

- I can *tell* my teacher how I found my answer.

- I can *explain* my working out.

Key Stage 2:

- I can *explain* clearly how I arrived at an answer.

- I can *convince* one of my friends that my maths is correct.

- I can *question* someone else's mathematical answers.

- I can *justify* my mathematical strategy or approach to a problem.

- I can *communicate* my mathematical thinking to other people.

Being able to construct mathematical tasks that involve reasoning requires that you are able to engage in mathematical reasoning yourself. Part of your development as a teacher should therefore involve some consideration of your own reasoning skills and your ability to spot opportunities for mathematical reasoning. Having spent some time reading this chapter and thinking about reasoning, you might now wish to see how well you can identify opportunities for developing children's reasoning skills.

Modelling reasoning in explanations

There is more to mathematical reasoning than simply getting children to explain a line of thinking that has led them to an answer. If you can engage in reasoning during your explanations, children are able to make more sense of their mathematics. Exploring and explaining concepts and processes in a reasoned way does two things.

- It enables your children to make more sense of the mathematics. In Edward's classroom, a reasoned explanation of why the adjustment needed would be to add one back or to take one away might have prevented Clare from becoming confused.

- It models the process of mathematical reasoning to the children and enables them to see what mathematical reasoning involves and the kind of language associated with it (see above). They will then be more inclined to engage in it themselves.

The development of children's reasoning skills requires teachers to design mathematical tasks where the need for mathematical reasoning is inherent in the task. Although the new National Curriculum implies that this is what teachers will do, you may see teachers addressing the learning objectives without engaging the children in reasoning because it is not explicit. Children taught in a way that focuses on outcomes rather than reasoning processes are only being given a partial mathematics education and are much less likely to pursue mathematics in the future, are less likely to see mathematics as relevant to their lives and are less likely to have a positive relationship with the subject (Boaler, 2010). Having a learning objective about reasoning will prompt you to include tasks that involve reasoning, to model mathematical reasoning in your explanations and to identify reasoning when your children engage in it.

Activity: Seeing opportunities for reasoning

Take a particular area of maths that you have recently taught, heard about or are about to teach and spend a few minutes considering the possibilities that it offers for developing reasoning.

This is a skill that all teachers can develop. It comes partly from experience and will grow the more you do it. The important thing is to try to find opportunities to develop reasoning in all the mathematical activities that your children engage in. To prompt you to do this, you might like to add a section to your maths planning proforma where you note opportunities for reasoning and specific questions to prompt it.

Some strategies for developing reasoning

1. Try to integrate it into all/most mathematical tasks; practise seeing opportunities for reasoning in all mathematical activity.

2. Have a 'reasoning' learning objective, which is communicated to the children.

3. Model mathematical reasoning yourself and draw the children's attention to it as you are doing so.

4. Be on the lookout for mathematical reasoning in your classroom and draw the children's attention to it when it happens.

5. Praise the children who engage in reasoning and be clear about why you are being so effusive.

6. Display a list of 'reasoning vocabulary' in the classroom to support the children who are struggling to explain and communicate their reasoning.

Teachers' reasoning

The discussion in the chapter so far has focused on the role of reasoning in children's understanding of mathematical ideas. We now move the focus of the discussion to the development of your own mathematical reasoning and how this might have an impact on the quality of your teaching.

Deborah Ball and her colleagues at the University of Michigan (Hill and Ball, 2009) have spent many years unpicking precisely what it is that mathematics teachers do and the kinds of knowledge that they need in order to be able to do it well. The knowledge needed to be a good primary mathematics teacher clearly extends well beyond that needed simply to 'do' the mathematics and come up with the right answer.

> *We realised that the capacity to see the content from another's perspective and to understand what another person is doing entails mathematical reasoning and skill that are not needed for research mathematics or for bench science.*

(p.69)

According to Ball and her colleagues, a key skill for you is to be able to see the mathematical world from the perspective of the learner. Developing children's mathematical understanding involves beginning from and building on individual children's current level of understanding. It also involves understanding why children have particular misconceptions and why they see the mathematical world in the way they do. Being able to make sense of children's answers and possible misconceptions is a starting point for helping. Ball and her colleagues suggest that this involves a particular kind of mathematical reasoning and give a good example to illustrate this.

Activity: Understanding children's mathematical responses

You are working with some children who are ten years old. The children in your class are multiplying decimals; the question under consideration is 0.3 x 0.2. A child comes up with 0.6 as an answer. What would you do to help this child?

To what extent does your own ability to reason mathematically affect the response to this situation?

Suppose that a child is multiplying 0.3 x 0.2 and gives the answer 0.6. This is an intuitively correct answer for a child who is confident that 3 x 2 comes to 6. It is also larger than either 0.2 or 0.3 and the child's prior experience with multiplication may have reinforced the idea that the result of a multiplication calculation is always greater than any of the numbers being multiplied. For you, simply knowing that the answer is

0.06 does not really help to develop the child's understanding further, or to get to the root of the misconception.

Providing a reasoned explanation as to why the answer is 0.06 is not straight-forward and involves considerable reasoning powers *from you, the teacher*, more sophisticated than those required simply to give the right answer. Your response to this misconception might be to offer a range of further examples to enable learners to explore their understanding of the mathematics. Being able to reason (and possibly being able to reason 'on-the-spot', in the classroom) will determine the quality and sophistication of such examples. Not all examples are equally effective at enabling learners to uncover misconceptions, or see flaws in their reasoning.

Consider the examples 0.3×0.4; 0.5×0.6; 0.1×0.5 and 0.2×0.4.

When multiplying 0.3×0.4, the learner with the misconception described above may give the correct answer of 0.12. This question would not reveal the child's misconception and would reinforce it, as the misconception has given the 'correct' answer. The following question (0.5×0.6) is potentially more instructive as the child is likely to give the answer 0.30. Your ability to see this answer and pursue the child's thinking a little further is dependent on your ability to reason. The final two examples are more instructive as they would both yield incorrect answers when calculated by a learner with the misconception. However, the first of these might be a much better choice in trying to help a child to understand the nature of the misconception. Multiplying 0.1 by 0.5, the child is likely to give the answer 0.5, which might, particularly with some prompting from you, give the child cause to reconsider.

Being able to provide useful prompts and explanations in this situation would require you to understand the mathematics from the child's point of view. Reasoning may help you to identify a misconception. Asking the child to reason and explain an answer might uncover a misconception that is not immediately obvious from what a child has written (the example of 0.3×0.4). Being able to provide the child with further questions, which illuminate the misconception (0.1×0.5), again requires you to reason why the child is giving a particular answer. In our example, the child may be uncomfortable with answering 0.5 to the question 0.1×0.5, but may be under the (common) misapprehension that multiplication cannot make an answer smaller than the numbers being multiplied.

Along with this ability to see the mathematics from a learner's point of view, Ball and her colleagues suggest various other key skills needed by primary mathematics teachers. Being able to conduct mathematical discussions with learners, which are effective in both drawing out understanding and building on it, is a key skill. It is difficult to see how this can be done without recourse to mathematical reasoning, to make sense of the learners' contributions and therefore to be able to build on them. A further skill, which clearly demands mathematical reasoning on the part of the teacher, is being able to give clear mathematical explanations.

Research Focus: Mathematical explanations

Charalambous et al. (2011) have written extensively about the development of teachers' mathematical explanations during the period of their teacher training. They followed a small group of pre-service teachers through their training, monitored the development of their mathematical explanations and explored the reasons for this development. The pre-service teachers' explanations at the beginning of their course were limited and tended to focus on how to carry out mathematical procedures, often reflecting the ways that they were taught themselves.

The teachers in the study progressed at very different rates in terms of their ability to give mathematical explanations. Those teachers who made the greatest gains in the quality of their explanations were those who, among other things, were able to develop their own ability to reason mathematically and to reconsider and refine their own ideas about what it means to reason mathematically. They said that being able to explain their ideas and thinking in a logical way was essential to improving their mathematical explanations.

It is important for teachers at all stages in their career, but especially for pre-service teachers, to consider their own mathematical reasoning. Detailed consideration of your own reasoning will help you to construct logical explanations of mathematical ideas and processes, to provide children with appropriate examples, and will enable you to consider how to respond to children's errors and misconceptions. These skills are discussed in greater detail in Chapter 9 on planning.

Curiosity

Children's curiosity is mentioned explicitly both in the Primary National Curriculum for mathematics (DfE, 2013) and in the Teachers' Standards (DfE, 2011). There is a growing body of literature dating back more than 50 years on children's curiosity. It contains a few central themes: children are naturally curious; curiosity is highly important for learning; children's curiosity is often wrung out of them by their experiences (often school experiences); there are clear behaviours (parent and teacher behaviours), which tend to reduce children's curiosity.

Much less has been written explicitly about mathematical curiosity than about reasoning. In the opening paragraph of the Primary National Curriculum for mathematics, curiosity is mentioned alongside the development of reasoning. Much of what has been said about the development of curiosity draws on ideas about the development of reasoning. There is a symbiotic relationship between curiosity and reasoning; curiosity is an essential starting-point for enticing children into engaging in mathematics which goes beyond the application of learned procedures and therefore engages them in reasoning. The mindset that is developed through engaging in reasoning will encourage children to become more curious about mathematics. What might mathematical curiosity look like in the classroom?

Case Study: Fostering mathematical curiosity

Jo is working with a group of Year 1 children who have been reading *Jack and the Beanstalk*. The mathematics topic for the week has been 'measures', so she has been combining the two. One of the children's activities involved them making 'Giant's Beer' by mixing specific quantities of ingredients. At the end of the week, they were going to bottle up the Giant's Beer into different containers. They were invited to see how many cupfuls of 'beer' would be needed to fill various bottles and containers. This could have been a fairly straightforward estimation and practical measuring task. Jo, however, spent a few minutes with the children prior to their beginning the task:

Jo: We are going to find out how many cupfuls of Giant's Beer we will need for these different bottles. I'm going to pass the cup round, so that you can all have a look at how big it is. (Jo passes round some of the cups, so that all the children have a 'feel' for how much a 'cupful' is.)

Jo: Now, before we get to pouring out the beer, let's have a look at all these bottles that we are going to fill with beer (children have a chance to look at the different bottles).

Jo: Now, in pairs, I'd like you to talk to your partner and decide how many cupfuls we are going to need to fill up this bottle (holds the bottle up).

Ned: We think it's seven.

Jo: How did you decide it would be seven?

Ned: Well, we tried to imagine each cup going in and counted them.

Jo: That's a very interesting idea. I wonder if it will actually take seven cupfuls to fill up the bottle. Did anyone have a different number?

Jill: We thought it would be 20.

Jo: Gosh, that's very different from Ned and Jimmy's number. What made you think it would take 20 cupfuls to fill the beer bottle?

Jill: The cup is only little and the bottle looks like it would need lots of cupfuls to fill it. We guessed 20.

Jo: Hmmm, good thinking too. I wonder which one will be closest to the actual answer. Did anybody else have a different number?

Aisha: We thought ten.

Jo: What made you think of ten?

Aisha: Well, seven seems not enough. I don't think that seven will fill the bottle, but 20 is way too many. We thought about how many cups would fit in the beer bottle and we got ten.

Jo: Well, I really like your thinking all of you. I'm really interested to know how many cupfuls it will take to fill the bottle. I think that I'd like to make an estimate. Shall I do that? (General assent from the children.)

→

Jo: I think that it will be 14. I think that we could fit in 14 of these cupfuls in this bottle. I'll write my estimate up on the board, so you can check it for me when you go off and do the measuring. Before you go off and see how many cupfuls we actually need, I'd like you to spend a few more minutes talking with your partner and deciding how many cupfuls we will need to fill these other bottles. You can come up and have a good look at the bottles before you make your estimate.

Investing the time before the children went to work by inviting the children to make reasoned and considered estimates created an atmosphere of curiosity about the outcome that might have otherwise been absent. The public discussion of the estimates appeared to add to the air of curiosity about the final outcome. By making an estimate herself, Jo was able to give the children an extra incentive to find out the actual number, as well as modelling the process of estimation. Estimation can be a highly useful device for developing curiosity, but some children can find it intimidating, as they are worried about getting the answer 'wrong'.

Factors that could diminish children's natural curiosity

Perry (2001) makes a strong case for children's curiosity being both natural and essential in their learning. Given children's inherent curiosity, the role of teachers is to build on it and nurture it. Perry highlights factors which are likely to diminish or crush children's natural curiosity: fear and disapproval. In thinking about the kinds of things that you might do to enhance and nurture curiosity, I will consider each of these factors in turn.

Fear

More is written elsewhere in this book (see Chapter 11) about mathematics anxiety. Here, it will suffice to say that anxiety about mathematics is a recognised fear, which is seen as being distinctive from general anxiety (trait anxiety) and anxiety about exams and tests (Hembree, 1990). For some children (and many adults), mathematics can produce feelings of unease, or even fear. Fear is the enemy of curiosity. Children who are fearful in a particular learning situation are unlikely to engage in any of the behaviours that characterise curiosity – asking questions, trying new things, taking risks. It is therefore your responsibility, as a primary mathematics teacher, to create a psychological environment in which children feel free to explore and be curious about mathematics without fear.

Research (Geist, 2010; Maloney and Beilock, 2012) has suggested that there are specific things about mathematics and the way that it is taught that tend to engender fear. The fact that mathematics is often perceived as a subject where there is a single correct answer (and thousands of incorrect answers) and therefore many different ways to be 'wrong' is thought to produce fear. While the importance of accuracy in mathematical calculation should not be diminished, throughout the book many ways of teaching mathematics are suggested that do not involve children having to produce a single correct answer. This approach to mathematics teaching can do a lot to reduce fear and therefore preserve children's mathematical curiosity.

Having to produce a correct answer under time pressure is also thought to contribute to anxiety about mathematics (Geist, 2010). Ashcraft and Moore (2009) found that adults' mathematical performance declined markedly when they were put under time pressure. It is important for children to quickly recall number bonds, multiplication facts, etc., but giving children a diet of time-pressured, high-stakes and performative tasks is likely to reduce curiosity. As 'fluency' is highlighted repeatedly through the Primary National Curriculum, there is a concern that fluency might be misinterpreted as 'speed' and children will be put under pressure to produce answers quickly, which might reduce curiosity.

Disapproval

Disapproval is linked to fear. Children's fear of being wrong in mathematics is fear of disapproval. In seeking to create classrooms which nurture children's mathematical curiosity, consideration needs to be given to the way that teachers respond to children's 'mistakes'. I am not talking about our mathematical responses, i.e. how you might use a 'mistake' as a vehicle for understanding the child's mathematical thinking more deeply. Here I am considering the words that are used to respond to a child who has made a mathematical 'mistake' and how they might have an impact on the extent to which the child feels a sense of approval or disapproval in mathematics and therefore on the child's level of mathematical curiosity.

Some strategies for fostering mathematical curiosity

1. Be genuinely curious about the mathematics that the children are engaged in.

2. Ask questions to which you don't know the answer.

3. Try to allow children who express curiosity in a particular piece of mathematics the time to pursue their curiosity.

4. Invite children to make estimates, or conjectures (where appropriate) about the mathematics they are about to engage in. This may increase their investment in the task and heighten their curiosity about the outcome.

5. Try to notice and celebrate children being curious about mathematics.

Research Focus: Dealing with mistakes

Santagata (2004; 2005) has investigated 'mistake handling' in different cultural contexts (the USA and Italy). She found that there was a considerable difference in the extent to which children's mathematical mistakes are discussed publicly or privately. In the Italian lesson she observed, the vast majority of children's mathematical mistakes (approximately 97 per cent) were discussed in public, whereas in the lessons observed in the

→

US, this occurred with only 63 per cent of them. Santagata cites research (Alexander, 2000) which suggests that the patterns of behaviour seen in American classrooms more closely resemble those typically seen in classrooms in the UK.

She explains a possible difference in the practices seen in the two countries as being deeply rooted in the prevailing cultural beliefs about the ways in which mathematics is learned and the role of mistakes in that learning process. In Italian schools, the prevailing belief is that children can learn from one another's mistakes and therefore that mistakes made and discussed in public can be used to enhance the learning of all the children. The belief in the American classrooms was more that children learn from individual instruction and that the focus of public debate should be on correct answers.

Santagata speculates about the role that learners' self-esteem plays in the teachers' decisions about how to handle mistakes. There is a predominant feeling in the USA that self-esteem is a prerequisite for learning and development and that the exposure of 'mistakes' could damage it. However, the USA and the UK have much higher levels of anxiety about mathematics (OECD, 2010) than many other OECD countries, so possibly acknowledging the inevitability of mathematical mistakes in the learning process and using them as a catalyst for learning is a better strategy in trying to foster a sense of curiosity about mathematics than trying to protect children from mistakes.

Learning Outcomes Review

This chapter has reviewed mathematical curiosity and reasoning and has explored what these look like in the classroom. The kinds of teacher behaviours that are likely to help children to engage in mathematical reasoning have been considered as well as some of the pitfalls which might lead you to, unwittingly, limit their reasoning. The chapter has also considered how mathematical curiosity could be developed and, again, looked at some pitfalls, which might hinder this process. This discussion is important as the new National Curriculum is explicit about the need for children to develop these skills, but is not explicit about how this is done. A key thought in the chapter is therefore about how you, as a primary mathematics teacher, can see and exploit opportunities to develop this kind of mathematical thinking, while still 'covering' the mathematical content in the curriculum.

Self-assessment questions

1. Identify three things that you could incorporate into your next mathematics lesson which will encourage the children to engage in mathematical reasoning.
2. How might children's reasoning lead to a deeper understanding of the mathematics that they are engaged in?
3. What are the barriers to reasoning and curiosity that exist among your class of children? What could you do to try and reduce these?
4. How might you develop your own curiosity about mathematics and convey this to your children?

References

Advisory Committee on Mathematics Education (2012) *Response to the draft Primary National Curriculum for Mathematics*. Available at www.acme-uk.org/media/10025/201 20807%20-%20acme%20ncr%20response%20part%20a%20-%20final.pdf (accessed 25/07/14).

Alexander, R. (2000) *Culture and pedagogy*. Oxford: Blackwell Publishers.

Ashcraft, M.H. and Moore, A.M. (2009) Mathematics anxiety and the affective drop in performance. *Journal of Psychoeducational Assessment*, 27(3): 197–205.

Askew, M. (2012) *Transforming Primary Mathematics*. London: Routledge.

Boaler, J. (2010) *The Elephant in the Classroom*. London: Souvenir Press.

Charalambous, C.Y., Hill, H.C. and Ball, D.L. (2011) Prospective teachers' learning to provide instructional explanations: how does it look and what might it take? *Journal of Mathematics Teacher Education*, 14(6) 441–463.

DfE (2011) *Teachers' Standards: Guidance for school leaders, school staff and governing bodies*. London: DfE. Available at: www.gov.uk/government/uploads/system/uploads/attachment_data/file/301107/Teachers__Standards.pdf (accessed 25/07/14).

DfE (2013) *National Curriculum in England: Mathematics programmes of study: key stages 1 and 2*. Available at: www.gov.uk/government/publications/national-curriculum-in-england-mathematics-programmes-of-study/national-curriculum-in-england-mathematics-programmes-of-study (accessed 25/07/14).

DfEE (1999) *The National Numeracy Strategy*. Suffolk: DfEE.

Geist, E. (2010) The anti-anxiety curriculum: Combating math anxiety in the classroom. *Journal of Instructional Psychology*, 37(1): 24–31.

Haylock, D. (2010) *Mathematics Explained for Primary Teachers*. London: SAGE.

Hembree, R. (1990) The nature, effects, and relief of mathematics anxiety. *Journal for Research in Mathematics Education*, 21: 33–46.

Hill, H. and Ball, D.L. (2009) The curious, and crucial case of mathematical knowledge for teaching. *Phi Delta Kappan*, 91(2): 68–71.

Maloney, E.A. and Beilock, S.L. (2012) Math anxiety: who has it, why it develops, and how to guard against it. *Trends in Cognitive Sciences*, 16(8): 404–406.

New Jersey Mathematics Coalition (1996) *New Jersey Mathematics Curriculum Framework*. Trenton, NJ: NJ Department of Education.

Nunes, T. and Bryant, P. (1996) *Children Doing Mathematics*. Oxford: Blackwell.

Nunes, T., Bryant, P., Sylva, K. and Barros, R. (2009) *Development of Maths Capabilities and Confidence in Primary School*. London: DCSF.

OECD (2010) *Mathematics Teaching and Learning Strategies in PISA*. OECD.

Perry, B.D. (2001). Curiosity: the fuel of development. *Early Childhood Today*, 15(6): 22–23.

Santagata, R. (2004) Are you joking, or are you sleeping? Cultural beliefs and practices in Italian and U.S. teachers' mistake-handling strategies. *Linguistics and Education,* 15: 141–164.

Santagata, R. (2005) Practices and beliefs in mistake-handling activities: A video study of Italian and U.S. mathematics lessons. *Teaching and Teacher Education*, 21(5): 491–508.

Vygotsky, L. (1978) *Mind in Society*. Cambridge, MA: Harvard University Press.

2 The Primary National Curriculum

Catherine Foley

Learning outcomes

In this chapter you will explore the context and nature of the statutory curriculum. The key learning outcomes are:

- to consider the key changes to the mathematics curriculum to set the context for teaching mathematics;
- to explore the aims of the National Curriculum and how they relate to the rest of the curriculum content;
- to examine the differences between the 'what' of the National Curriculum and 'how' it might be taught;
- to reflect upon the demands of the National Curriculum for your own subject and pedagogical knowledge.

TEACHERS' STANDARDS

3. Demonstrate good subject and curriculum knowledge
4. Plan and teach well-structured lessons

Part Two

- Teachers must have an understanding of, and always act within, the statutory frameworks which set out their professional duties and responsibilities.

Introduction

Secure understanding of the nature of the Primary National Curriculum for mathematics will allow you to make well-informed decisions about your mathematics teaching – what you teach and why, how you teach it and when. The National Curriculum sets out minimum expectations for the mathematics children must be taught, leaving decisions about approaches to teaching and learning, underlying progression and how to integrate the aims of the curriculum into teaching to the professional judgement of the teacher. This chapter will explore key issues to consider when planning to implement the National Curriculum, will support you in interpreting and 'reading between the lines' of the statutory curriculum, and will lead into the subject knowledge and key issues to be explored in later chapters.

The National Curriculum became statutory from September 2014 and represented a fundamental shift not only in content but in the underlying messages about the nature of mathematics (see Chapter 1). The role of this chapter is to help you see the style of the curriculum, with its emphasis on what should be taught rather than how, as an opportunity rather than as a problem to be solved.

> ## Activity: Accessing the National Curriculum for mathematics
>
> In order to engage with this chapter you will need to refer to the National Curriculum, published in September 2013 (See Appendix 2). You will need to become familiar with this document, so try answering the following questions as you browse through.
>
> - How are the programmes of study laid out (in key stages, year groups, areas of mathematics ...)?
>
> - Are there any recurrent ideas or phrases? You may find it useful to highlight ideas which seem to appear frequently.
>
> - Do you find anything surprising, for example in terms of how early or late children need to understand concepts or be able to carry out calculations?
>
> - What is the role of the non-statutory guidance as opposed to the statutory content?
>
> - What messages are given in the introductory text, for example about connections between areas of mathematics or pace and progress through the programmes of study?

The introduction of the 2014 National Curriculum for mathematics

The mathematics curriculum intentionally sets out to raise expectations of what can be achieved in mathematics, as explained by Michael Gove MP in a speech to Parliament: *Our new National Curriculum is explicitly more demanding – especially in mathematics – it's modelled on the approach of high-performing Asian nations such as Singapore* (Gove, 2013). The evidence for the need for this increase in standards remains controversial. On the one hand, in 2013 figures show the proportion of children in England attaining the 'required' level 4 was 85 per cent, up one percentage point from the previous year and at its highest ever level (DfE, 2013b). On the other hand, employers' frequent frustrations at the lack of numeracy among school leavers (CBI, 2013) and international test results published by the Organisation for Economic Co-operation and Development (OECD) showing UK pupils ranked 26th among developed countries were seized upon by both politicians and press alike (OECD, 2013) as evidence that something needed to change. In the meantime, ministers are visiting high-performing parts of the world such as Shanghai to discover *what has made jurisdictions in the Far East the most successful in the world in teaching the subject* (DfE, 2014b), although you might like to consider the implications of the exclusion of the children of migrant workers from their figures when reading this kind of statement, for example see Kaiman (2014).

Dissatisfaction with the mathematics curriculum and its outcomes is nothing new, with fluctuating tensions between procedural and conceptual approaches to mathematics teaching, different philosophies about the degree of autonomy teachers should have within their planning for mathematics and ever-increasing pressure on teachers to 'raise standards'. These 'swings and roundabouts' are laid out in Brown's (2010) introductory chapter to Ian Thompson's key text, *Issues in Teaching Numeracy in Primary Schools*.

The different structures of the previous and current curricula make them difficult to compare directly – because of this, the non-statutory 'Primary Framework for Mathematics' (DfES, 2006), which underpinned many schools' planning and is set out year-by-year, is used as a comparison. Some of the more noticeable changes include:

- clearly articulated aims with three focus areas of fluency, reasoning and problem solving underpinning not only the rest of the curriculum but also its assessment;

- knowledge of multiplication tables up to 12 x 12 by Year 4;

- progression to formal written methods from Year 3 for multiplication and division;

- specific stipulation of calculation methods (e.g. short and long division) rather than simply what children have to be able to calculate (e.g. HTU ÷ TU);

- an increased emphasis on fractions throughout the curriculum, including a greater emphasis on links between fractions and division from Key Stage 1, and on calculation with fractions;

- rapid progression in children's ability to not only 'tell' but represent the time by Year 3;

- more links between algebra and the rest of the curriculum (e.g. geometry);

- reduced emphasis on data handling, with exploration of continuous data occurring earlier than previously, less descriptive statistics (no mode or median) and the removal of probability from the primary curriculum.

These changes have proved controversial, and are challenging for teachers and mathematics subject leaders alike. As you are entering the teaching profession, it is important that you form your own views. You might like to gauge your own reaction to the following statements.

Our children already struggle to reach the expectations. If we try to go any faster they will simply be left behind. (Year 2 teacher)

Mathematics should be about preparing children for real life. So shouldn't they spend most of their time using money, and reading graphs and charts? (Mathematics subject leader)

There's plenty of good practice out there in our schools, but one of the issues is that internationally in many ways our competitors are moving ahead of us in mathematics – we've got to keep abreast of that. (Charlie Stripp, Director of the NCETM, 2013)

I knew my times tables by the time I was seven because we chanted them every day – so why shouldn't my children too? (Parent)

Surely the most important thing is that children can calculate quickly and accurately – does it matter how they do it? (Trainee teacher)

Case Study: Parvinder

Parvinder is the mathematics subject leader in her primary school, a one-form intake school in a socially deprived area. As well as leading the implementation of the new curriculum, she has responsibility for supporting newly qualified teachers (NQTs). When she was visited she was planning how she would be implementing the new curriculum, and was considering the key changes for her school and what she would be looking for in the NQT they were seeking to appoint.

Working together, Parvinder and her colleagues have been comparing the previous and 2014 National Curricula. Key differences they have identified include a greater emphasis on fractions linked with division right from Year 1, earlier competence in key skills such as telling the time and greater emphasis on standard written methods, with no mention of informal and expanded methods. To meet the earlier expectations of knowledge of number facts (such as times tables, related division facts and number bonds within 20), they are considering building in additional time each day dedicated to developing rapid recall.

'Although we draw on schemes to support our planning, we want to hold onto our belief in mathematics as a practical subject in implementing the new curriculum. A lot of our children don't have much experience with number and the language of mathematics when they start at our school, so we need to build their fluency based on ensuring they all have equity of experience, and that we bring mathematical ideas to life for them.'

Although the school is working hard alongside other local schools to develop their own scheme of work based on the new curriculum, Parvinder knows that teaching the curriculum will prove challenging for newly qualified and established teachers alike. She is looking for teachers who:

- are confident being creative and practical in their mathematics teaching rather than needing to rely on a scheme;

- understand progression within and connections between areas of mathematics, frequently marking and assessing children's progress to ensure targeted teaching;

- can base their teaching on the three aims of the curriculum, using the objectives to provide context rather than simply delivering the objectives themselves;

→

- can look for and take opportunities to teach and apply mathematics across the curriculum rather than thinking purely in terms of mathematics lesson time.

Parvinder sees the next few years as a key time for her school, as she and her colleagues work to meet the demands of the new curriculum while taking the opportunity to build confidence and fluency in children and teachers alike. Where do you think you are against the characteristics Parvinder is looking for in her NQTs?

The aims of the primary National Curriculum

The aims of the National Curriculum for England, published in its final version in the autumn term of September 2013, relate to Key Stages 1, 2 and 3 (DfE, 2013a).

The National Curriculum for mathematics aims to ensure that all pupils:

- *become **fluent** in the fundamentals of mathematics, including through varied and frequent practice with increasingly complex problems over time, so that pupils develop conceptual understanding and the ability to recall and apply knowledge rapidly and accurately;*

- ***reason mathematically** by following a line of enquiry, conjecturing relationships and generalisations, and developing an argument, justification or proof using mathematical language;*

- *can **solve problems** by applying their mathematics to a variety of routine and non-routine problems with increasing sophistication, including breaking down problems into a series of simpler steps and persevering in seeking solutions.*

(p.3)

The guidance on new testing arrangements make clear that these aims will be used as the basis for national assessments (DfE, 2014c). As a general principle, every lesson should target these aims as the backdrop to the specific lesson content. The emphasis on solving problems within these aims is revealed by using the web-based tool Wordle™ to represent them (see Figure 2.1).

The third aim challenges teachers to ensure that their children are capable of solving not only routine but also non-routine problems, leading to much discussion about the nature of problem solving and in particular requiring a definition of non-routine problems and the skills needed to solve them. Perhaps a routine problem could be typified by the type of question typically presented in the statutory assessment tests tackled by children in England at the end of their primary schooling, for example:

30 children are going on a trip. It costs £5 including lunch.

Some children take their own packed lunch. They pay only £3.

The 30 children pay a total of £110. How many children are taking their own packed lunch?

(KS2, 2003, Paper A)

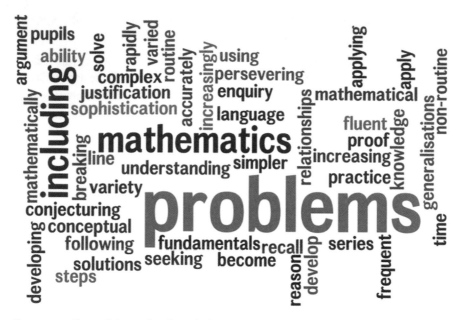

Figure 2.1 Aims of the National Curriculum

Such questions are often tackled by heuristics (rules) such as RUCSAC (**R**ead the question, **U**nderline the key information (or understand what you need to do), **C**hoose the calculations necessary, **S**olve the problem, **A**nswer the question, **C**heck whether your answer makes sense, and generally have a well-defined solution).

In contrast, non-routine problems demand a more open-ended approach combining the fluency, reasoning and problem-solving skills described by all three aims. An example of these is provided by the type of 'Fermi questions' attributed to the Nobel-prize-winning physicist, Enrico Fermi (Peter-Koop, 2005). These are questions which seek a quick, rough estimate which is difficult or impossible to calculate directly, yet which demand a well-justified and thought through estimate drawing on a wide variety of mathematical skills from approximation and converting between measures to presenting and justifying solutions (Peter-Koop, 2004).

Activity: Tackling non-routine problems

Try out the following Fermi-style question. Allow yourself one minute to record an initial estimate. Then, take a further ten minutes or so to work through the problem, developing a response you could explain and justify to a partner.

How many cars will there be in a two-mile long traffic jam?

Now, go back through your notes, analysing the knowledge, skills, understanding and attitudes towards mathematics you needed to tackle this problem. These might have included:

- jotting down some known facts;

- estimating the length of a car;

- deciding on the type of road (one, two or three lanes);

- predicting the proportion of vehicles using the road at any one time that are cars;

- converting between measures;

- rounding and approximating;

- trying different ideas and persevering.

With more time, you should find you can refine and improve your estimate (and if you try out this approach in the classroom you could get children working in groups to see who can produce the most convincing argument for their solution).

Finally, compare your list against the National Curriculum programmes of study. Can you see how this type of activity might be used to deliver some of the more content-based objectives while meeting the overarching curriculum aims? What about questions such as 'How many ice creams are sold in England each year?' or 'How long would it take you to cycle around the United Kingdom?' Try generating some Fermi-style questions of your own and considering how they might cover different aspects of the new curriculum.

The NRICH website provides an excellent source of 'low-threshold, high-ceiling' problems and activities which fit perfectly with the aims of the National Curriculum. This approach provides a way in for all children, while allowing those who are high attaining to be challenged. See the article by Lynne McClure at http://nrich.maths.org/7701 for an introduction.

Research Focus: Procedural and conceptual change

Voutsina (2012) explored the interaction between procedural and conceptual knowledge and how children combine knowledge, procedural fluency and understanding when engaging with addition problem-solving tasks.

The study involved ten 5–6 year-old children who were asked to work over a series of five sessions taking place on five consecutive days on problems involving finding all possible pairs of number bonds that add up to a given number, with target numbers increasing throughout the research. Children were observed and were asked to describe how they completed each step and their strategies. Observations revealed changes in how effectively children organised their approaches and articulated their findings.

→

Firstly, the results revealed a *dynamic interplay between children's developing representation of the task, improved . . . procedures and their gradually more explicit grasp of the conceptual aspects of their strategy* (Voutsina, 2012, p.211). In other words, rather than first teaching facts and procedures then using these to develop conceptual understanding, or focusing on teaching concepts then introducing arithmetic procedures, the research supported the 'iterative model' hypothesis that children develop their problem-solving ability best when tasks allow them to apply different types of knowledge and explore connections between them. Secondly, the study recommended that tasks build on previously successful strategies, allowing for reflection and requiring reasoning.

This research links to and exemplifies the aims of the National Curriculum for mathematics (2013), such as the importance of fluency in both conceptual und   erstanding and factual knowledge, and following lines of enquiry, persevering when presented with increasingly complex problems. It also illustrates some of the guidance in the curriculum that it is easy to miss – for example, within the introduction to the curriculum the importance of children's ability to move fluently between representations of mathematical ideas is established as vital.

Reading between the lines – the nature of the National Curriculum

Viewed at its extremes, the word 'curriculum' can be interpreted as either *incorporating all the experiences that students have in school both in and out of the classroom* or as *a dry two-page statement of a prescribed National Curriculum* (Brown, 2014, p.151). Although the mathematics curriculum in England runs to considerably more than two pages, the distinction between the intended (set out), implemented (what pupils experience) and attained (what they actually learn) curriculum is useful.

This need to look beyond the statutory curriculum to the wider picture is reinforced by Jo Boaler (2009) in her popular text *The Elephant in the Classroom: Helping Children Learn and Love Maths*. For her, the mathematics curriculum provides neither links to the real world of the children's lives nor a basis for further mathematical study: *In many maths classrooms a very narrow subject is taught to children, that is nothing like the maths of the world or the maths that mathematicians use* (Boaler, 2009, p.2). It is easy to assume that mathematics is the preserve of the mathematics classroom, with the role of homework to consolidate this learning, and to consider mathematics across the curriculum and links with the real world as an afterthought to try to make your mathematics teaching more meaningful. You might want to consider the following assertion from Masingila, studying Kenyan children's mathematical lives: *... students need in-school mathematical experiences to build on and formalise their mathematical knowledge gained in out-of-school situations* (Masingila, 2002, p.30). The following section uses the topic of time to illustrate some of the processes involved in 'reading between the lines' of the curriculum.

Interpreting the curriculum (the 'what' and the 'how')

Any experienced primary teacher will tell you that one of the trickiest areas of the curriculum to teach is time, possibly because it is the least easily perceived property that we measure (Barmby et al., 2009). Children enter school with understanding as diverse as being able to 'tell the time' through to having little concept of past, present and future let alone experience of interpreting times on an analogue clock face. As well as being confusion difficult, the awkward numbers involved (12, 24, 60, ¼, 7, etc.), the confusion between digital and analogue time and having to interpret two scales (minutes and hours) superimposed onto one circular scale will always make this a difficult area to teach. Haylock and Cockburn (2013) point out the dangers of focusing too much on 'telling the time' at the expense of exploring time intervals – the time that passes between events or two recorded times. Looking at the National Curriculum we find the statements that pupils should be taught:

- in Year 1, to compare, describe and solve practical problems for time (for example, quicker, slower, earlier, later); measure and begin to record time (hours, minutes, seconds); and tell the time to the hour and half past the hour and draw the hands on a clock face to show these times;

- in Year 2, to compare and sequence intervals of time; tell and write the time to five minutes, including quarter past/to the hour and draw the hands on a clock face to show these times; know the number of minutes in an hour and the number of hours in a day;

- in Year 3, to tell and write the time from an analogue clock, including using Roman numerals from I to XII, and 12-hour and 24-hour clocks; estimate and read time with increasing accuracy to the nearest minute; record and compare time in terms of seconds, minutes and hours; use vocabulary such as o'clock, a.m./p.m., morning, afternoon, noon and midnight; know the number of seconds in a minute and the number of days in each month, year and leap year; compare durations of events (for example to calculate the time taken by particular events or tasks).

Apart from references to using the language of time, introducing o'clock times before half past, and laying the foundations in Year 3 for reading digital time, the non-statutory guidance provides little further support for translating this part of the curriculum into reality. You can interpret this either as being problematic, or as an opportunity. The following activity is designed to begin the process of questioning the assumptions underpinning the explicit curriculum.

Activity: Considering the 'how'

Put yourself in the position of a class teacher planning some lessons on telling the time. Jot down your responses to the following questions and return to them as you build your experience throughout your training year and beyond.

- How will you get parents and carers involved?

- How could your classroom environment support teaching about the time? For example, is your clock labelled with minutes in multiples of five, as well as quarter past, half past and quarter to? Could children make their own clocks?

- What procedural fluency do you need to work on, for example counting in 5s or quarters, bridging through multiples of 60 to find time intervals?

- What kind of resources will be most beneficial? When are geared clocks (ones which move the hour hand on automatically when the minute hand is rotated) useful, and when are ungeared clocks more appropriate?

- Will you incorporate a focus on reading Roman numerals within your teaching of time, or tackle this within a cross-curricular history topic?

- Will your teaching of time be restricted to within the mathematics lesson? Or will you take opportunities to work on it throughout the school day, for example within science or PE?

- What will you do with the child who is already adept at telling the time, or who is still grappling with sequencing numbers?

Although you won't find answers to any of these questions in the statutory curriculum, they are key to establishing the ethos and approach of your mathematics teaching, how you work with parents, and the attitudes your pupils develop towards the subject. More detailed support for planning is given in Chapter 9: Planning with discernment.

Subject knowledge and the mathematics curriculum

Much writing about subject knowledge in relation to education relates back to the work of Lee Shulman in the mid-1980s and his emphasis on the importance of subject-matter knowledge – understanding the content of the subject, as well as pedagogical content knowledge (Rowland, 2014). Despite numerous studies, links between previous levels of mathematical subject knowledge and quality of teaching are unproven (Murphy, 2006). In fact one recent study emphasises the importance of people preparing to teach prioritising empathy towards those who find mathematics difficult (Hobden and Mitchell, 2011). The frequently cited *Effective teachers of numeracy report* (Askew et al.,

1997) found that being of a connectionist orientation – valuing connections between aspects of mathematics, representations, and with children's methods – was the strongest indicator of effectiveness. This research is echoed in the introductory section to the mathematics curriculum:

> *Mathematics is an interconnected subject in which pupils need to be able to move fluently between representations of mathematical ideas. The programmes of study are, by necessity, organised into apparently distinct domains, but pupils should make rich connections across mathematical ideas to develop fluency, mathematical reasoning and competence in solving increasingly sophisticated problems.*

(DfE, 2013a)

While acquiring strong subject knowledge is an essential part of developing your confidence and competence as a teacher, how you approach not only your subject knowledge but the challenges presented by learning and teaching the mathematics curriculum will dictate your future success.

Research Focus

Murphy (2006) investigated the views of generalist primary trainee teachers about subject knowledge audits and their role in their developing mathematics teaching. It involved a combination of questionnaires using Likert-scales to explore questions based on two areas, confidence in mathematics and the implications of the audit. Further evidence was captured through the use of semi-structured telephone interviews with nine trainees to further explore their perceptions. Responses were analysed, coded and compared to draw out themes.

Although all trainees felt that subject knowledge was important to the teaching of primary mathematics, trainees valued pedagogical and curricular knowledge over subject knowledge development. Being exposed to the audit process was useful to the extent that it built confidence, in particular through prompting and refreshing subject knowledge. However, the findings suggest that taking a list/test approach to auditing subject knowledge may be less helpful than connecting ideas within and across age ranges. As you work through the remainder of the book, think about how to challenge your subject knowledge by considering planning decisions, including how you will extend children who are quick to grasp concepts, and support those who need detailed, step-by-step progression in ideas. (See Chapter 9 for a discussion about planning maths lessons.)

Case Study: Subject knowledge and the curriculum

A trainee I worked with taught a good lesson to children in Year 1, focused on establishing language around the properties of 2-D shapes. She used an excellent starter based on 'Shaun the shape-eating sheep' to engage their interest, then took children on a shape hunt to find shapes that had been hidden in their outdoor environment. After finding shapes, children were challenged to sort them into labelled sorting hoops, explaining how they were recognising the shapes by comparing them with the photographs on the labels. The lesson was memorable for the children, fun and engaging, and well resourced. With subject knowledge which moved beyond the 'sound' level of knowledge of shapes and their attributes, it could have been outstanding.

In the post-lesson discussion, we talked about some of the opportunities more in-depth subject knowledge underpinning the lesson could have provided. Images of shapes used during the starter could have been presented in non-horizontal orientations to prompt discussion about common misconceptions, for example 'that can't be a triangle; it doesn't have a flat base'. Squares could have been presented as special kinds of rectangles, rather than their 'differences' being emphasised, and children could have been encouraged to generalise their findings about shape properties, laying the foundation for later work on classification.

The new curriculum poses challenges for subject knowledge for training and experienced teachers alike, with some areas being included within the primary curriculum for the first time.

Before or during your training programme you will be asked to audit your subject knowledge and identify targets for development. Sometimes these targets may relate to underpinning mathematical subject knowledge (what exactly is a composite number?). Alternatively they may relate to pedagogical subject knowledge (how will I help children understand the difference between 2-D and 3-D shapes?). Before getting into detail, take a step back and look at the curriculum as a whole and the challenges and opportunities it provides.

Activity: Challenges and opportunities

Using your copy of the National Curriculum, choose at least one year group: you may like to look at one in Key Stage 1 and one in Key Stage 2.

1. What challenges will teaching the content in this year group present? Will you need to research mathematical vocabulary and concepts, or are the challenges more about how to explain or make connections between key ideas?

2. What opportunities does the new curriculum offer for you and your future teaching? How can you use it as an opportunity to build your confidence in your own mathematics, identify your strengths or support your peers? Most people know far more about mathematics than they think they do when entering initial teacher training.

The National Centre for Excellence in the Teaching of Mathematics provides self-evaluation materials to support you in developing your subject knowledge (see www.ncetm.org.uk/self-evaluation/) and the rest of this book will allow you to pinpoint and explore key areas.

Linking the Early Years Foundation Stage and the National Curriculum

At first glance you may find it challenging to uncover links between the Early Years Foundation Stage (EYFS) and the National Curriculum for Years 1 to 6 in mathematics. With its 'areas of learning and development' and Early Learning Goals backed up by non-statutory guidance via the 'Development Matters' documentation, the structure of the EYFS can feel very different. Children work towards two Early Learning Goals in mathematics relating to numbers and shape and space, with an emphasis on counting and early calculating, using language to talk about comparison in measures and describing shapes and their characteristics. Looking more closely, links can be found both in terms of content and flexibility to make connections, develop reasoning and represent ideas.

Activity

Reflecting upon this chapter so far, in particular what you have learnt about the aims of the curriculum, consider the characteristics of effective learners set out in the EYFS:

- *playing and exploring* – *children investigate and experience things, and 'have a go';*

- *active learning* – *children concentrate and keep on trying if they encounter difficulties, and enjoy achievements; and*

- *creating and thinking critically* – *children have and develop their own ideas, make links between ideas, and develop strategies for doing things.*

(DfE, 2014a, p.9)

In order to ensure a smooth transition between the EYFS and Year 1, children need continuity not only in terms of progression of mathematical knowledge, skills and understanding, but also through the teaching and learning approach. What similarities are there between the EYFS effective learner characteristics and the aims and introductory section of the mathematics curriculum?

Learning Outcomes Review

Over the course of this chapter you have become aware of the context for the new mathematics curriculum and its implications for training and practising teachers. You have engaged with the aims, in particular considering the nature and role

(Continued)

(Continued)

of non-routine problems and how these might be used across the rest of the mathematics curriculum. You have reflected on the difference between the 'what' specified by the statutory curriculum and the 'how' of how it might be taught to establish your own approach and beliefs as a teacher of mathematics. Finally, you have begun the process of reflecting upon the demands of the National Curriculum for your own subject knowledge.

Self-assessment questions

1. What are the implications of the key changes to the National Curriculum?
2. Jot down key words from the three aims of the National Curriculum. How can you ensure that these aims underpin all of your planning and children's learning?
3. What messages are given in the introductory text to the mathematics programme of study? How will you use these ideas (for example, moving between representations, making connections) to meet the higher expectations embedded in the curriculum?
4. Where do the main challenges lie for your subject knowledge in its widest sense? Identify three key areas.

References

Askew, M., Rhodes, V., Brown, M., Wiliam, D., and Johnson, D. (1997) *Effective Teachers of Numeracy: report of a study carried out for the Teacher Training Agency*. London: King's College.

Barmby, P., Bilsborough, L., Harries, T., and Higgins, S. (2009) *Primary Mathematics: teaching for understanding*. Maidenhead: Open University Press.

Boaler, J. (2009) *The Elephant in the Classroom: helping children learn and love maths*. London: Souvenir Press Limited.

Brown, M. (2010) Swings and roundabouts, in Thompson, I. (ed.) *Issues in Teaching Numeracy in Primary Schools*, 2nd edition. Maidenhead: Open University Press. pp.3–26.

Brown, M. (2014) Debates in mathematics curriculum and assessment, in Leslie, D. and Heather, M. (eds) *Debates in Mathematics Education*. Abingdon: Routledge. pp.151–162.

CBI (2013) *Changing the Pace: CBI/Pearson education and skills survey 2013*. London: CBI.

DfE (2013a) *National Curriculum in England: Mathematics programmes of study: key stages 1 and 2*. (DFE-00180–2013). Available at: www.gov.uk/government/uploads/system/uploads/attachment_data/file/239129/PRIMARY_national_curriculum_-_Mathematics.pdf (accessed 25/07/14).

DfE (2013b) *National Curriculam Assessments at Key Stage 2 in England, 2013 (Revised)*. (SFR 51/2013). Available at: www.gov.uk/government/uploads/system/uploads/attachment_data/file/264987/SFR51_2013_KS2_Text.pdf (accessed 25/07/14).

DfE (2014a) Early Years Foundation Stage Framework. Available at: www.gov.uk/government/publications/early-years-foundation-stage-framework--2 (accessed 25/07/14).

DfE (2014b) *Experts to visit Shanghai to raise UK maths standards*. Press release, 18 February 2014. Available at: www.gov.uk/government/news/experts-to-visit-shanghai-to-raise-standards-in-maths (accessed 25/07/14).

DfE (2014c) *Key Stage 2 Mathematics Test Framework (draft): National Curriculum tests from 2016*. (STA/14/7103/e). Available at: www.gov.uk/government/uploads/system/uploads/attachment_data/file/295174/2016_Key_stage_2_Mathematics_test_framework.pdf (accessed 25/07/14).

DfES (2006) *Primary Framework for Literacy and Mathematics*. DfES 02011–2006BOK-EN.

Gove, M. (2013) Secretary of State for Education Michael Gove's statement in the House on the OECD's 2012 PISA results. Press release, 3 December 2013. Available at: www.gov.uk/government/speeches/2012-oecd-pisa-results (accessed 25/07/14).

Haylock, D. and Cockburn, A. (2013) *Understanding Mathematics for Young Children*, 4th edition. London: SAGE Publications Ltd.

Hobden, S. and Mitchell, C. (2011) Maths and me: using mathematics autobiographies to gain insight into the breakdown of mathematics learning. *Education as Change,* 15(1): 33–46. DOI: 10.1080/16823206.2011.566572.

Kaiman, J. (2014) Nine-hour tests and lots of pressure: welcome to the Chinese school system. *The Observer,* 23 February. p.29.

Masingila, J. (2002) Examining students' perceptions of their everyday mathematics practice. *Journal for Research in Mathematics Education*, 11: 30–39.

Murphy, C. (2006) 'Why do we have to do this?' Primary trainee teachers' views of a subject knowledge audit in mathematics. *British Educational Research Journal*, 32(2): 227–250.

OECD (2013) *PISA 2012 Results in Focus: What 15-year-olds know and what they can do with what they know*. Available at: www.oecd.org/pisa/keyfindings/pisa-2012-results-overview.pdf (accessed 25/07/14).

Peter-Koop, A. (2004) Fermi problems in primary mathematics classrooms: pupils' interactive modelling processes. Paper presented at the *Mathematics Education for the Third Millennium: towards 2010*. Townsville, 27–30 June.

Peter-Koop, A. (2005) Fermi problems in primary mathematics classrooms: fostering children's mathematical modelling processes. *Australian Primary Mathematics Classroom*, 10(1): 4–8.

Rowland, T. (2014) Mathematics teacher knowledge, in Andrews, P. and Rowland, T. (eds) *MasterClass in Mathematics Education: International perspectives on teaching and learning*. London: Bloomsbury. pp.87–98.

Stripp, C. (2013) The big picture. Available at: www.ncetm.org.uk/resources/41229 (accessed 25/07/14).

Voutsina, C. (2012) Procedural and conceptual changes in young children's problem solving. *Educational Studies in Mathematics*, 79: 193–214.

3 Early number, counting and place value

John Smith

Not everything that can be counted counts, and not everything that counts can be counted.

(attributed to Albert Einstein among others)

Learning outcomes

In this chapter, we will explore how young children develop counting and other early number skills and understanding, and the ways in which teachers and other adults can help with this development. The key learning objectives for the chapter are:

- to explore the nature of counting and what this involves for children;
- to consider the ways that teachers can help children to develop their counting skills;
- to consider the obstacles children encounter as they develop an understanding of 'place value' and the ways that teachers can help them.

Note about terminology: For the sake of simplicity, the word 'number' is used throughout this chapter although many writers use the word 'numerosity' to refer to the number of items in a set. The word 'numeral' will be used when the written symbol for a number is being specifically referred to.

TEACHERS' STANDARDS

2. Promote good progress and outcomes by pupils
3. Demonstrate good subject and curriculum knowledge
4. Plan and teach well-structured lessons
5. Adapt teaching to respond to the strengths and needs of all pupils
8. Fulfil wider professional responsibilities

Introduction

What is involved in counting and how does it develop? How does it lead on to more complex procedures and understanding and how can teachers, parents and other adults support this process? Although this section of the mathematical journey will be different for every child, there are certain things which are common in the experiences of most children. Good teachers carefully combine what they know about their own particular children with what they know about the understanding of children who are at the same stage of development (note 'stage' not 'age' – a point which will be returned to in due course). It is vital that children's needs are met at this point since all of their future development will rest upon the foundations built here, not only in terms of their skills, knowledge and understanding but also in terms of their enthusiasm and confidence in tackling mathematical ideas.

Curriculum Link

The areas of teaching and learning addressed in this chapter will typically be undertaken in the Foundation Stage (Nursery and Reception) and in Key Stage 1 (Years 1 and 2). It is therefore important to bear in mind the official guidance relating to both age phases.

By the end of the Reception year children should have acquired the following knowledge, skills and understanding:

Numbers: children count reliably with numbers from 1 to 20, place them in order and say which number is one more or one less than a given number. Using quantities and objects, they add and subtract two single-digit numbers and count on or back to find the answer. They solve problems, including doubling, halving and sharing.

(DfE, 2014)

The principal focus of mathematics teaching in Key Stage 1 is to ensure that pupils develop confidence and mental fluency with whole numbers, counting and place value. This should involve working with numerals, words and the four operations, including with practical resources (for example, concrete objects and measuring tools).

(DfE, 2013)

The National Curriculum specifies three aims, all of which are evident when children develop their knowledge, skills and understanding in this area. While it is clear that *fluency* is inherent in children's early number work, the other two aims, for children *to reason mathematically* and to *solve problems*, are also vital.

Opportunities and reasons for counting

Make sure that children have many opportunities to count and alert them to the purposes of counting. Nunes and Bryant stress the importance of children using *mathematical thinking meaningfully and appropriately in situations* (Nunes and Bryant, 1996, p.17), so be constantly on the lookout for suitable contexts for counting. Sometimes this will arise naturally through the structured play opportunities that you can set out – role play areas, 'small world' play area, in the sand and water areas, etc. – and you should make sure that you talk to the children about what they are counting, for example 'How many starfish are there in the water, Jack? Can you count them for me so we can be sure?' Sometimes you can set out items in a more structured way for them to count. Make sure that you and the children also count in other settings. A walk to the park, for example, will give many opportunities for counting.

Discussing the purposes of counting with children can be very helpful. From interviews with young Scottish children, Penny Munn (2008) discovered that many children associated counting solely with their school work, often seeing it as simply something that adults wanted them to do. The implication of this is that we must be constantly looking for opportunities to help children connect abstract concepts with the practical, concrete problems they can use mathematics to solve. To have a full understanding of what counting entails and the world it gives access to, they must appreciate the usefulness of counting in virtually every area of life. With a little ingenuity on the part of the teacher, counting-rich problem-solving activities can be engaging and enjoyable and can require reasoning too. For example: 'How many coats are on the pegs? Can we work out how many children are absent today?'

Activity: The complexity of counting

Work with a partner and scatter a number of countable items onto the table in front of you. Medium-sized items like cubes or beads will work best. The total number is not crucial – 30 will be fine. Then take it in turns to play the roles of 'Counter' and 'Observer'. The Counter should count *three* items – physically separate them from the group and then return them. The Observer should watch out for any words, actions, facial expressions, etc. which accompany this activity. Then Counter and Observer should exchange roles and repeat this procedure. Counter and Observer should exchange roles twice more but during this second pair of trials, each Counter should count *13* items. Finally, discuss with one another what the Observer noticed on each occasion. What sort of behaviours were evident? Did the Counter say anything while counting? Can the Counter add anything to this account – for example, what was the Counter thinking while the counting was going on?

When you did this task you probably discovered something fairly remarkable when you 'counted' three items; you probably didn't need to count them at all. Most people report that they 'just saw three' and removed them from the group without counting (although you may have counted just to check). This ability is called 'subitising'. Thirteen was almost certainly too large a number for you to do this, so you would have needed to count in a more conventional way. You probably touched each item and counted aloud as you did so. You may have used a strategy to speed up the count such as counting in pairs and then adding one at the end. Some people recognise that 13 can be made another way, for example by three 3s and a 4, which might allow them to repeat the strategy they used to 'count' three. Others recognise that it is ten and three so they will count the items in this way. Some people count aloud, others mouth the number words silently, while others report that they count in their heads (and perhaps nod for each number). What does this tell us?

Here are a few conclusions which all primary teachers need to be aware of.

- Counting is a more complex activity than we first imagine.

- Physical actions and thoughts are synchronised as we count.

- There is not a single way of counting. (The *act of counting* is meant here, rather than the simple reciting of numbers.)

- There is a range of ways that counting can go wrong and skilled counters build in checks to try and ensure accuracy.

- It is unsurprising that many children struggle to master this skill. It cannot be acquired 'in one go'.

- Although it is often performed in concrete situations, there is a very abstract aspect of counting which children must come to terms with if they are to master the skill.

- Counting is not separate from calculation but is the beginning of calculation. Moreover, counting persists as a vital strategy which must be practised and developed at increasingly sophisticated levels throughout and beyond a child's primary education.

Why is counting so difficult?

Many researchers have considered this question and some of the results of this research will be considered in this section. There is a piece of freely accessible video called 'Every child counts' , which you will find extremely helpful in your study of these ideas. The link to it is given at the end of the chapter and it will be referred to at a number of points below.

Research Focus: Gelman and Gallistel's counting principles

We have already pointed out that counting is far more complex than it appears initially. Two American researchers, Rochel Gelman and Charles Gallistel, analysed this complexity and they suggested that, in order to count, children needed to understand what they referred to as five 'principles' of counting. Although their work was first published about forty years ago, it is still widely regarded as offering the most comprehensive analysis to date of the counting process and its difficulties for children (Gelman and Gallistel, 1978). In the video 'Every child counts', Rochel Gelman explains these principles and demonstrates some of them in experiments and discussions with young children. The five principles identified by Gelman and Gallistel are as follows.

$\longrightarrow$

The one-one principle

This is the central principle on which all the others rest and it is also referred to as 'one to one correspondence'. As Gelman observes, counting is not simply the reciting of numbers. To count we must synchronise the actions of counting – identifying the set of items to be counted, generally by touching them – and the systematic assigning of one number to each item.

The stable-order principle

The numbers in the count must be used consistently. The child must know the order of the numbers and must recognise that they need to be recited in exactly this order every time they are used.

The cardinal principle

The child must recognise that the final number recited is the total number contained in the set.

The abstraction principle

This involves understanding that anything countable can be counted. (Not everything can be as we shall see.)

The order-irrelevance principle

This is clearly, if somewhat uncomfortably, demonstrated in the video when the young girl is unable to make the middle toy in a row of five toys become the last item to be counted. Once children's counting skills have developed, however, they can count the same set of items starting or finishing at any point, although some arrangements will clearly be easier than others.

These five principles are not consciously followed by children, but until they understand them they will not be able to count with accuracy and confidence.

How can we help children to develop their counting skills?

Not all children will be at this stage at the same age. The Foundation Stage is where you are most likely to see this set of skills and understanding developing. However, some children arrive in Reception or even in Nursery as confident counters but you are very likely to see others at the same stage in Key Stage 1. Sadly, many children will pass into Key Stage 2, and even beyond that point, without having fully mastered this skill. Be alert to the fact that some children will be at an early stage while their peers will be counting more confidently. The skills and understanding described in the following sections will take a long time to be assimilated and they will develop through a mixture of direct teaching and children's own investigation and discovery. The latter may be structured or semi-structured by you or other adults in your classroom — working together to count and sort objects in games or construction or pattern work, for example — or it may be completely independent – you might observe a child choosing to sell tickets in the class shop or airport and there are many other examples.

Returning to the five principles, here are some difficulties that children can encounter and some of the experiences which teachers can offer to help them. An important point is that the five principles are not acquired sequentially but in parallel. Progress will be subtle and often uneven so teachers must be patient, encouraging and careful in their assessment. Although the names given to these principles may be very useful in guiding your assessments, it would not be useful to share them with children.

The one-one principle

Possible errors

A child may touch more than one item while saying a single number, touch an item more than once or say more than one number for a single touch.

Teaching strategies

Model counting where you touch or move each object that has been counted. When counting piles, or randomly arranged items, move those that have been counted aside, or arrange them in groups or piles of ten.

The stable-order principle

Possible errors

Children will sometimes get numbers in the wrong order or they will repeat or miss out numbers.

Teaching strategies

As well as simple counting, use stories, songs and rhymes that you know with number sequences in them. You have probably thought of stories like *Goldilocks and the three bears* and *The three little pigs,* songs like *Ten green bottles, There were ten in the bed, Five little speckled frogs* and rhymes like *Round and round the garden.* These can be used in the classroom as well as at home and they help to develop children's knowledge of the counting numbers. There are also many wonderful children's books in which counting is explicitly or implicitly featured. *The Very Hungry Caterpillar* by Eric Carle and *Handa's Surprise* by Eileen Browne are just two examples and these and others are available in multi-media formats.

Children should also see numbers around the classroom – number tracks and washing lines with numbers pegged on to them can be very useful for younger children, and number lines for older children. Using a washing line of numbers can create opportunities to teach a puppet the number order: 'Someone has mixed up our numbers at play-time. Can you help to put them in the right order so that we can teach them to Joey the Parrot?' This is an un-threatening activity which most young children will enjoy and can be a whole class activity.

The cardinal principle

Possible errors

In some ways, this can appear to be the most mystifying principle to acquire. How can children not understand that the last number they say when counting is the total number in the set? A good example of secure understanding in the video can be seen when a child who has counted five items is not persuaded by a puppet that there are six. Like all of the other principles, however, this is an idea which has to be understood through repeated exposure and practice.

Teaching strategies

It is important for you to model this principle. When you are modelling counting, reinforce the principle: '1, 2, 3, 4, 5, 6 … there are six apples.'

Make sure that you ask children questions related to their activities which will draw their attention to the total number in the set – the cardinal value. Use questions like 'How many cubes have you used in your model, Sajid?' and 'How many tiger cubs can you see in the picture?' Use a variety of contexts to ask children if they would give you a number of items, 'Could you give me five pencils please, Sacha'.

As well as helping children to understand the *cardinal* value of numbers, i.e. their use in counting, you should set up activities to help them to understand the *ordinal* value of numbers too, i.e. their use in ordering. Readers of this book can easily see the connection between, for example, *one* and *first* or between *21* and *21st* but this is another area of learning for children. Use a variety of contexts to develop the use of this aspect of numbers: 'Which lorry came down the slope first, Sara's or Imran's? So Sara's was first and Imran's was second. Which one came third?'; 'This is the last day of November. It's the thirtieth of November. How many days does November have?'; 'Red Table can go out to play first because they went out last yesterday. Who should go out second today?' Sports and other competitive activities can of course create a context for discussing order but you should take care when using this context – the child who always comes last in the race will probably not enjoy having this pointed out. A safer context, which can be adapted as children get older, is the ordering of winners which arises from large sporting events: the Olympics, the World Cup, football tournaments involving local teams and so on.

The abstraction principle and the order-irrelevance principle

We have combined these final principles as they are quite closely linked and highlight the abstract nature of counting. They also draw our attention to the fact that children are reasoning when they count.

Possible errors

The abstraction principle might be evident in children's inability or reluctance to transfer counting skills from one situation to another. The order-irrelevance principle is evident when children can only count in a linear manner and when changes in that order become difficult obstacles.

Teaching strategies

Children must recognise at some point that not everything can be counted. At the seaside, for example, the deckchairs can be counted but the sand and sea cannot. Of course we can find ways of quantifying the sand and the sea. From a young child's perspective this might involve filling buckets or other containers with sea or sand and at a later stage, measuring (some) sand and sea using standard units like grams and litres. However, unless we do this, we must ask 'How much sand and sea is there?' which is a different sort of question to those we can ask about things which can be counted. We usually begin those questions with 'How many ...' So children have to realise that some things can be counted and some things cannot and this is itself an abstract notion. Once they have grasped this notion, they are ready to recognise that we can count items we cannot see ('close your eyes and count how many people are with you in the room, or how many times I clap my hands'). We can also count items which are too far away to touch: 'Look at that building; how many square windows can you see?' Look for as many different and imaginative opportunities for counting as you can find. These might include your children counting sounds like tambourine or drum beats, physical movements like hops or jumps, or more abstract things like the number of school days left till the weekend.

If we think back one more time to the girl in the video who could not make the toy in the middle of a row the final item to be counted, we recognise that it is a good idea to give children practice at counting that is not always along a row of items. In real life, objects do not always fall into such neat arrangements for counting and this is something that children need practice at coping with – can they count a circle of objects or pick out one type of object from a group: the lorries from a group of toy vehicles, for example? Set up a variety of situations but be prepared, as ever, to simplify the context if a child is struggling.

Subitising – identifying numbers without counting

We now return to the task you undertook at the beginning of this chapter to count three and 13 items. How was it possible to 'just see three items' without counting? For many years, researchers have observed this aptitude which has been given a name: *subitising*. When we subitise we are able to recognise the number of items before us without needing to count them. Butterworth (2000) has produced some extremely interesting work about this area of mathematical ability. There are several points which seem to be true about this ability.

- It only works with a relatively small number of items – beyond about five is out of reach for most people.

- It is an innate ability that almost everyone has and which can be observed from birth. (Those who are unfortunate enough not to have this skill may well experience significant mathematical difficulties in later life.)

- It is generally considered to be a separate skill from counting but it can usefully be combined with it.

Reading and writing numbers

As well as seeing numbers in the environment, children need opportunities to make their own written representations of mathematical ideas. Eventually, the goal is for them to use the standard number system and this will be developed through exposure to numbers in context as described in this chapter. Children should be introduced to these alongside the letters which they are learning and you should provide as wide a range of materials as you can for them to practise using them, such as tracing numbers in sand, making play-dough numbers, using magnetic numbers and other tactile resources like the many fabric numbers that are now available. They should also have opportunities to use pens and pencils to write numbers on paper.

In the early stages of number (and letter) acquisition, children's performance can vary greatly from day to day. Never force children to use materials that they find difficulty in using – give large pieces of paper and chunkier pens if these are more suitable, for example – and never scold a child for poor writing, even if you feel that you have seen better examples on other occasions. Many children will also reverse numbers such as 5, even when they have used them for some time. While most difficulties that children experience will resolve themselves over time without specific intervention, you should be alert to unusual, severe or persistent difficulties as these might signify a learning difficulty and the child will need appropriate support. Once again, good communication with parents and carers is essential, as is close communication with your school SENCO and other relevant staff.

There is an important stage which runs alongside the process of learning to use standard numbers and symbols and this is referred to by Carruthers and Worthington as 'mathematical graphics' (see Worthington and Carruthers, 2003, and the excellent article on the NRICH website, cited at the end of the chapter). Here, children will devise their own representations of numbers and mathematical ideas such as scores in a game, shopping lists, etc. These will probably include standard numbers combined with their own, idiosyncratic marks which may look meaningless to the adult observer. For many years this stage of development was dismissed as 'scribble' but research has revealed that it is a vital stage in children's development. You should ensure that structured play environments – shops, airports, doctors' surgery, etc. – include examples of numbers (such as the till and telephone in Figure 3.1 and other items such as posters and leaflets) and materials for children to record their own representations. Numbers often have significance to all of us beyond their functional use (Alex Bellos has discovered that seven appears to be the most popular number among the large number of people who responded to his survey: Bellos, 2014) so try to use numbers which are significant for children wherever possible. After a child's birthday, for example, a parent might offer to bring in their child's birthday cards which will show the numeral written in a variety of ways and might include other images linked to it, such as four candles on a cake.

Case Study: Young children's calculation strategies

Maths educator Ian Sugarman interviewed many young children to explore their calculation strategies. In one of his interviews Ian presented a girl of about five with the following problem, presented on a card: 5 – 3. The young girl, who seemed confident mathematically, answered without hesitation that the answer was 5. This answer is clearly puzzling to an adult and seems completely illogical. When Ian probed her answer, however, she explained that the 3 was taken away, so the 5 was left intact. The child's literal interpretation of 'take away the 3' should remind us that language is often ambiguous. Teachers must therefore probe meaning and not just presume meaning from a single response. This lovely episode also reminds us that children are generally creative in their reasoning and that, although it may take some effort to understand, they often show remarkably logical thinking. As we have seen repeatedly, until they have had a great many practical experiences, children may understand rather abstract terms like 'take away' very differently from the way we intend them to.

Figure 3.1 Try to ensure that structured play settings give opportunities for children to use numbers for a variety of purposes

Activity

Plan a structured play area for children in a Reception class (although this could be used with other ages too). If possible, use a real setting where you can try out your ideas. Try to ensure that there are rich and interesting resources to stimulate mathematical thinking and for children to record any mathematical ideas they wish to express.

- What opportunities for mathematical thinking will your area provide?

- What opportunities for talk and reasoning will your area provide?

- What role(s) can adults take in this area?

- If you have the opportunity to actually set this up for children, take careful note of the kinds of 'play' they undertake. How much does this match your expectations? What might you change next time?

Place value

Once children can count successfully, they have begun to familiarise themselves with what we often call the 'number system', but once they encounter larger numbers, they will need to understand that our numbers are organised in a way that allows them to be used efficiently and economically. At the heart of the number system is a set of conventions that we refer to as 'place value'.

Curriculum Link

If we look at the Year 1 expectations within the National Curriculum, we can see how crucial this understanding is.

Year 1 Pupils should be taught to:

- *count to and across 100, forwards and backwards, beginning with 0 or 1, or from any given number;*

- *count, read and write numbers to 100 in numerals; count in multiples of twos, fives and tens;*

- *given a number, identify one more and one less;*

- *identify and represent numbers using objects and pictorial representations including the number line, and use the language of: equal to, more than, less than (fewer), most, least;*

- *read and write numbers from 1 to 20 in numerals and words.*

(DfE, 2013)

In most Year 1 classes there are longer periods of focused study than in the Foundation Stage, reflecting the increased ability of children to sustain such activities, but a note of caution should be sounded here. Once children have reached Year 1, there should not be an abrupt change of approach. Practical approaches and experiences are vital for this age group and for older children as well as for the younger children in the Foundation Stage. Concerns have also been raised by Ofsted and others about a rapid trend towards children being passive for long periods, on the carpet or at their tables, while teachers demonstrate particular points, or working at their seats, often in near silence, completing written work for significant periods of time.

The development of children's understanding of place value begins once they understand that the value of a number with more than one digit can only be calculated if each digit, reading from left to right, is understood to be ten times the value of the one beside it. In other words, the *place* of each digit determines its *value*. Like most concepts, this cannot be fully conveyed to children by simply telling them how this system works, but children must be given many, varied opportunities to develop this understanding in practice.

What are the advantages of place value within our number system?

It is important for teachers to realise that the number system we share and which we help our children to use is not an English invention. A brief and useful introduction to its origins can be found in Jennifer Piggott's article, on the NRICH website (see the link at the end of this chapter). The central feature of this system is that any number, no matter how large or small, can be represented using some or all of just ten symbols: 0 to 9. The significance of zero cannot be overstated. Without zero, it would be impossible to differentiate between 1, 10, and 100 or between 11 and 101. The number system can also be adapted to show numbers smaller than one, or containing elements smaller than one, by the use of the decimal point. Further extensions and enhancements can be added by the introduction of signs to indicate negative numbers, powers and so on. All of this complexity, though, rests on the use of the ten symbols from 0 to 9 to represent numbers and successful use depends on an understanding of place value. We will look at this in more detail in the next section of this chapter.

How can we help children to understand place value?

The number line will become an invaluable aid at this stage. The transition from number track to number line is an important one. As has already been noted, children in Nursery are likely to see and use a number track or washing line with numbered items which is very useful for developing their recall of the order of numbers. In Reception, or certainly by Year 1, children should use number lines. The difference between number tracks and number lines is not immediately apparent since both represent the number order for a given range – probably up to 10 or 20 in the earliest stages. Whereas the number track shows the numbers occupying spaces – often accompanied by illustrations (one doll, two beach balls, etc.) – the number line shows each number (technically each *integer*) as a point along the line. Other important numbers and number domains – zero, negative numbers, etc. – can eventually be represented too and, crucially, the line can be adapted to demonstrate, at a later stage, the fractional numbers between the integers (0.5, 2.2, 21.6, etc.). This gives the number line a far more lasting value in the primary (and secondary) classroom as you will appreciate later in the book.

Try to ensure that the questions you ask are varied, that you regularly use the mathematical terms which the National Curriculum stipulates at this age and that there are frequent opportunities for children to use this vocabulary themselves and to hear and say numbers, as well as seeing them. They will also need opportunities to practise writing the numbers, both as numerals and as words, so make sure that your displays and other visual aids contain both. As well as static number lines on the classroom wall, make sure that smaller versions are available as long as children need them. This 'scaffolding', as it is often called, should be gently withdrawn when children can manage without it but it should be used as long as it is needed. You should also try to get the children to act as 'human number lines' carrying numbers on cards or wearing stickers. This engagement of kinaesthetic approaches to learning as well as visual and auditory approaches is important. Be sure to include games and puzzles as part of the mathematics curriculum. These have many advantages, being unthreatening and engaging and offering opportunities for talk and reasoning. Dice games and variations of traditional board games such as 'snakes and ladders' (which uses a type of number line) are two possibilities.

It is common practice to begin lessons with a 'mental and oral starter' to warm children up and to practise key skills. Use this time for counting games and activities and for adding and subtracting questions that children can answer using number fans or arrow/digit cards (see Figure 3.2). This gives you a much clearer picture of the children's developing understanding than a 'hands-up' routine for answering questions. Try to take group counting beyond 100 so that children do not develop the sense that there is an insurmountable wall at that point. Another development in children's counting is their ability to count in multiples: twos, fives and tens are likely to arise first. These skills can also be practised during this first section of a lesson.

There are a wide range of approaches that you can use to help children to develop their knowledge and understanding of these number patterns but try to ensure that, when considered as a whole, your approach is multi-sensory and varied. Visual images are extremely important. In addition to the number line there are other useful images and resources. The hundred square is a very useful image and you can find examples that are 'free standing', wall mounted and computer based. If children are able to manipulate the numbers – taking them off and replacing them – this will enhance their understanding of patterns. An advantage of the hundred square is that the relationships between numbers ending in the same digit can be easily seen. This can assist children in finding mental strategies for calculations, as you will see in later chapters. If asked, for example, 'How much must I add to 27 to make 47?' the child can use the visual arrangement of the hundred square to answer '20' since 47 is two squares 'below' 27 in the same column. A good classroom technique devised by Ruth Merttens is to attach a plastic spider above the hundred square in such a way that it can be lowered down a column. This image can be used to show the route of the spider when moving from, say, 27 to 47, or vice versa, and can be a useful memory aid which can eventually be internalised. Arrow cards and number fans can also be used to demonstrate the value of numbers in relation to place value.

Number fans can show two-digit numbers (except for those using the same digit twice) and their design makes them ideal for use by children from Nursery to Year 1. Beyond this point, arrow cards/place value cards and other devices can be used. The advantage of arrow cards is that the shapes and colours of the cards reduce the possibility of error, such as thinking that one hundred and two should be written as 1002. They are an excellent resource for developing children's understanding of place value, seeing how numbers are written (for example, what would 200, 50 and 3 look like when written together?) and for 'partitioning' numbers into hundreds, tens and ones. Arrow cards and other place value apparatus are available in large versions for teachers to use with groups of children or the whole class and in smaller versions for children themselves to use.

Figure 3.2 A variety of images and equipment should be used regularly to develop children's understanding.

Why is place value so challenging for children?

The following activity (a composite of many actual examples of this kind) and the research focus which follows give us an insight into this difficulty.

Activity: Confusing 37 and 73

In a Year 2 class, a child struggles to tell the difference between two-digit numbers like 37 and 73. He will often put the digits the wrong way around for the number required and you feel that, rather than being a simple error, this indicates a complete misunderstanding of the order and value of the digits in a number. His peers are beginning to use column methods for addition and subtraction but the difficulties this child is experiencing make it impossible for him to use these methods effectively.

Stop and think about methods that you might use to help this child to overcome his difficulties.

Research Focus

You may have decided in the activity above that an explicit reference to place value is required. You might ask the child to write the numbers on a sheet with columns marked T and U for tens and units so that he can see that 73 is seven tens and three units and that 37 is the reverse of this. You might think of using materials like the 'Deines' apparatus shown in Figure 3.3 (on the left of the photograph – often called 'tens and units' blocks). These allow numbers to be modelled with single cubes for units, sticks of cubes for tens and squares of cubes for hundreds. Money is another good model if you restrict the coins available to single pence, ten pence pieces and pound coins. Numicon – the resource shown on the right of Figure 3.3 – can be used to model smaller and larger numbers too. All of these approaches have been commonly used in primary classrooms for many years and they are valuable resources. However, Ian Thompson (2003) has argued that children do not acquire an understanding of place value all at once. According to Thompson, children typically go through two phases which he calls 'quantity value' and 'column value' under-standings. When children are at the 'column value' stage, they recognise the value of the digits in a number and they can appreciate how the number system works in this respect. However, at the 'quantity value' stage, which is where the child in the Activity above appears to be, they will not have such a full understanding but they will appreciate that, for example, 73 is greater than 37 and they might be able to order the two numbers correctly on a number line. The number line is, once again, invaluable because the teacher can help the child demonstrate what he already knows and can lead him on to new understanding: 'Good, you have shown me where 37 is. What is the next multiple of 10 after 37? How many multiples of 10 are there between 37 and 73? So 37 is 7 more than 30 and 73 is 3 more than 70.' The important implication for the teacher, from Thompson's research, is that, in any class beyond those with the youngest children, there are likely to be children at both of these stages of understanding and some who have not yet reached either stage. We must be patient and sensitive and provide children with resources and explanations which will be helpful for them at any particular time.

$\longrightarrow$

Figure 3.3 These and many other resources can assist children as they try to understand place value and the number system

Figure 3.4 Try to find as many ways as possible of helping children understand the value of the digits in two and three digit numbers

Learning Outcomes Review

In this chapter you have examined the ways in which young children learn to count, the obstacles they must overcome to do this and the ways which you, and the other adults you work with, can help children develop confidence and fluency in this vital area. You have also examined the difficulties which children encounter when they begin to understand the concept of place value, which is at the heart of our number system. You should hopefully have realised the importance of creating a good classroom ethos in pursuing these goals. You should aim to make your classroom interesting and stimulating, with many multi-sensory opportunities for learning and many opportunities for purposeful talk and reasoning. Finally, you should have recognised that it is very important to be alert to the stage that a child's understanding has reached if you are going to offer appropriate support for that child.

> ### Self-assessment questions
>
> 1. How might you ensure that children understand all five of Gelman and Galistel's counting principles?
> 2. What are some of the barriers to children understanding place value.
> 3. What could you do to help children to overcome these barriers?

Further Reading

Tammet, D. (2012) *Thinking in Numbers. How maths illuminates our lives.* London: Hodder and Stoughton.

Useful websites

www.youtube.com/watch?v=OBsjbpFjiAk 'Every child counts' (Extract from the 1985 BBC *Horizon* programme *Twice five and the wings of a bird*)

http://nrich.maths.org/5598 *A Story About Absolutely Nothing* by Jennifer Piggott

http://nrich.maths.org/6894 *Children's Mathematical Graphics: understanding the key concepts* by Elizabeth Carruthers and Maulfry Worthington

References

Bellos, A. (2014) *Alex Through the Looking-Glass: How life reflects numbers and numbers reflect life.* London: Bloomsbury.

Butterworth, B. (2000) *The Mathematical Brain*. London: Papermac.

DfE (2013) *National Curriculum in England: Mathematics programmes of study: key stages 1 and 2.* Available at: www.gov.uk/government/publications/national-curriculum-in-england-mathematics-programmes-of-study/national-curriculum-in-england-mathematics-programmes-of-study (accessed 25/07/14).

DfE (2014) *Statutory Framework for the Early Years Foundation Stage.* Crown copyright.

Gelman, R. and Gallistel, C.R. (1978) *The Child's Understanding of Number.* Cambridge, MA: Harvard University Press.

Munn, P. (2008) Children's beliefs about counting, in Thompson, I. (ed.) *Teaching and Learning Early Number.* Maidenhead: Open University Press.

Nunes, T. and Bryant, P. (1996) *Children Doing Mathematics.* Oxford: Blackwell.

Thompson, I. (2003) Place value: the English disease?, in Thompson, I. (ed.) *Enhancing Primary Mathematics Teaching.* Maidenhead: Open University Press.

Worthington, M. and Carruthers, E. (2003) *Children's Mathematics. Making marks, making meaning.* London: SAGE.

4 Addition and subtraction

Jane McNeill

Whether browsing the web, interpreting medical records, administering medicine to children, reading the news, working with finances or taking part in elections, 21st century citizens need mathematics.

(Boaler, 2010, p.9)

Learning outcomes

In this chapter you will:

- consider different models for addition and subtraction;
- appreciate that addition and subtraction are linked and that it is important to develop this understanding with children;
- recognise how addition and subtraction skills build on prerequisite knowledge and skills including counting, number sense and place value;
- explore the range of mental strategies that can be used to add and subtract and consider how to develop these;
- develop insight into progression from mental to written methods;
- appreciate the value of addressing errors and misconceptions;
- consider opportunities for developing reasoning through addition and subtraction and for linking learning to real life.

TEACHERS' STANDARDS

3. Demonstrate good subject and curriculum knowledge
5. Adapt teaching to respond to the strengths and needs of all pupils

---

Introduction

This chapter aims to clarify some of the key concepts underpinning addition and subtraction and to explore progression and breadth in the teaching and learning of addition and subtraction.

Many aspects of our everyday lives involve quantities and measures. Using mathematics frequently involves more than just counting or assigning numbers; it involves calculating. When we combine, compare, reduce or increase amounts, these actions can be represented by the mathematical operations of addition or subtraction. Helping children to develop confidence and proficiency in working with these additive relations is therefore an important element of the primary mathematics curriculum.

Different models for addition and subtraction

Curriculum Link

The National Curriculum statutory requirements for Year 1 state that children should solve one-step problems using practical equipment. Guidance adds that children should experience problems that involve a range of vocabulary including *altogether, total, take away, difference between, more than and less than.* In order to solve problems involving this range of vocabulary, children should develop flexibility in how they understand addition and subtraction.

Case Study: Understanding addition and subtraction

Jess has just started her NQT year in a Year 1 class. She is working with a guided group and has planned practical activities to help assess the children's understanding of addition and subtraction. Jess gives each child a tray containing rulers and asks them to label their tray to show the number of rulers it contains. She then asks the children to work in pairs to find how many rulers are in their two trays altogether:

Bilal tips the rulers from his tray onto the table and tells his partner, Hayley, to do the same. They then count how many rulers are in the pile altogether.

Alex and Devi work in a different way.

Devi: My tray has seven rulers. What's in yours?

Alex: Five.

Devi starts to move rulers one by one from Alex's tray into hers, counting on from 7 as she does so:

Devi: So, that is 8, 9, 10, 11, 12. Is that right?

The pair then check by counting the 12 rulers that are now in the tray.

Later in the session, Jess asks Devi how many rulers would be left in her tray if five children took a ruler each.

Devi remembers that there are seven rulers in her tray and puts up seven fingers. She then puts down the five fingers of one hand, looks at the two fingers which are left and says, 'There will be two.'

Jess asks Alex the following question: 'How many more rulers are in Devi's tray than yours?'

Alex is not sure how to start so Jess suggests he puts the rulers from his tray (five) in a line on the carpet. Jess then prompts him to line up Devi's rulers (seven) above his. Alex does this, points to the two extra rulers in Devi's line and says, 'There are two more.'

Activity: Understanding addition and subtraction

Consider the different ways in which the pairs of children approached the problems. Think about what this reveals about the children's understanding of addition and subtraction.

In the case study, children demonstrate different conceptions of addition and subtraction. We will consider here the two main models for addition and for subtraction.

Addition as aggregation

The aggregation model of addition involves finding the total after combining two sets. Early aggregation strategies involve children combining sets of objects and then counting the total, which is a 'count all' approach. Such strategies do not require complex arithmetic, only accurate counting skills. 'Count all' strategies, however, become inefficient with large numbers. Bilal and Hayley use an aggregation strategy when they tip out the rulers to find how many rulers are in both trays together.

Addition as augmentation

Addition as augmentation involves starting from the known quantity in one set and counting on. Devi uses this model for addition. She recognises that she does not need to count the rulers in her tray as she already knows there are seven. She therefore adds Alex's rulers one by one to this set, counting up from 7 as she does so. This 'count on' approach is more efficient than a 'count all' approach but requires a greater level of sophistication in terms of counting skills. In order to use it children need to be able to count on from any start number and, alongside this, to keep track of the total as they count.

Nunes and Bryant (2009) consider this change in behaviour from using a 'count all' to a 'count on' strategy to be a critical step in children's emerging understanding of calculation. Teachers working with children at this stage in their learning may need to structure learning opportunities carefully in order to encourage children to make this transition. This might involve teaching strategies such as covering up the first set of objects or placing the first set of objects in a labelled container and asking the child to say how many objects are in the first set. Initially teachers may also scaffold the counting on process by asking prompt questions such as 'If you add in another object, how many are there now?' This physical experience of adding objects into a known set is an important precursor to the more abstract skill of counting on in your head.

Subtraction as 'take away'

Devi uses this approach to find how many rulers would be left in her tray if five children each took a ruler. To answer this problem she models it on her fingers, putting up seven fingers to represent the rulers in her tray then taking away five fingers to represent the five rulers that are removed. This take away model for subtraction can develop towards a 'counting back' strategy. One way to work out 7 subtract 5 is to start at 7 and count back 5.

As with counting on strategies for addition, counting back strategies for subtraction involve sophisticated counting skills and children are likely to need carefully structured experiences in order to use such strategies effectively.

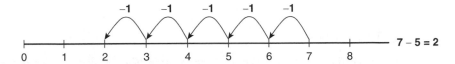

Figure 4.1

Subtraction as 'difference'

Jess supports Alex in creating a visual representation to work out how many more rulers are in Devi's tray than his. By placing the rulers into two lines and matching one of Devi's rulers to each of his, he can see that there are two extra rulers in Devi's tray. These two 'extra' rulers represent the difference between 7 and 5. The difference model for subtraction is linked to counting on. One way to work out 7 subtract 5 is to start at 5 and count up to 7.

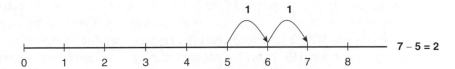

Figure 4.2

Understanding the relationship between addition and subtraction

Addition and subtraction are inverse operations. Using a trio of numbers such as 3, 5 and 8, which are linked through a part-whole relationship, it is possible to write two addition and two subtraction facts: $3 + 5 = 8$, $5 + 3 = 8$, $8 - 5 = 3$ and $8 - 3 = 5$.

Figure 4.3

Understanding the inverse relationship between addition and subtraction is important in enabling children to use both operations effectively. In particular it allows us to check answers to calculations. For example, if we work out that $43 - 18$ gives 25 then we can check that the related addition, $25 + 18$, gives the expected answer of 43. This inverse relationship is also important within the 'difference' model of subtraction. Children can work out the subtraction $32 - 25 = ?$ by considering instead the related addition $25 + ? = 32$. The missing number can therefore be found by counting up from the smaller number (25) to the bigger number (32), keeping track of the count to find the difference between the two numbers.

Curriculum Link

To acknowledge the importance of the inverse relationship between the two operations, the National Curriculum sets the expectation that, by the end of Year 2, children should *recognise and use the inverse relationship between addition and subtraction and use this to check calculations and solve missing number problems* (DfE, 2013, p.12).

Research Focus: Key Understandings in Mathematics Learning

Terezhina Nunes and Peter Bryant are part of a team of educationalists from the University of Oxford commissioned by the Nuffield Foundation to review the available research literature on how children learn mathematics. Their findings were published in 2009 in eight papers, together titled *Key Understandings in Mathematics Learning*. This section refers to the findings presented by Nunes and Bryant in Paper 2 of the series.

According to Nunes and Bryant (2009) the majority of five-year-olds appreciate that if three sweets are added to a set and then taken away again, the number of sweets in the set remains the same. Thus, even young children can understand that addition and subtraction in some sense 'undo' each other. However, they also suggest that children find it harder to work in the abstract when the numbers are not related specifically to a quantity of objects. Although children may use an intuitive understanding of the inverse nature of addition and subtraction when carrying out practical activities, it takes longer to formalise this understanding to a point where they can identify linked addition and subtraction facts such as $10 + 5 = 15$ and $15 - 5 = 10$.

In order to meet the expectations of the National Curriculum by Year 2, it will therefore be necessary for teachers to find strategies to bridge this gap between the practical and the abstract. One approach is to use resources and images to model the interaction between addition and subtraction and to link this explicitly to the related number facts.

Activity: Coat hanger and pegs

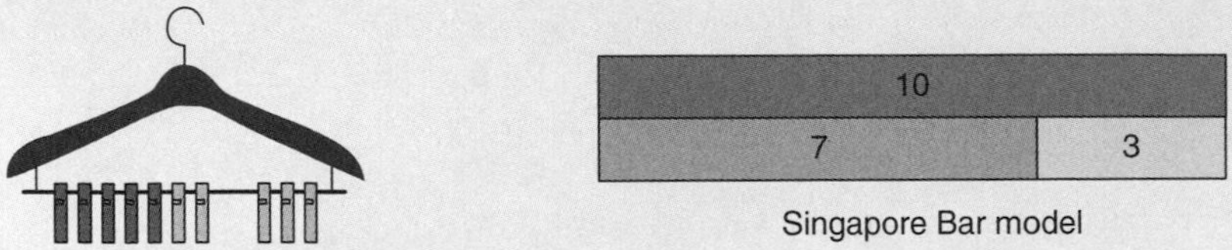

Singapore Bar model

Figure 4.4

Consider the coat hanger and pegs resource and the Singapore Bar model above. Write down the possible addition and subtraction number sentences they could represent. Reflect on how each model could be used to develop understanding of related addition and subtraction facts and consider advantages and disadvantages of each model.

Mental addition and subtraction: prerequisite knowledge, skills and understanding

Once children start to solve calculations involving two-digit and larger numbers, strategies that involve counting in ones will become inefficient and may lead to errors. Children will need to extend the range of calculation strategies they use beyond counting strategies. Gray (2008) calls this move from counting in ones towards more efficient approaches *compressing the counting process*. Mental calculation can involve many small steps. If a child takes significant time to consider and work through each of these small steps in turn, the calculation as a whole will become unwieldy and the child may become lost in the process. In order to become efficient when using mental methods children therefore need to build up a repertoire of knowledge, skills and understanding about numbers and arithmetical operations which they can draw on to carry out each small step in a calculation quickly. The activity below is intended to help you identify key elements of this repertoire of knowledge, skills and understanding.

Activity: Mental method

Work out this calculation using a mental method: 56 + 37. As you work, identify each step in your method. Reflect on the range of knowledge, skills and understanding you use.

There are many different approaches you may have taken to work out 56 + 37. However, most strategies will include several of the following elements:

(Continued)

(Continued)

- using understanding of arithmetical operations;

- counting in ones, tens, hundreds, etc.;

- recalling and using known facts;

- partitioning numbers in various ways;

- using understanding of place value, including to add (and subtract) multiples of tens, hundreds, etc.;

The knowledge, skills and understanding above constitute important prerequisite learning which children need to secure in order to move from counting strategies towards efficient mental strategies for addition and subtraction.

Curriculum Link

The National Curriculum reinforces the notion that providing children with opportunities to carry out addition and subtraction will not, on its own, be enough to promote efficient mental methods when it states that:

The principal focus of mathematics teaching in lower key stage 2 is to ensure that pupils become increasingly fluent with whole numbers and the four operations, including number facts and the concept of place value. This should ensure that pupils develop efficient written and mental methods and perform calculations accurately with increasingly large whole numbers.

(DfE, 2013, p.17)

In his article 'Mathematical Fluency', Askew (2009) specifies that the focus on developing fluency detailed in the National Curriculum does not imply a return to a 'drill and practice' pedagogy but is best achieved through regular, short but meaningful practice tasks which sit alongside rich problem-solving opportunities. An example he gives is 'Find 50', where children are presented with a set of specially chosen numbers and given a set time to find as many ways as they can to make the total 50. The nature of this activity encourages children to work strategically, for example using approximation to identify sensible combinations to try. Thus, alongside the rehearsal of facts and skills, an activity such as this can help children develop and extend their problem-solving strategies. Askew advocates that practice activities should be simple to set up and do; be done little and often; keep everyone focused on the maths; and help children see their progress.

Mental strategies for addition and subtraction and how to support them

Mental calculation forms an important part of the toolkit that will equip children to become flexible and efficient solvers of mathematical problems. Ian Thompson has written extensively about the development of calculation methods. In *Issues in Teaching Numeracy in Primary Schools* (2010, p.147) he suggests four important reasons for teaching mental methods.

- Most calculations in real life are done in the head rather than on paper.

- Mental work develops a sound number sense.

- Mental work develops problem-solving skills.

- Mental work promotes success in later written work.

Curriculum Link

National Curriculum aims and guidance for Key Stage 2 promote the development of mental and written calculation methods alongside each other. The expectation is that children will continue to develop and refine their mental calculation methods in all four operations throughout Key Stage 2. The National Curriculum does not, however, specify explicitly what range of mental strategies children might be expected to develop. Although some approaches could be described using widely accepted terminology such as 'partitioning' or 'bridging', these terms do not describe fixed strategies but instead flexible approaches that may be used in different ways by different children and may be combined within one calculation. It is also the case that children (and adults) may well devise idiosyncratic strategies for particular calculations. Haylock (2010, p.60) describes these informal non-standard calculation methods *where the method used is dependent on the particular numbers in the problem and the relationship between them* as *adhocarithms*.

Although it is not possible to provide a definitive list of addition and subtraction strategies, it may be helpful to consider some common approaches in order to get a feel for the range of strategies that children might usefully develop. We will also consider the kinds of learning activities teachers might provide and explore the role of the teacher in supporting children's developing mental calculation strategies. The next section of this chapter focuses on these areas.

Appreciating the range and variety of mental addition and subtraction strategies

The National Strategies booklet, *Teaching Children to Calculate Mentally* (DfE, 2010, p.26) identifies the following mental strategies for addition and subtraction:

- counting forwards and backwards;

- reordering;

- partitioning – using multiples of 10 and 100;

- partitioning – bridging through multiples of 10;

- partitioning – compensating (also often called 'rounding and adjusting');

- partitioning – using 'near' doubles;

- partitioning – bridging through numbers other than 10.

Anghileri (2006, p.6) considers instead two categories of mental addition and subtraction strategies: 'sequencing' methods and 'splitting' methods. Sequencing methods involve keeping one of the numbers in the calculation whole while separating the other number into suitable chunks to add or subtract. Splitting methods involve partitioning both numbers in the calculation into helpful chunks, often tens and units.

Sequencing method example:

$56 + 37 = 56 + 30 + 7$

$= 86 + 7$

$= 93$

Splitting method example:

$56 + 37 = 50 + 6 + 30 + 7$

$= 50 + 30 + 6 + 7$

$= 80 + 13$

$= 93$

Figure 4.5

Activity: Common calculation strategies

Think back to how you answered the calculation $56 + 37$. Reflect on whether you used any of the strategies listed in the National Strategies booklet (DfE, 2010) and whether your strategy was based on a 'sequencing' or a 'splitting' method.

Consider whether it would be useful to have access to lists of common calculation strategies such as those in *Teaching Children to Calculate Mentally* (DfE, 2010) to ensure that you recognise and promote use of a breadth of strategies within your future planning and teaching. Also reflect on the value of identifying different classifications of strategies such as sequencing versus splitting methods. This may be particularly helpful to identify possible next steps for children who are using inefficient methods or making repeated errors with a particular approach.

Using resources to promote conceptual understanding

Drews and Hansen (2007) suggest that mathematical resources have an important role to play in supporting children's mathematical thinking. Thoughtful use of manipulatives (structured resources) and models supports children in developing conceptual understanding of some of the approaches used in mental calculation. A widely used model is the hundred square where the numbers from 1 to 100 are arranged in a ten by ten grid starting in the top left corner. Thus, counting in tens involves moving vertically within a hundred square. Learning to count forwards and backwards in tens is an important early skill that supports many mental addition and subtraction strategies. Children may initially use a physical hundred square and keep track of the answer when they add or subtract tens by moving their finger vertically within the grid. The arrangement of the numbers in the grid reinforces the patterns that occur when we count in tens and repeated experience of such activities will enable children to predict answers without the need to physically handle the resource. Indeed, a power of many mathematical models is that, over time, they become tools for thinking in their own right.

Activity: Mental addition and subtraction calculations

Consider some of the manipulatives and models you have seen children use to support them in carrying out mental addition and subtraction calculations. Reflect on the way in which the resource supported the child's conceptual understanding and how this related to the structure of the manipulative or model.

Making jottings to record steps in mental calculations

One important, and sometimes misunderstood, aspect of mental calculation is that the calculations are not always completed 'in your head'. Trying to hold all the small steps involved in a calculation 'in your head' can put a strain on working memory and lead to children becoming 'lost' in a calculation. So, in order to become proficient at using mental methods for increasingly complex calculations it is important for children to develop the skill of recording the steps they are working through and the interim answers. Such recording may take many forms including number sentences, number lines and other diagrams. The fact that children are free to record steps in a way that makes sense to them is often recognised in the term 'jottings'. One of your roles when teaching mental calculation is to model 'jotting' and then support children in developing their own recording approaches. Worthington (2012, p.51) discusses evidence that suggests children's calculation methods become increasingly efficient as they integrate symbols and ways of recording they have been shown by adults and peers with their own personal notations.

Choosing, explaining and comparing methods

Activity: Subtraction calculations

Consider each subtraction calculation in turn. Look carefully at the numbers involved and decide on a mental strategy which you feel will be accurate and efficient:

$103 - 97$ $103 - 7$

After you have worked through the calculations, reflect on your choices. Consider which features of the numbers involved in each calculation affected your choice.

It is not only the size of numbers involved in a calculation that influences our choice of strategy but also the relationship between the numbers.

- For example, 103 and 97 are numbers that lie close together. Counting up from 97 to 103 can be completed in a few steps, particularly if known facts are used to 'bridge' on 100. Thus, one efficient approach to answering $103 - 97$ is to 'find the difference' between the two numbers by counting up from 97 to 103.

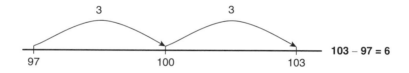

Figure 4.6

- Counting up from 7 to 103, however, is likely to involve more steps. Since 7 is a small number, one efficient strategy to work out $103 - 7$ is to start at 103 and count back 7. Again, this is particularly efficient if known facts are used to bridge on 100.

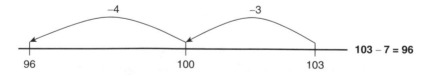

Figure 4.7

It is evident that some strategies may be more efficient than others for particular calculations because of the properties of the numbers involved. However, it is important to acknowledge that there is no 'right' choice of strategy for any particular calculation. While a sensible aim for all children is to build up a bank of calculation strategies that they are able to use confidently and accurately, the particular choice of strategy that children make will depend on many factors including: the facts they can recall at speed; their security and fluency with particular underpinning skills; their conceptual understanding of the operations they are using; and their personal preference.

One of the National Curriculum's stated aims is for children to develop conceptual understanding. The intention is not, therefore, for children to learn mental strategies and procedures by rote, but instead with deep understanding of the processes and steps involved. Sir Peter Williams' *Independent Review of Mathematics Teaching in Early Years Settings and Primary Schools* (2008, p.5) stressed *the critical importance of engaging children in discussing mathematics* and suggested that high quality discussion should underpin all mathematical learning activity. Encouraging children to describe their methods will involve them in clarifying key steps and selecting the appropriate mathematical language to make their strategies transparent to others.

Case Study: Subtraction strategies

Amanda is working with two Year 5 pupils, Jake and Beckie, who have been targeted for small-group intervention. She has decided to carry out an assessment activity to identify which subtraction strategies the children are able to use accurately. She has put a range of different subtraction calculations onto card and spread these out in front of the children.

Amanda: We are going to choose a calculation and see if we can explain how we worked it out. I will start.

I am going to choose 75 subtract 32.

So . . . I am going to start with 75 and then take away 32. This is too difficult to take away in one go. So I am going to partition it into 30 and 2 and take each part away in turn.

I can use counting in tens to work out 75 – 30. This gives me 45 (writes 75 – 30 = 45 onto her whiteboard).

The answer so far is 45 but I still need to take away the 2, so I need to work out 45 take away 2 which gives 43 (writes 45 – 2 = 43).

This means the answer is 43.

Jake, can you take a turn? Choose a calculation you feel confident with.

Jake: Right, 61 – 20. That is 41.

Amanda: How did you work that out? What did you do first?

Jake: Well I know that 61 is 60 and 1.

Amanda: So, you partitioned the 61 into 60 and 1. Okay. What did you do next?

Jake: I counted back in tens to work out 60 take away 20. That makes 40.

Amanda: Good, and then?

Jake: I put the 1 back on, so that is 41.

Describing the steps in calculations methods accurately is a challenging activity and it takes time to develop the ability to do this. One key teaching skill for you to develop is therefore the ability to model precise use of the language of calculation. In the case study above, Amanda models precise use of language through vocalising her thought processes as she chooses a strategy and works through stages to answer a particular calculation. Even after this example, Jake still struggles to explain his method so Amanda supports him by scaffolding his explanation. She offers prompts such as 'What did you do first?' to help Jake focus on the sequence of steps involved. She also reframes his explanation, using the term 'partition' to describe the process of breaking 61 into 60 and 1.

Being able to explain methods clearly to others, orally and through written recording, is an important skill in its own right but explaining a method also helps children develop a deep understanding of the steps and processes involved. Another important benefit of children explaining their calculation methods is that they will be able to compare and refine their approaches in the light of hearing the approaches taken by others. Discussion and comparison of calculation methods is therefore valuable in supporting children towards being able to choose an efficient method for any given calculation or problem.

Addressing errors and misconceptions

In addition to recognising the importance of children explaining and comparing strategies, the National Curriculum identifies another important role of teacher–pupil discussion – that of identifying and addressing any misconceptions the pupil may have. Where pupils make errors in calculations, this may be simply due to an arithmetical 'slip' such as misremembering a number fact. However, other errors may reveal more serious underlying misconceptions. Hansen (2014) considers the forming of misconceptions to be a natural part of children's conceptual development. She promotes a shift from planning lessons that avoid misconceptions towards actively planning lessons which address misconceptions by including challenge and talk to enable children to restructure their thinking.

Case Study: More subtraction calculations

Amanda continues to work with Jane and Beckie. She has deliberately included some of the types of subtraction calculations that can lead to common errors.

Amanda: You have worked out that 75 – 32 is 43. How did you work that out?

Jake: I used partitioning. 70 take away 30 is 40. 5 take away 2 is 3. So the answer is 43.

Amanda: Okay, can you have a look at another calculation now and see how you would answer this one? (82 – 46)

Jake: Right, well this will be the same. So, 80 take away 40 is 40 and 6 take away 2 is 4. So the answer is 44.

→

Amanda:	Beckie, you have worked out that 65 – 9 is 54. Can you tell me how you worked this out?
Beckie:	Well, 65 – 10 is 55. 9 is one less than 10. So the answer is one less. That makes 54.
	Amanda uses the rest of the session to address the misconceptions revealed. We are going to look at how she starts to do this with Jake:
Amanda:	So, you have said that 82 – 46 is 44 (writes this down). Let's look at this calculation with equipment (base ten apparatus). Show me how you would start.
	(Jake takes 8 ten sticks and 2 one cubes)
	What will you do now?
Jake:	I need to take away 46 (takes away 4 tens sticks and then stops).
Amanda:	You look like you are thinking really hard. What are you thinking?
Jake:	There are not enough ones to take away 6 . . . The answer isn't 44 . . .
Amanda:	Shall we jot down what you have done so far? (writes 82 – 40 = 42 on a whiteboard) What will you do next?
Jake:	I need to take away 6. So, I need to use a ten . . .

Amanda decides to encourage Jake to use a manipulative to show his thinking. This use of a physical resource promotes what is sometimes called 'cognitive dissonance', that is a situation where someone realises that they are trying to hold two contradictory beliefs at the same time. In this case Jake appreciates that, since he has correctly represented the 2 in 82 with 2 unit blocks and this does not give him enough units to instantly take away 6, his initial answer of 44 cannot be correct. Amanda's ongoing scaffolding, through using probing questions and prompts, enables Jake to move towards an appropriate strategy he can use to work out the answer correctly.

Activity: Subtraction misconceptions

Reflect on the explanations that Beckie gave for how she worked out 65 − 9. Consider what misconceptions are revealed. Think about what interactions and learning activities you would plan to help Beckie appreciate that her method contains an error and to overcome the misconception that underpins this error.

Developing written methods

One of the overall aims of the National Curriculum is that children leave primary school able to select appropriate calculation methods to solve a wide range of problems. This will involve calculating with large numbers so, alongside a range of mental strategies, children will need to develop efficient written methods or algorithms (often simply referred to as 'written methods'). These do not replace, but augment, mental methods which children also continue to use and extend.

Prerequisite knowledge and skills for written methods of addition and subtraction

The Ofsted *Good practice in primary mathematics report – summary: evidence from 20 successful schools* identified common features of practice in ten state primary schools and ten independent schools all of which had a strong track record of high achievement in mathematics. The report found that:

> *Understanding of place value, fluency in mental methods, and good recall of*
>
> *number facts such as multiplication tables and number bonds are considered by*
>
> *the schools to be essential precursors for learning traditional vertical algorithms*
>
> *(methods) for addition, subtraction, multiplication and division.*

(2011, p.2)

This reinforces Thompson's (2010) suggestion that secure understanding of mental mathematics is a precursor for success with written calculation methods; this includes insight into place value. However, Fuson (2004) identifies research that suggests many children do not demonstrate secure understanding of place value when using written algorithms. The most complex aspect of the algorithms for addition and subtraction is the 'exchange' between columns involved in 'carrying' for addition and 'decomposition' for subtraction. This exchange is based on a fundamental place value concept – that 10 units are equivalent to 1 ten, 10 tens are equivalent to 1 hundred and so on. If children's understanding of place value is not secure then it is unsurprising that this can lead to errors in written methods as documented by Hansen in *Children's Errors in Mathematics* (2011).

Activity: Common subtraction errors

Look at these examples of common subtraction errors. Try to work out what the child has done at each stage, and where and why the error has occurred. Identify misunderstandings or misconceptions the child demonstrates.

$$
\begin{array}{r}
6\,7\,2 \\
-1\,3\,5 \\
\hline
5\,4\,3
\end{array}
\qquad
\begin{array}{r}
{}^{2}\cancel{4}\,{}^{1}0\,{}^{1}0 \\
-1\,3\,7 \\
\hline
1\,7\,3
\end{array}
$$

The first example involves the same confusion as that demonstrated earlier by Jake. The minuend (start number) contains 2 units whereas the subtrahend (the number being subtracted) contains 5 units. There are many reasons why a child may write the partial answer 3 in the units column. The child may not appreciate that the answer to 2 − 5 is different to the answer to 5 − 2. Alternatively, they may simply have 'read' the calculation the wrong way round. Such misunderstandings may sometimes, inadvertently, be fuelled by imprecise teaching points such as 'Always take the smaller number away from the big one.'

The second example demonstrates confusion about the process of exchange. Here the child has realised that the partial calculation in the units column is 0 − 7. They have appreciated that they need to carry out exchange in order to provide sufficient units to take away 7. However, as there are no tens in the minuend they have taken 1 from the hundreds column and exchanged this for 10 units. Of course this is not mathematically valid as 1 hundred is not equivalent to 10 units.

Progressing towards written methods with understanding

In order to try to minimise errors like the ones above, it will be necessary to help children move towards use of written methods with a deep conceptual understanding of the underpinning mathematical processes involved. As with mental methods, the use of resources can be valuable in promoting this understanding. As part of its remit to provide professional development materials for teachers, the National Centre for Excellence in the Teaching of Mathematics (NCETM) produced a suite of video material to support implementation of the National Curriculum (see web address at the end of this chapter). These clips include examples of teachers and children using place value counters alongside their recording of written methods to develop understanding of the mathematical processes underpinning each step.

The National Strategies *Guidance paper – Calculation* (2007, p.3) reviewed the use of 'expanded methods' to support children towards using written methods with understanding. Expanded methods are described as *staging posts* that bridge the gap between mental methods and written algorithms (see Figure 4.8).

However, the 2007 *Guidance paper – Calculation* commented that, at that time, some schools included such a strong focus on the use of expanded methods that many children did not progress beyond these onto the formal written method and suggested this was inappropriate as *the great majority are entitled to learn how to use the most efficient methods* (p.3). This strong focus on efficient written methods is mirrored by the National Curriculum which states that by the end of Key Stage 2 children should be able to solve a wide range of problems that require efficient written and mental methods for addition and subtraction. While no specific mention is made of expanded methods, use of them is not proscribed. Thus the National Curriculum leaves to individual schools the decision about how to ensure their children progress smoothly and with understanding towards effective use of written addition and subtraction methods and to what extent this should include a focus on expanded methods as interim steps.

Expanded method for addition

```
      3 4 7
    + 1 2 5
    ───────
        1 2
        6 0
      4 0 0
    ───────
      4 7 2
    ───────
```

Formal written method for addition

```
      3 4 7
    + 1 2 5
    ───────
      4 7 2
    ───────
          1
```

Expanded method for subtraction

```
                    50
  365 →    300 + 60 + ¹5
− 127 →  − 100 + 20 +  7
         ────────────────
          200 + 30 +  8
         ────────────────
```

Formal written method for subtraction

```
      ⁵6¹
    3 ⁄0 5
  − 1 2 7
  ───────
    2 3 8
  ───────
```

Figure 4.8

Activity: Written methods of addition and subtraction

Reflect on the teaching and learning of written methods of addition and sub-traction you have seen in schools. Consider how use of resources such as base ten equipment or place value counters could promote understanding of the underly-ing processes. Reflect on the use of expanded methods as interim steps in the progression from mental approaches to written methods. Identify implications for your future practice.

Choosing appropriate addition and subtraction approaches

If schools are to meet the National Curriculum expectation that children leave primary school able to solve a range of problems using mental and written calculation methods, they will not only need to ensure that children develop accurate and efficient mental and written strategies but also that children are able to select an appropriate strategy to solve any particular problem. This will involve making discerning choices about whether a mental strategy or a written method is appropriate for any given calculation. As with the choice between mental strategies, this wider choice will vary from child to child depending on their level of confidence and facility with different methods.

Research Focus: Calculation strategies

Alison Borthwick and Micky Harcourt-Heath have carried out the same research activity four times over recent years. Their research analyses the range of strategies that a large group of Year 5 children choose to use to answer four particular calculations in a QCA paper and the success rates for each approach. The table below, taken from their 2012 article *What Can Year 5 Children do Now?*, shows the outcomes when 999 Year 5 children answered the subtraction: 317–180.

Subtraction

69% correct/31%incorrect

317–180	Number Correct	Number Incorrect	Percentage Correct	Percentage Incorrect
Not attempted		11		
Standard Algorithm – decomposition	106	71	60%	40%
Standard Algorithm – equal addition	0	2	0%	100%
Number Line	484	70	87%	13%
Negative Number	13	5	72%	28%
Counting Up	20	65	24%	76%
Counting Back	16	1	94%	6%
Answer only	28	9	76%	24%
Other	24	74	24%	76%
Totals	691	308	69%	31%

Table 4.1: Results from 999 children for subtraction question.

Activity: Relative accuracy rates

Look at the number of children choosing each approach and the relative accuracy rates. Compare this with your own school experience. Consider whether the research shows the kinds of results you would expect or whether there are some surprises. Consider also the possible implications of these results for your future teaching of subtraction methods.

There are many interesting reflections which might be prompted by Borthwick and Harcourt-Heath's (2012) data. Out of approximately 1000 pupils, under 200 chose to use a written method algorithm to work out 317 − 180. About 60 per cent of these children obtained the correct answer, compared to 87 per cent of the much bigger group who used a number line. Such findings would appear to reinforce the value of

(Continued)

(Continued)

children maintaining a strong focus on developing and using mental methods throughout Key Stage 2 and the importance of helping children to make informed choices about the most appropriate method based on the particular numbers involved in a calculation or problem. In reviewing outcomes, Borthwick and Harcourt-Heath comment that some children used partitioning of both numbers incorrectly for subtraction, reinforcing the suggestion in the earlier case study that 'sequencing' methods appear to be more reliable for mental subtraction than 'splitting' methods.

Opportunities for using and applying addition and subtraction and connecting learning to real life

The Ofsted *Good practice in primary mathematics report – summary: evidence from 20 successful schools* states that:

> *Pupils' confidence, fluency and versatility are nurtured through a strong emphasis on problem solving as an integral part of learning within each topic.*

(2011, p.3)

This suggests that when children learn about addition and subtraction, their learning will be enriched by the provision of regular opportunities to apply their developing calculation strategies within problems and other contexts.

Learning about addition and subtraction through solving problems and puzzles

Many teachers assume that 'problem solving' in the context of calculation refers to solving 'word problems'. Askew (2003, p.82) suggests that solving word problems involves three steps: First children translate the problem into a mathematical model. Next they identify and work through any calculations they need to do in order to solve this mathematical model. Finally they reinterpret the solution in terms of the original problem. It is important that children have experience of solving word problems in this way. These experiences help them to develop insight into the kinds of scenarios that may be represented by the operations of addition and subtraction and this in turn will extend their understanding of the mathematical operations. This can further be developed by asking children to construct their own word problems, which provides an excellent vehicle to deepen their understanding of operations and allows teachers to assess understanding and identify and address any misconceptions.

However, word problems are not the only type of problem that provides valuable opportunities to extend children's insight into addition and subtraction. Exploring patterns within addition and subtraction calculations, problems and puzzles allows children to make and test predictions and can lead towards their making and justifying generalisations. Such opportunities to consider what is known about addition and subtraction and to use known facts and ideas to make predictions and to explain and apply relationships provide rich opportunities for promoting and developing mathematical reasoning. The mathematical thinking involved in such activities will also enrich children's calculation skills and understanding of the operations of addition and subtraction.

Activity: Reasoning and understanding about addition and subtraction

Work through the following problems and consider how each problem could be used to promote reasoning and understanding about addition and subtraction:

Problem 1: Number pyramids

The number in each brick is the total of the numbers in the two bricks underneath it (apart from the bottom row). If the numbers 3, 1 and 5 are placed in the bottom row as shown, the top brick contains the number 10. Find other combinations on the bottom row that will give the number 10 at the top.

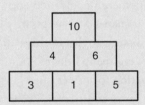

Figure 4.9

Problem 2: Subtraction gap calculation

Place a digit in each box to make the calculation correct.

Find as many different ways to complete the calculation as you can. What do you notice?

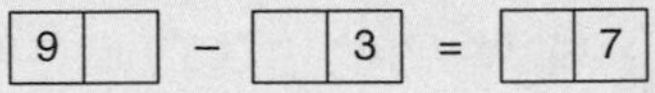

$$9\ \square\ -\ \square\ 3\ =\ \square\ 7$$

Figure 4.10

Problem 3: Hundred square diagonal totals

Choose any 2 by 2 square from a hundred grid. Find the totals of the pairs of numbers in each diagonal.

(Continued)

For example:

67	68
77	78

Figure 4.11

$67 + 78 = ?$ $77 + 68 = ?$

Try other examples.

What do you notice? Why does this happen?

Opportunities to apply addition and subtraction across the mathematics curriculum, the wider curriculum and in real life

Opportunities to rehearse, extend and apply addition and subtraction skills are by no means restricted to units of work involving calculation. The National Curriculum states that children should be encouraged to make connections across the curriculum. Many aspects of the mathematics curriculum provide meaningful contexts within which children will need to apply their emerging addition and subtraction skills. For example, exploring the perimeters of linear shapes will necessarily involve addition of lengths. Using angle properties to find missing angles in shape diagrams will involve addition and subtraction of angles. Following many lines of enquiry involving handling data will involve addition and subtraction to answer questions such as 'How many more ...?' Measures activities frequently involve addition and subtraction, for example adding prices of individual items to work out the total cost or finding the difference between a start and end time to find the duration of an event. Addition and subtraction of time can provide particular challenges to children as the units of time are not decimal.

The National Curriculum sets the expectation that teachers should develop pupils' mathematical fluency through using and applying mathematics across the primary curriculum. Science experiments and investigations involve taking measurements to collect data and then analysing this data. Addition and subtraction are frequently needed to support this analysis, for example to calculate the changes in a particular measure over time. All aspects of the primary curriculum and many cross-curricular topics provide a wealth of opportunities to carry out contextualised calculation.

In order to help children appreciate how fundamental the operations of addition and subtraction are to their everyday lives, it would seem important that teachers take opportunities to solve real-life problems that involve addition and subtraction. There are many situations teachers can exploit to give children opportunities to apply their addition and subtraction skills to answer important questions and explore relevant and motivating lines of enquiry. For example, teachers can ask children to work out the budget for a school trip or to find out how much money can be saved by reducing waste in school. Applying addition and subtraction skills across the mathematics curriculum and wider school curriculum will help children towards an understanding that, as the National Curriculum suggests, *a high-quality mathematics education ... provides a foundation for understanding the world* (DfE, 2013, p.3).

Learning Outcomes Review

In this chapter you have considered some of the different conceptions of addition and subtraction, the relationship between them and some of the ways in which you could help children to understand them. You have also considered ways in which mental addition and subtraction strategies can be developed through jottings into more formal written methods of calculation. You have reflected on some of the knowledge that children need in order to be able to perform written addition and subtraction calculations and have considered some of the key misconceptions that you should be aware of as you come to teach these skills. Finally, the chapter has considered ways in which an understanding of addition and subtraction might be developed through other areas of the curriculum.

Self-assessment questions

1. Reflecting on your own practice, what are the key areas for you to develop in your teaching of addition and subtraction?
2. What strategies could you use to help incorporate opportunities for reasoning into your teaching of addition and subtraction?

Useful websites

www.ncetm.org.uk/resources/40529 National Centre for Excellence in the Teaching of Mathematics (NCETM) video material to support the implementation of the National Curriculum.

References

Anghileri, J. (2006) *Teaching Number Sense*. London: Continuum International Publishing Group.

Askew, M. (2003) Word Problems: Cinderellas or wicked witches? in Thompson, I. (ed.) *Enhancing Primary Mathematics Teaching*. Maidenhead: Open University Press.

Askew, M. (2009) *Mathematical Fluency*. Available at: www.mikeaskew.net/page3/page2/page2.html (accessed 25/07/14).

Boaler, J. (2010) *The Elephant in the Classroom: Helping Children Learn and Love Maths.* London: Souvenir Press Limited.

Borthwick, A. and Harcourt-Heath, M. (2012) Calculating: What can Year 5 children do now? in Smith, C. (ed.) *Proceedings of the British Society for Research into Learning Mathematics*, 32(3), November 2012. Available at: www.bsrlm.org.uk/IPs/ip32-3/ BSRLM-IP-32-3-05.pdf (accessed 25/07/14).

DfE (2010) *Teaching Children to Calculate Mentally.* Available at http://dera.ioe. ac.uk/778/ (accessed 25/07/14).

DfE (2013) *National Curriculum in England: Mathematics programmes of study: key stages 1 and 2.* Available at: www.gov.uk/government/publications/national-curriculum-in-england-mathematics-programmes-of-study/national-curriculum-in-england-mathematics-programmes-of-study (accessed 25/07/14).

Drews, D. and Hansen, A. (2007) *Using Resources to Support Mathematical Thinking.* London: Learning Matters SAGE.

Fuson, K. (2004) Pre-K to grade 2 goals and standards: achieving 21st-century mastery for all, in Clements, D.H., Sarama, J. and DiBiase, A. (eds) *Engaging Young Children in Mathematics: Standards for Early Childhood Mathematics Education.* Mahwah, NJ: Larence Erlbaum Associates.

Gray, E. (2008) Compressing the Counting Process: strength from the flexible interpretations of symbols, in Thompson, I. (ed.) *Teaching and Learning Early Number.* Maidenhead: Open University Press. pp.82–93.

Hansen, A. (2014) *Children's Errors in Mathematics*, 3rd edition. London: Learning Matters SAGE.

Haylock, D. (2010) *Mathematics Explained for Primary Teachers.* London: SAGE.

National Strategies (2007) *Guidance paper – Calculation.* Available at: www. nationalstemcentre.org.uk/elibrary/resource/4556/guidance-paper-calculation (accessed 25/07/14).

Nunes, T. and Bryant, P. (2009) *Key Understanding in Mathematics Learning – Paper 2: Understanding extensive quantities and whole numbers.* London: The Nuffield Foundation.

Ofsted (2011) *Good Practice in Primary Mathematics Report – summary: evidence from 20 successful schools.* Manchester: Ofsted. Available at: www.ofsted.gov.uk/resources/good-practice-primary-mathematics-evidence-20-successful-schools (accessed 25/07/14).

Thompson, I. (ed.) (2010) *Issues in Teaching Numeracy in Primary Schools.* Maidenhead: Open University Press.

Williams, P. (2008) *Independent Review of Mathematics Teaching in Early Years Settings and Primary Schools.* Nottingham: DCSF Publications.

Worthington, M. (2012) Children Becoming Expert Symbol Users, in McAteer, M. (ed.) *Improving Primary Mathematics Teaching and Learning.* Maidenhead: Open University Press. pp.39–57.

5 Multiplication and division

Balbir Ahir

Learning outcomes

By reading this chapter you will develop:

- an understanding of the concepts related to multiplication and division;
- an awareness of the progression for multiplication and division;
- an awareness of the different informal and formal methods to solve multiplication and division calculations.

TEACHERS' STANDARDS

2. Promote good progress and outcomes by pupils
3. Demonstrate good subject and curriculum knowledge
4. Plan and teach well-structured lessons

Introduction

Good planning is the key to good mathematics teaching (and it is common knowledge that there is never enough time in teaching). While a good plan will not guarantee a good lesson, poor or non-existent planning will almost certainly guarantee a poor lesson.

Being proficient in multiplication and division is fundamental for children to be competent mathematicians. Over the past 15 years the teaching of multiplication and division methods has been under scrutiny. At a national, local and school level the introduction of the National Numeracy Strategy (NNS) (DfEE, 1999) and then later the revised Primary National Strategy (PNS) (DfES, 2006) frameworks brought with them detailed content and policies with supporting materials (DfE, 2010; DSCF, 2008) demonstrating the progression of multiplication and division from mental methods to informal written methods, then moving on to more 'efficient or 'traditional' methods (Ofsted, 2011; Benson, 2014; Murphy, 2004). In the Primary National Curriculum increased emphasis is placed on children using 'efficient methods'. As Benson (2014) indicates, efficiency can be achieved in many ways and can include a *range of approaches: formal and informal, mental and written, electronic and non-electronic* (p.31).

Research Focus

Ofsted (2011) examined the work of 20 schools with a high level of mathematical achievement. The focus in mathematics was on the effective learning and teaching of arithmetic which encompassed both mental and traditional methods across the four operations. The key teaching approaches that supported conceptual understanding were as follows:

- the importance of practical activities, using models and images to develop an understanding of mental methods, structures and relationships in number;

- correct mathematical language;

- understanding of place value, number facts such as multiplication and division facts and number bonds;

- understanding of the inverse operation which should be taught alongside the corresponding operation;

- developing an understanding of calculation across the mathematics curriculum, particularly through problem solving;

- addressing children's errors and misconceptions;

- moving quickly towards more efficient methods;

- a clear school calculation policy and guidance.

The above are underpinned by good subject and pedagogical knowledge in mathematics.

The aim of this chapter is to identify some key concepts in the development of a secure knowledge and understanding of multiplication and division. The above findings place a great emphasis on the efficiency of the calculation method but less on a deep understanding of the method. Some children may not be at the stage of performing the multiplication or division calculation, with understanding, with the least number of steps. Exploring some of the 'interim' methods towards efficient, traditional methods will be valuable stepping stones for many children's learning. Misconceptions, use of language as well as how multiplication and division can be communicated through models and images will be addressed throughout the chapter.

What do we mean by multiplication and division?

Children find multiplication and division difficult; this is partially due to not having a clear understanding of what is meant by multiplication and division

(Anghileri, 2000b). Multiplication is about replication; Julie Anghileri (2000a) refers to the representation of multiplication as a *two dimensional operation*. The first input in a multiplication number sentence represents the size of a set and the second input represents the number of replications of that set.

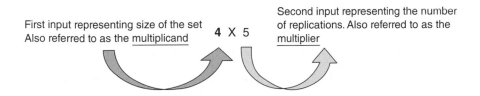

I have four oranges in a pack (the size of the set), I have five packs of oranges (number of replications of the first set, also thought of as equal grouping). How many oranges altogether? The terminology used to describe multiplication includes multiplicand, multiplier, product or multiple and the symbol x is used to represent the calculation.

Of all the four number operations, division is the one that most children are least confident with but it is also one that many teachers are less confident in teaching. This is partly due to the high level of conceptual understanding required to do division (Cotton, 2010; Thompson, 2005; Anghileri, 2000b) but also *this higher level concept is reliant on children's understanding of addition, subtraction and multiplication* (Back, 2005, p.19).

The terminology used to describe division includes dividend, divisor and quotient and the symbol ÷ is used to represent the calculation as a division: 15 ÷ 3.

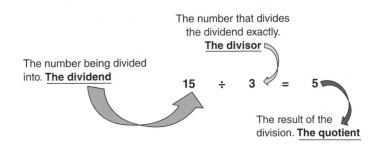

Division can also be represented as $3\overline{)15}$, which is often used in a more formal written method. What may cause misconceptions or confusion is the fact that the numbers are in the reverse order in the later representation for division compared to the first one (Thompson, 2005).

When fostering a conceptual understanding of multiplication and division it is important that a variety of representational systems are shared, discussed and understood by children (Harris and Barmby, 2007; Miller and Hudson, 2006). Writing mathematical statements using the multiplication (×), division (÷) and equals (=) signs is introduced in Year 2 in the National Curriculum. The calculations 4 x 5 or 15 ÷ 3 will have very little meaning for children unless they are put within a context. The introduction of multiplication and division needs to be carried out using a range of practical experiences; talking about and describing patterns and calculations; using the appropriate language; manipulating visual representations, as well as applying these to real-life problems and objects and mathematical equipment.

Curriculum Link

The significance of using and applying multiplication and division, in the context of problem solving and with the use of models and images to assist that understanding, is emphasised and reinforced across all the year groups in the National Curriculum.

Year 1	*solve one-step problems involving multiplication and division, by calculating the answer using concrete objects, pictorial representations and arrays with the support of the teacher* (DfE, 2013, p.8)
Year 2	*solve problems involving multiplication and division, using materials, arrays, repeated addition, mental methods, and multiplication and division facts, including problems in contexts* (DfE, 2013, p.13)
Year 3	*solve problems, including missing number problems, involving multiplication and division, including positive integer scaling problems and correspondence problems in which n objects are connected to m objects* (DfE, 2013, p.19)
Year 4	*solve problems involving multiplying and adding, including using the distributive law to multiply two digit numbers by one digit, integer scaling problems and harder correspondence problems such as n objects are connected to m objects* (DfE, 2013, p.25)
Year 5	*solve problems involving addition, subtraction, multiplication and division and a combination of these, including understanding the meaning of the equals sign* *solve problems involving multiplication and division, including scaling by simple fractions and problems involving simple rates* (DfE, 2013, p.33)
Year 6	*solve addition and subtraction multi-step problems in contexts, deciding which operations and methods to use and why* (DfE, 2013, p.39)

Harris and Barmby (2007) highlight that different representations emphasise different aspects of a concept. The development of a concept comes with providing a range of representations and allowing children to move both within and between them.

The concept that multiplication is repeated addition is introduced to develop a basic understanding of multiplication. Both the number line or number track provide a visual model and an image of multiplication as repeated addition 4 x 5 = 4 + 4 + 4 + 4 + 4 = 20; four repeated five times.

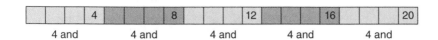

4 and   4 and   4 and   4 and   4 and

Images of sets and replications should be related to real-life examples such as:

2 x   pairs of hands, feet, ears, eyes, pockets, shoes, bicycle wheels

3 x   three sides to a triangle, three-legged stool, tricycle

4 x   wheels on cars, four sides to a square, legs on an animal

5 x   fingers on hands or toes on feet. I have five fingers on one hand – how many fingers on two hands; three hands; four hands …? (5 + 5 + 5 …) (5, 10, 15 …)

6 x   insects' legs, eggs in a pack

7 x   seven days of the week

8 x   spiders' legs

10 x   'digits' on both hands or both feet

The understanding of multiplication as sets or lots of is further extended and represented as arrays. Arrays describe multiplication in rows and columns, 4 rows x 5 columns or 5 rows x 4 columns. Getting children to look for multiplication as arrays and relate to real-life images such as eggs in a box, pages of stamps and stickers, or floor tiles and bricks would be a valuable starting point (Haylock and Coburn, 2008). The image of arrays can become a powerful visual model to gain a better understanding of the written strategy of 'grid multiplication', which relies on a visualisation of a blank grid which progresses onto a more formal method of long multiplication (Harris and Barmby, 2007).

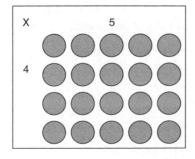

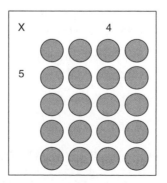

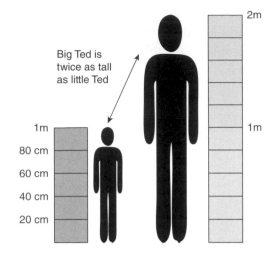

Big Ted is twice as tall as little Ted

Another structure associated with multiplication is scaling by a factor frequently used in everyday life in the context of comparing quantities or measurements. The key language used within this structure is times, as many, scale factor and so many times bigger related to enlargement. At primary level this would be increasing by a factor of 2 (doubling) or twice as many. For example, Beth has four cards and Sharon has twice as many. How many cards does Sharon have? It also relates to the idea of rate, to percentage increases, and to scale drawings. This discussion is developed further in Chapter 6.

Case Study: Year 2 – Solving problems involving multiplication and division, using materials, arrays, repeated addition

Peter, a student teacher on his final placement in Year 2, is introducing his class to multiplication and visually representing the multiplication in different ways. He has set up his classroom so that images and 3-D objects reflect multiplication. He took pictures of real-life images such as equal sets of children lining up in the playground; piles of books on a shelf; equal numbers of crayons in a pot; rows of counters.

He started the lesson with one of the images: six children standing in a line – how many children are there in two lines? In talk partners he encouraged children to:

- discuss and talk about the image mathematically, so they had to use mathematical vocabulary;

- relate it to a calculation;

- think of a word problem;

- think about a mathematical way to represent the image.

Children also had whiteboards to jot down thoughts. He highlighted responses which included the language pairs: twos, even numbers, rows, counting in twos and doubling. He then asked them to express the image as a number sentence and to find more than one way to do it. Responses included:

- 6 + 6 = 12

- 2 + 2 + 2 + 2 + 2 + 2 = 12

Peter took the responses and modelled repeated addition on the number line.

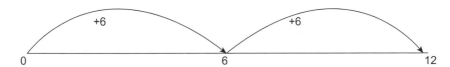

He then asked children to model: two children standing in a line – how many children are there in six lines? as a number sentence, 2+2+2+2+2+2, and show it on the number line.

For the main activity he asked children to work in groups on big paper, using the images provided to:

- talk mathematically about the image;

- think of a word problem;

- relate it to a maths calculation (repeated addition and multiplication);

- think about a mathematical way to represent it.

He then went back to the image of 6 children standing in 2 lines, the number line and repeated addition and expressed the image as a multiplication modelling 6 children x 2 rows = 6 x 2 = 12, and drew an array to show 6 x 2. Children were asked to model back to him 2 children in 6 rows 2 + 2 + 2 + 2 + 2 + 2 and to say the number sentence as a multiplication: 2 children x 6 rows. He emphasised that the order of the numbers being multiplied did not matter in terms of the answer, although the different order represented different situations. For the main teaching and learning activity children were encouraged to express the image given to them and images they spot around the classroom as a multiplication emphasising the commutative property. They also had counters and cubes to build the image as an array.

Peter did an extended 'review and next steps to learning' to develop the concept of multiplication as repeated addition, reinforcing the commutative property through the rectangular representation for multiplication. He also went back to 2 x 6 = 12 to ask children to think about 12 ÷ 2 = 6 for the next lesson.

There are two structures, or ways of conceptualising division. It is important that children are exposed to practical situations that mirror both of them. The first structure is that of 'sharing based on a 1:1 correspondence model: 15 ÷ 3 = 5 is interpreted as 15 shared equally between three groups; how many in each group? 5.

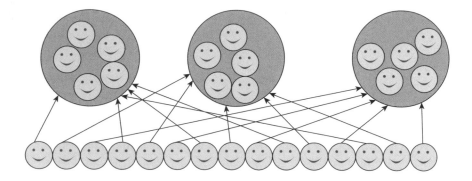

The second structure, inverse of multiplication, is based on grouping according to the divisor: 15 ÷ 3 = 5 is interpreted as 15 divided into groups of 3 and the answer is given by the number of groups. The grouping structure involves repeatedly subtracting the divisor from the dividend until there is nothing left or the remainder is too small to subtract the divisor again. How many groups of 3 go into 15 (15 ÷ 3), which as a multiplication is expressed as 3 x ? = 15 (3, 6, 9, 12, *15*; 5 lots of 3 make 15).

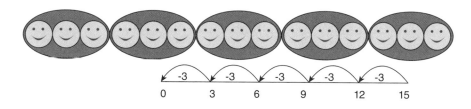

The later structure for division relates to the knowledge and understanding that multiplication and division are linked. The equal sharing structure has its limitations. The divisor must be a whole number, for example 15 ÷ 0.3 would be difficult to work out using the equal sharing as the number of items which the dividend is being shared by is not a whole number. In the grouping structure you can use a number line and subtract 0.3 from 15 or even subtract multiples of 0.3 from 15 (10 groups of 0.3 is 3, so 50 groups of 0.3 is 15 = 50 x 0.3 = 15).

The visual and verbal representation of both multiplication and division are areas for possible confusion. In multiplication the symbol x is also referred to as 'lots of' or 'groups of' and in the context of the above multiplication would be verbalised as 5 lots of 4 (5 representing the number of replications and 4 would be the size of the set), which is the reverse order to the symbolic representation (Haylock, 2010). The complications of relating the vocabulary to symbols to visualise the representation indicate that the connections are not always easy to make. The understanding that multiplication has commutative properties may alleviate some of the confusion, so 4 x 5 would refer to 4 lots of 5 (5 + 5 + 5 + 5), which is equal to 5 lots of 4 (4 + 4 + 4 + 4 + 4). The order of the numbers in a multiplication makes no difference to the outcome/product and in this context it is an important teaching point in the understanding of multiplication. Haylock notes that the *meaning of the symbol is determined by how it is used* and that *one symbol can have more than one meaning* (2014, p.136). The above understanding allows you to choose which of the two numbers in a multiplication will be the multiplier and multiplicand.

In division the verbal calculation 15 divided by 3 or 15 shared by 3 relates well to the symbolic representation of $15 \div 3$. However, when discussing division as grouping, the verbalisation of that calculation can also be: how many groups of 3 are there in 15? Division is not commutative and some children will write $3 \div 15$ for how many groups of 3 go into 15, which is mathematically incorrect. Using and emphasising the correct language and relating it to models and images of multiplication and division will support teachers' explanations as well as children's understanding (Hansen and Ahir, 2014).

Properties of multiplication and division

The other important aspects of multiplication are the commutative and associative properties, and for both operations, the distributive property. Having a secure understanding of these properties provides a good basis for developing mental calculations.

- As mentioned earlier, the commutative property of multiplication states that the order of the multiplicand and multiplier does not change the product, $4 \times 5 = 5 \times 4$ or $a \times b = b \times a$. The understanding of the commutative property allows children to learn multiplication facts more efficiently. The National Curriculum introduces the concept of the commutative property for multiplication in Year 2. It also highlights the misconception that some children may have in applying it to division calculations as being a key objective to communicate to children.

- The associative property of multiplication allows the order of the multiplication to be switched. For example: $4 \times 2 \times 5 = (2 \times 5) \times 4$, multiply 2×5 first to get 10 and then multiply by 4 to get 40. This property reinforces the mental strategies where *numbers are factorised*, in a calculation, *before multiplying them* (Taylor and Harris, 2014, p.159), for example $24 \times 5 = 12 \times 2 \times 5 =$ associate the 2 with the 5 first (2×5) to get 10, then multiply 10 by 12 to get 120.

- The distributive property of multiplication and division allow the calculation to be partitioned to make it easier to multiply or divide smaller groups and then recombine. The model of an array is a valuable image when explaining the distributive property (Harris and Barmby, 2007). For multiplication the multiplicand can be partitioned, for example for 24×5 this could be $20 + 4$ and then each part is multiplied by 5; $(20 \times 5) + (4 \times 5) = 100 + 20 = 120$. For division the dividend is often partitioned into multiples of the divisor, for example $132 \div 6 = (60 \div 6) + (60 \div 6) + (12 \div 6)$ or $(120 \div 6) + (12 \div 6) = 20 + 2 = 22$. In division only the dividend can be partitioned whereas in multiplication either the multiplicand or the multiplier can be partitioned ($24 \times 5 = (24 \times 2) + (24 \times 2) + (24 \times 1) = 48 + 48 + 24 = 120$).

Activity

Below are a number of word problems related to division and multiplication. For each word problem identify the following:

- the model/image you would use to describe it;

- the understanding of multiplication and division you would expect children to have;

- any links to the concepts, structures and properties for multiplication and division mentioned above.

1. I have 120 children going on a school trip to the museum. One coach seats 40 children. How many coaches will I need?

2. What is the price of 4 CDs at £4.50 each?

3. In a school there are seven classes with 30 children in each. Each child has two pencils as a Christmas present from the head teacher. How many pencils does the head teacher need to buy?

4. I have 28 children in my class. How many groups of four can I have working together on a maths puzzle?

5. Tom bakes eight cakes. He has 40 chocolate buttons. How many chocolate buttons can he put on each cake?

Mental methods for multiplication and division

Confidence and understanding of a range of mental methods to solve multiplication and division calculations is valuable for everyday mathematics. There is no single 'correct' mental method for a given calculation (see Chapter 4 for a detailed discussion). Murphy (2004) argues that informal, individual approaches demonstrate conceptual understanding of multiplication and division, which can be encouraged and refined through discussion and scaffolding of children's ideas. The introduction of the NNS placed great emphasis on the *potential and power of mental calculation strategies* (Benson, 2014, p.31) and although some strategies may not be taught and are child initiated, some mental methods would need to be taught so that all children have access to them.

Haylock (2010) highlights a number of prerequisites for children to be competent at developing and refining mental calculation methods. The first is that all approaches to multiplication and division calculations rely on having a secure understanding and rapid recall of number facts and derived facts which allow children to manipulate numbers mentally (Benson, 2014).

Curriculum Link

In the National Curriculum the recall of number facts progresses across the primary mathematics programmes of study as follows.

Year 2	recall and use multiplication and division facts for the 2, 5 and 10 multiplication tables, including recognising odd and even numbers (DfE, 2013, p.13)
Year 3	recall and use multiplication and division facts for the 3, 4 and 8 multiplication tables (DfE, 2013, p.19)
Year 4	recall multiplication and division facts for multiplication tables up to 12×12 (DfE, 2013, p.25)
Year 5	identify multiples and factors, including finding all factor pairs of a number, and common factors of two numbers

know and use the vocabulary of prime numbers, prime factors and composite (non prime) numbers

establish whether a number up to 100 is prime and recall prime numbers up to 19

multiply and divide whole numbers and those involving decimals by 10, 100 and 1000 (DfE, 2013, p.32) |
| Year 6 | identify common factors, common multiples and prime numbers (DfE, 2013, p.39) |

Below are some strategies that can be shared with children across the years in supporting the recall of multiplication and division facts. Providing a strategic approach to the learning of multiplication and division facts can help *children to make connections and reduces the burden on their memory* (Askew, 2009, p.29).

- 2, 4 and 8 times tables can be accessed using children's knowledge of doubles and facility with doubling. Multiplication by 4 involves doubling and then doubling again, etc.

- 10 times table: place value (move the digits one place value to the left, 4 x 10 = 40; know that multiples of 10 end in 0).

- 5 times table: counting in 5s; multiplying by 10 and then halving; halving the 10 times table (5, 10, 15, 20, 25 ... know that multiples of 5 end in 0 and 5).

- 3 times table: counting in 3s (3, 6, 9, 12 ...).

- 6 times table: double the 3 times table (4 x 3 = 12 so 4 x 6 = 24; there is a lot of mathematical reasoning involved in these processes).

- 7 times table: commutativity (much of the 7 times table can be derived from the facts that the children have already learned).

Other strategies include:

- visual representations of the multiplication square;

- apply the property that multiplication is commutative, 4 x 8 is the same as 8 x 4, and that it is easier to work out 8 x 4 as it results in less counting 8, 16, 24, 32 than 4 x 8 (4, 8, 12, 16, 20, 24, 28, 32);

- emphasise the inverse operation and trio of number facts to derive other facts: 8 x 4 = 32, so 32 ÷ 4 = 8 and 32 ÷ 8 = 4;

- develop auditory approaches that include chanting, counting forwards and backwards, looking for patterns in the count 10, 20, 30, 40 ... what other numbers will be in the 10 x table?

- develop a range of strategies and ideas for testing multiplication facts such as follow me/loop cards, target boards, bingo, prepared cards.

Case Study: Year 4 – probe multiplication test

Milly, the Year 4 class teacher, uses a range of strategies to support children in learning, remembering and recalling number facts across all four number operations. For multiplication she carries out a multiplication test regularly, as one of the activities. To combat the fact that children are at different stages in learning multiplication facts she has devised a probe card (see Figure 5.1) Most children have a target of completing 25 multiplications that they are working on, in a minute. They have to meet the target three times before they can move onto the next multiplication of their choice. Children write the answers on a tracing paper which sits over the card so that the card could be used over and over again. If children are practising their 2 times table they would write the answers 12, 6, 18, etc. on the top line; if they are practising their 6 times table they would write the answers 36, 18, 54, etc. on the top line.

Name						
Tick the times table achieved – x2, x3, x4, x5, x6, x7, x8, x9, x10						
Target 25 to achieve in 1 minute						
x6	x3	x9	x2	x5	x8	x1
x4	x7	x10	x1	x6	x9	x5
x2	x3	x8	x9	x10	x6	x4
x6	x5	x9	x10	x7	x2	x3
x8	x10	x3	x4	x3	x1	x5

Figure 5.1 Multiplication 'probe card'

Some children complete this test orally. This probe is also sent home and shared with parents.

The other prerequisites for a comprehensive understanding of mental calculation methods are having knowledge of place value and knowing how to use informal jottings or recordings. A secure combination of the above allows freedom and flexibility to select a range of informal, mental strategies (Robinson and LeFevre, 2012).

When using mental methods to solve 28 x 4, some possibilities include the following.

Use factors of 4 (2 x 2) to multiply by 2 or to double and double again: (28 x 2) x 2 = 112.

> **Method 1: Use of factors**
>
> 28 X 4 =
>
> 28 x 2 = double 28 to get 56.
>
> 56 x 2 = double 56 to get 112.

This strategy is most effective with factorising multiples in the 2, 5 and 10 times tables (Haylock, 2010). Links to the National Curriculum include for Year 3 *develop efficient mental methods, for example ... associativity* (DfE, 2013, p.20) and for Year 4 *recognise and use factor pairs ... in mental calculations* (DfE, 2013, p.25).

Partition 28 into 20 + 8 and multiply each part by 4, then add the partial products 80 + 32 to get the answer. This strategy applies the distributive property, which gives children the freedom to partition the calculation in any way. Links to the National Curriculum include for Year 4 *use place value, known and derived facts to multiply and divide mentally* (DfE, 2013, p.25), for example: use known facts 2 x 4 = 8 to work out derived facts 20 x 4 = 80.

> **Method 2: Partition and recombine**
>
> 28 X 4 =
>
> (20 x 4) + (8 x 4) =
>
> 80 + 32 = 112

Compensate by rounding 28 to the nearest multiple of 10 which is 30, working out 30 x 4 then subtracting 2 lots of 4 as you have over compensated in 30 x 4. Links to the National Curriculum include in Year 6 *perform mental calculations* (DfE, 2013, p.39).

> **Method 3: Compensation**
>
> 28 X 4 =
>
> (30 x 4) – (2 x 4) =
>
> 120 – 8 = 112

When using mental methods to solve 132 ÷ 6, some possibilities include the following.

The mental strategy for division relies on partitioning the dividend according to the divisor and an understanding of the application of the distributive law. Ian Thompson (2008b) highlights a number of misconceptions and errors in this mental method. In multiplication distributivity is both left and right (for example, 28 x 4 = (20 x 4) + (8 x 4); it can also be

> **Method 1: Partition and recombine**
>
> 132 ÷ 6
>
> (120 ÷ 6) + (12 ÷ 6) =
>
> 20 + 2 = 22

(28 x 2) + (28 x 2)). In division it can only be one way as you cannot partition the divisor. The other area, open to difficulty, is that for many other calculations children are encouraged to use knowledge of place value to partition, but in division they are required to make 'non-canonical partitions' (Thompson, 2008b, p.6), often grouping

the dividend into multiples of the divisor. Partitioning the above calculation according to place value $(100 \div 6) + (30 \div 6) + (2 \div 6)$ makes it a very difficult calculation to solve mentally.

Factors can also be used to solve division calculations mentally. You can only factorise the divisor – use the factors of 6 which are 2 and 3. Divide 132 by 2 first as it is easier to halve, this gives the partial answer of 66 which is then divided by the remaining factor 3.

Method 2: Use of factors
$132 \div 6$
$132 \div 2 = 66$
$66 \div 3 = 22$

Activity: Mental methods

Solve the following calculations. Identify what knowledge, skills and information you needed to be able to solve the problem.

	How I solved it?	Knowledge, skills and prior information needed to solve the calculation
$35.7 \div 7$		
16×24		
$96 \div 8$		
29×12		
$104 \div 5$		

Using approximation to check the reasonableness of the answer

Relating the answer back to the calculation and checking its reasonableness can be done through approximation. Approximation encourages children to develop a number sense when carrying out both mental and written calculations. It is particularly important when solving formal written calculations. When solving 432×7 the calculation can be rounded to 400×7 and using related facts ($4 \times 7 = 28$) it is clear that the answer will be over 2800. To be able to approximate effectively the following knowledge is required:

- how to round to the nearest …;
- which number to round for a sensible approximation, one or both;
- how to use related facts and place value to approximate quickly;
- the value and importance of checking the reasonableness of the answer to the calculation.

Formal written algorithms for multiplication and division

Curriculum Link

The National Curriculum emphasises the teaching of formal written algorithms with the appendix setting out a range of examples of formal written methods for multiplication and division exemplifying the progression across the key stages.

Year 4	*multiply two-digit and three-digit numbers by a one-digit number using formal written layout* (DfE, 2013, p.25)
Year 5	*multiply numbers up to 4 digits by a one- or two-digit number using a formal written method, including long multiplication for two-digit numbers* *divide numbers up to 4 digits by a one-digit number using the formal written method of short division and interpret remainders appropriately for the context* (DfE, 2013, p.32)
Year 6	*multiply multi-digit numbers up to 4 digits by a two-digit whole number using the formal written method of long multiplication* *divide numbers up to 4 digits by a two-digit whole number using the formal written method of long division, and interpret remainders as whole number remainders, fractions, or by rounding, as appropriate for the context* *divide numbers up to 4 digits by a two-digit number using the formal written method of short division where appropriate, interpreting remainders according to the context* (DfE, 2013, p.39)

The debate about the teaching of formal written methods has been an interesting one with many studies and educationalists indicating the *cognitive passivity and suspended understanding* as a disadvantage in the way traditional algorithms were taught and used (Norton, 2012, p.2; Clarke, 2005; Thompson, 2005; Anghileri, 2000b). The learning of written methods has sometimes been associated with memorising sequences of procedures which make little sense to the learner. Instead greater emphasis in supporting children's mental methods was recommended (Norton, 2012).

Clarke highlights some of the advantages of using formal methods. If the procedure is applied correctly the written method will always give the correct answer; they are efficient and can be applied to any number. They can be carried out automatically so that concentration can be directed towards the development of new ideas in which that particular calculation plays a minor role. However, compact methods can be difficult to understand which can affect children's self-confidence, especially if the understanding is built on memorising basic facts without understanding the underlying concepts related to the calculation (Miller and Hudson, 2006; Plunkett, 1979). Children are prone to error when they use mechanically methods they do not fully understand (Clarke, 2005; Norton, 2012).

Research Focus: Calculation strategies used by Year 5 children (Borthwick and Harcourt-Heath, 2007)

Borthwick and Harcourt-Heath undertook a study exploring Year 5 children's use of calculation strategies based on the mathematical education programme provided by the NNS on calculation strategies. Children were given four questions, one question for each of the four number operations. (For this chapter the outcomes for multiplication and division will be discussed; see Chapter 4 for a discussion of the results for addition and subtraction). The children often found it *difficult to choose the most efficient and effective method in order to answer the question* (p.12).

For the multiplication 56 x 24 the majority of the children chose the grid method compared to the standard algorithm, expanded vertical methods or other strategies. When using the grid method, Borthwick and Harcourt-Heath found that twice as many children got the answer right than those using other strategies. When the answer was incorrect, the method was secure but the mental maths that was required was incorrect.

When calculating 222 ÷ 3 a variety of strategies were used, including the standard algorithm, chunking down, chunking up and using a number line. The majority of the children did not attempt this calculation.

Borthwick and Harcourt-Heath came to the following conclusions.

- Children did not have a secure concept of multiplication as arrays and were not able to relate the grid method to other written methods (for example, 56 x 24 was attempted by multiplying 50 x 20 and 6 x 4, giving an incorrect answer).

- A high proportion of children (68 per cent) did not attempt to do division.

- Children who did attempt the division calculation used a wide range of methods ranging from 'intuitive' to showing a stronger understanding of division as sharing rather than grouping.

- Many children did not appear to have a strategy for the multiplication or division.

- When children did choose a strategy which was based on mental methods they usually got the right answer. However, they often did not have any strategies to draw upon. especially if the mental strategies had not been taught.

The findings of the research clearly indicate a need to adopt a structured approach when introducing formal written methods which are securely built on previous knowledge of the properties, structures, language, mental facts and children's own informal mental methods. Doug Clarke notes that formal written methods *encourage children to give up their own thinking leading to a loss of ownership of ideas* (2005, p.94). It is important that compact, 'efficient' calculation strategies are built on a strong conceptual understanding of the underlying mathematics.

The following section explores some written calculation strategies for multiplication and division.

The grid method as a formal written method can be seen as an interim stage towards a more traditional short multiplication (see stage 2) or long multiplication see stage 3).

The grid method builds on a visual image of arrays and mental strategies of partitioning as well as drawing upon the distributive properties for multiplication (Cotton, 2013).

The jump from mental methods and the grid method to the formal written method for short multiplication requires a number of key teaching points.

You are requiring children to work from right to left starting off with the least significant digit first: 2 x 7.

Children are required to work with numbers in columns whereas in mental methods and the grid method children are working with quantities and not digits *with specific column values* (Thompson, 2008a, p.35). Norton argues that formal written methods *unteach place value and hinder children's development of number sense* (2012, p.3), this is further supported by Clarke who states that *it does not correspond to the way people think about number* (2005 p.94). The digit 4 in the number 342 is treated as a 4 and not 40.

This method relies on carrying place value digits which need to be added on, 2 x 7 is 14, carry the 1 ten and put the 4 in the unit column. Children need to remember to add on the 1 ten to the answer to the calculation 4 tens x 7; an error that children can make is to forget to add on the 1 ten or to just add on 1.

The progression towards long multiplication requires children to multiply up to 4 digits by two digits. The grid method could be used as an interim strategy, or the expanded long multiplication in columns can also be used. This interim method does retain the column

---

Interim written method (Stage 1)

1a The grid method 23 x 7

X	20	3	
7	140	21	161

23 x 7 =

(20 x 7) + (3 x 7)

140 + 21 = 161

1b The grid method 24 x 16

X	20	4	
10	200	40	240
6	120	24	144

24 x 16 = 200 + 120 + 40 + 24

= 384

Formal written method for short multiplication (Stage 2)

Links to examples of formal written methods for multiplication in the National Curriculum (DfE, 2013, p.46)

342 x 7 becomes

```
    3 4 2
  ×     7
  2 3 9 4
    2 1
```
Answer: 2394

Interim written method (Stage 3)

Expanded long multiplication 24 x 16

```
        2 4
      × 1 6
      2 4 (6 x 4)
    1 2 0 (6 x 20)
      4 0 (10 x 4)
    2 0 0 (10 x 20)
    3 8 4 = 16 x 24
```

layout and allows children to work out the partial products starting from the left-hand side. The partial products are then added to find the product to the multiplication calculation.

The progression towards the formal written method for long multiplication requires the process of 'carrying'. In the example 124 x 26, 6 x 4 = 24, the 2 tens are carried over the tens column and the 4 ones are retained in the units column. Children then have to remember to add on the 2 tens when solving (6 x 2 tens) + 2 tens is 14 tens; put the 4 tens in the tens column and carry the 1 hundred over the hundreds column.

> **Formal written method for long multiplication 124 X 26**
>
> 124 x 26 becomes
>
> ```
>       1 2
>     1 2 4
>   ×   2 6
>   -------
>     7 4 4
>   2 4 8 0
>   -------
>   3 2 2 4
>       1 1
> ```
>
> Answer: 3224

The difficulty in explaining the formal written method for long multiplication indicates the complexity of the ideas that underpin it (Suggate et al., 2006).

This method of short division can be seen as an interim stage towards a more traditional short division (see below). This interim stage builds on the 'non-canonical partitions' (Thompson, 2008b) as well as drawing upon the distributive properties for multiplication.

> **Interim written method – short division**
>
> 427 ÷ 7 becomes
>
> ```
>        6 0 + 1
>   7 | 4 2 0 + 7
> ```

When moving onto the written algorithm for short division the concept of place value is forgotten and the number is split into its digital parts (Cotton, 2013; Thompson, 2008). So rather than how many 7s in 423 (the whole number) it becomes how many 7s in 4, 2 and 7.

In the example given in the National Curriculum appendices, 98 ÷ 7, the remainder 2, which is moved over to the 8, has to be interpreted back to place value of 2 tens which is carried across to the 8 to create 28, making the next calculation how many 7s in 28.

> **Formal written method for short division**
>
> 427 ÷ 7 =
>
> ```
>      0 6 1
>   7 | 4 ₄2 7
> ```
>
> Approximate of the answer:
>
> If you just take the first two digits in the division 42 ÷ 7 =6
>
> 6 x 7 = 42 so
>
> 60 x 7 = 420
>
> Answer to 427 ÷ 7 is going to be about 60

It is clear that the written method does not progress and lead on from mental methods or even the interim method for division. However, the understanding of estimation and approximation of the calculation is a vital link between the mental methods for division and this written method. If you emphasise the inverse of division and draw upon multiples in the 7 times table and derived facts, children can make that link back to the answer.

> **Link to examples of formal written methods for division in the National Curriculum (DfE, 2013, p.47)**
>
> **Short division**
>
> 98 ÷ 7 becomes
>
> ```
>      1 4
>   7 | 9 ²8
> ```
>
> Answer: 14

The progression within the written method for short division moves onto remainders and then interpreting remainders. Remainders are the amount left over in a division calculation. For example, $432 \div 5 = 86$ groups of 5 with 2 left over not in a group, or two-fifths of a group, which is written as r2 (Haylock, 2010).

By Year 6 children are required to interpret remainders as fractions, understanding the answer to the division as a mixed number and making the connection that $432 \div 5$ can also be understood as an improper fraction $432/5$.

After finding how many 5s go into 432 the remainder is left as a fraction $2/5$. The remainder in a division calculation is always represented as a fraction where the divisor is the denominator. Using their knowledge of equivalent fraction and decimals, two-fifths can also be interpreted as a decimal, 0.4, giving a more accurate answer of $86\ 2/5$ or 86.4. Making links and connections to the programme of study related to fractions and decimals is vital in interpreting remainders as a fraction or as a decimal (see Chapter 6).

The progression within the written methods for long division relate to the interim method called 'chunking', based on subtracting multiples of the divisor, or 'chunks' (DfES, 2006). Initially children subtract several chunks, but with practice they should look for the biggest multiples of the divisor that they can find to subtract. This method does allow for differentiation, where the more confident learner can take larger chunks and the less confident can take away smaller chunks depending on understanding (Thompson, 2008b).

The formal written method for long division uses the language of the grouping structure for division in terms of how many groups of 15 can I make from 432. Relating to the 15 times table, I know that 15 x 2 is 30, so 15 x 20 is 300. I take this from 432 to be left with 132. I know 15 x 2 is 30, so 15 x 4 is 60 and 15 x 8 = 120 which is closest to 132. I subtract 120 from 132 to be left with 12 fifteenths. The equivalent fraction to $12/5$ is $4/5$. The equivalent decimal to $4/5$ is 0.8. The answer to $432 \div 15 = 28.8$ or $28\ 4/5$.

The examples above demonstrate the difficulties that can be posed with the transition from mental informal methods to formal written methods. The interim methods, although not strongly advocated in the National Curriculum, may be valuable stepping stones in developing children's 'relational' understanding (Skemp, 1972). This would certainly support the recommendations put forward by the Williams review in supporting understanding in mathematics (DCSF, 2008). One of the biggest differences is that:

Formal written method for short division with remainders

$432 \div 5$ becomes

```
        8 6 r2
    5|4 3 ³2
```

Answer: 86 remainder 2

Links to examples of formal written methods for division in the National Curriculum (DfE, 2013 p.47)

Interim written method – long division

```
              2 8 r12
       15|4 3 2
        1 5 0  (15 x 10)
          2 8 2
        1 5 0  (15 x 10)
          1 3 2
           7 5  (15 x 5)
            5 7
            4 5  (15 x 3)
             r 12
```

the aspect of place value underpinning mental calculation methods and informal written procedures is different from that which underpins the standard (or 'column') written algorithms: the former methods involve 'quantity value' (where 56 is interpreted as fifty plus six*), whereas the latter procedures involve 'column value' (where 56 is interpreted as* five in the tens column and six in the ones column*).*

(Thompson, 2008, p.35)

Learning Outcomes Review

Plunkett describes written algorithms as *teaching a method rather than an idea*, compared to children's mental informal methods which he illustrates as *requires understanding all along . . .* and *holistic in that they work with compete numbers* (1979, p.3). The research carried out by Dave Benson (2014) summarises some of the key teaching points when fostering an understanding of all four number operations but particularly multiplication and division, and although his research explored how children *developed efficient calculation methods in division* (p.31), many of the outcomes and next steps are pertinent for multiplication too.

- Strong links need to be made between the inverse nature of multiplication and division.
- The efficiency of the method used to solve the calculation often depended on the question. What is required is that children need to be taught to read and understand the question before applying a preferred method to solving it. Benson shares the strategy of being a calculation 'detective', which involves looking for clues in the question, as well as *connections between the numbers involved as a vehicle for deciding* whether to use mental or written methods or a calculator (p.32).
- Children need to have a secure knowledge of related multiplication and division facts to be able to apply to the calculation. This also includes knowledge of multiplication and division of whole and decimal numbers by 10, 100, 1000.
- Greater emphasis needs to be given to estimation and approximation skills before actually solving the calculation. Benson referred the teachers to using the question 'Does it look right?' (p.34).
- Children need to have an understanding of formal written methods and know that many methods can be used to solve the calculation but some are more efficient than others.

Self-assessment questions

1. Look at the National Curriculum 'Mathematics Appendix 1: Examples of formal written methods for addition, subtraction, multiplication and division' (DfE, 2013, p.46). Note the errors, misconceptions and difficulties that some children may have with the suggested formal written methods. What strategies could you put in place to address these?

2. Access the school's calculation policy and note down the progression of teaching multiplication and division across Key Stages 1 and 2.
3. What opportunities are provided for children to develop informal methods of multiplication and division during guided sessions and/or independent work?
4. Identify two key points that you wish to develop in your practice.

Further Reading

Anghileri, J. (ed) (2003) *Children's Mathematical Thinking in the Primary Years: Perspectives on Children's Learning*. London: Continuum.

DfE (2006) *Calculation Guidance Paper*. Available at: http://webarchive.nationalarchives. gov.uk/20110202093118/http:/nationalstrategies.standards.dcsf.gov.uk/ node/47364?uc=force_uj (accessed 25/07/14).

Haylock, D. (with Manning, R.) (2014) *Mathematics Explained for Primary Teachers*, 5th edition. London: SAGE.

References

Anghileri, J. (2000a) *Teaching Number Sense*. London: Continuum.

Anghileri, J. (2000b) British research on mental and written calculation methods for multiplication and division, in Askew, M. and Brown, B. (eds) *Teaching and Learning Primary Numeracy: Policy, Practice and Effectiveness: A review of British research for the British Educational Research Association in conjunction with the British Society for Research in the Learning of Mathematics*. BERA. Available at: www.bera.ac.uk/wp-content/ uploads/2014/01/numeracyreview.pdf (accessed 25/07/14).

Askew, M. (2009) *On the Double*. London: BEAM.

Back, J. (2005) *Difficulties with Division*. Available at www.atm.org.uk (accessed 25/07/14).

Benson, D. (2014) *Division: What Do We Mean By 'Efficient Methods'?* Available at www. atm.org.uk (accessed 25/07/14).

Borthwick, A. and Harcourt-Heath, M. (2007) Calculation strategies used by Year 5 children. *Proceedings for the British Society for Research into Learning Mathematics*, 27(1): 12–17.

Clarke, D.M. (2005) Written algorithms in the primary years: undoing the 'good work'? *Making Mathematics Vital: proceedings of the twentieth Biennial Conference of the Australian Association of Mathematics Teachers*. University of Technology, Sydney, 17–20 January, pp.93–98.

Cotton, T. (2010) *Understanding and Teaching Primary Mathematics*. Harlow: Pearson.

Cotton, T. (2013) *Understanding and Teaching Primary Mathematics*, 2nd edition. Harlow: Pearson.

DCSF (2008) *Independent Review of Mathematics Teaching in Early Years Settings and Primary Schools*. London: DCSF.

DfE (2010) *Teaching Children to Calculate Mentally*. London: DfE.

DfE (2013) *National Curriculum in England: Mathematics programmes of study: key stages 1 and 2*. Available at: www.gov.uk/government/publications/national-curriculum-in-england-mathematics-programmes-of-study/national-curriculum-in-england-mathematics-programmes-of-study (accessed 25/07/14).

DfEE (1999) *The National Numeracy Strategy*. Suffolk: DfEE.

DfES (2006) *The Primary National Strategies*. Norwich: DfES.

Hansen, A. and Ahir, B. (2014) Mathematics, in Smith, P. and Dawes, L. (eds) *Subject Teaching in Primary Education*. London: Sage Publishers.

Harries, T. and Barmby, P. (2007) Representing and understanding multiplication research. *Mathematics Education*, 9(1): 33–45.

Haylock, D. (2010) *Mathematics Explained for Primary Teachers*, 4th edition. London: SAGE.

Haylock, D. and Cockburn, A. (2008) *Understanding Mathematics for Young Children: a Guide for Foundation Stage and Lower Primary Teachers*. London: SAGE.

Miller, S.P. and Hudson, P.J. (2006) Helping students with disabilities understand what mathematics means. *Teaching Exceptional Children*, 3 (1): 28–35.

Murphy, C. (2004) How do children come to use a taught mental calculation strategy? *Educational Studies in Mathematics*, 56: 3–18.

Norton, S. (2012) *The Use of Alternative Algorithms in Whole Number Computation*. Griffith University. Available at: www.cimt.plymouth.ac.uk/journal/ (accessed 25/07/14).

Ofsted (2011) *Good Practice in Primary Mathematics: evidence from 20 successful schools*. London: Ofsted.

Plunkett, S. (1979) Decomposition and all that rot. *Mathematics in School*, 8(3): 2–5.

Robinson, K.M. and LeFevre, J-A. (2012) The inverse relation between multiplication and division: Concepts, procedures, and a cognitive framework. *Education Studies in Mathematics*, 79: 409–428.

Skemp, R.R (1972) *Relational Understanding and Instrumental Understanding*. Warwick: Department of Education: University of Warwick.

Suggate, J. Davis, A. and Golding, M. (2006) *Mathematical Knowledge for Primary Teachers*, 4th edition. Abingdon: Routledge.

Taylor, H. and Harris, A. (2014) *Learning and Teaching Mathematics 0–8*. London: SAGE.

Thompson, I. (2005) Division by complementary multiplication. *Mathematics in School*, 34(5): 5–7.

Thompson, I. (2008a) Deconstructing calculation methods, Part 3: multiplication. *Mathematics Teaching Incorporating Micromath*, 206: 34–36.

Thompson, I. (2008b) Deconstructing calculation methods, Part 4: division. *Mathematics Teaching Incorporating Micromath*, 208: 6–8.

6 Fractions, decimals, percentages, ratio and proportion

Alice Hansen and Jonathan Leeming

Learning outcomes

This chapter aims to develop your understanding of:

- fractions, decimals, percentages, ratio and proportion;
- the relationship between fractions, decimals, percentages, ratio and proportion;
- how to teach fractions, decimals, percentages, ratio and proportion effectively.

TEACHERS' STANDARDS

1 Set high expectations which inspire, motivate and challenge pupils.
2 Promote good progress and outcomes by pupils.
3 Demonstrate good subject and curriculum knowledge.
4 Plan and teach well-structured lessons.
6 Make productive and accurate use of assessment.

Introduction

In this chapter you will explore what fractions, decimals, percentages, ratio and proportion (FDPRP) are, why they are important and how you can teach them effectively.

FDPRP are presented together in this chapter because of their interconnected nature. However, the majority of this chapter will focus on fractions because they are one of the most difficult aspects of mathematics to understand and teach, and fractions dominate this section of the Primary National Curriculum. Then, in turn, decimals, percentages, and ratio and proportion will be discussed.

Fractions

Research Focus: The importance of teaching fractions in primary school

Siegler et al. (2012) carried out a longitudinal study to examine the predictors of secondary school students' achievement in mathematics. They found that, in the UK, the strongest predictor of mathematical performance at 16 was pupils' understanding of fractions

→

and division when they were ten years old. This was greater than the contributions of whole number arithmetic knowledge, verbal and non-verbal IQ, working memory, and family education and income. Siegler et al. suggest improving the teaching and learning of fractions in primary school could yield 'substantial improvements' in later mathematics.

What is a fraction?

Quantities represented by natural numbers are easily understood. For example, we can say how many sweets are in our pocket. Fractions, however, are not easy to define succinctly. They cause difficulties because they involve relationships between quantities. 'What is $\frac{3}{4}$?' $\frac{3}{4}$ of what? A fraction, depending on the context in which it is being used, can be defined or interpreted in five different ways. These are explained below, using $\frac{3}{4}$ as an example. In each case, the development of children's understanding of fractions is also discussed.

Activity

While you are reading the five interpretations, think about:

- how the interpretations challenge your own understanding of fractions;

- the various contexts you could use to set up fractions problems for children in your class.

Fractions as part-whole

Part-whole fractions partition a continuous quantity or a set of discrete objects into a number of equal-sized parts. In this interpretation, the numerator must be smaller than the denominator, for example a pie is divided into four equal parts (quarters) and three are eaten, so $\frac{3}{4}$ of the pie has been eaten.

When using the part-whole representation, children should understand that (a) the parts into which the whole is partitioned must be of equal size; (b) the parts, when taken together, must equal the whole; (c) the more parts the whole is divided into, the smaller the parts become; and (d) the relationship between the parts and the whole is conserved, regardless of the size, shape or orientation of the equivalent parts (Leung, 2009).

Fractions as quotient

The quotient interpretation is the result of a division. It results in a number that can be placed on a number line, for example $3 \div 4 = \frac{3}{4}$.

For this interpretation, children should be able to identify fractions using division and understand the role of the dividend and the divisor in this operation (Leung, 2009).

Fractions as measurement

In a measure interpretation a unit fraction is identified (for example, $\frac{1}{4}$) and the number of repeated units determine the distance from a predetermined starting point (for example, $3 \times \frac{1}{4} = \frac{3}{4}$).

In this interpretation, children should be able to give a distance from the origin as a fraction. They should also be able to locate a fraction on a number line and identify a fraction represented by a point on the number line (Leung, 2009) or region (Pantziara and Philippou, 2012).

Fractions as ratio

A fraction can be seen as a ratio of two quantities; in this case it is seen as a part-part interpretation and it is considered to be a comparative index rather than a number (Carraher, 1996), for example three parts out of every four are red.

For this interpretation, children need to understand the relative nature of the quantities. They also need to know that when two quantities in the ratio are multiplied by the same positive number the value of the ratio is unchanged (Leung, 2009).

Fractions as operator

A fraction is interpreted as an operator that acts upon a number, set or object. In operator situations, children understand the relative nature of fractions. They realise that the same fraction symbol may actually refer to different quantities (for example, $\frac{1}{2}$ of 6 is not equivalent to $\frac{1}{2}$ of 14) and that different fraction symbols may be equivalent because they refer to the same quantity (for example, $\frac{1}{2}$ and $\frac{2}{4}$) (Nunes, 2006; Mamede et al., 2005).

In operator situations involving the area representation, children understand that fractions are transformers (Lamon, 1999). They can take a figure in the geometric plane and map it onto a larger or smaller figure of the same shape (Charalambous and Pitta-Pantazi, 2007). This is called scaling and is discussed in more detail later in this chapter. They are also referred to as a *stretcher/shrinker* (Behr et al., 1983). When using sets of objects, children understand that fractions can increase or decrease the number of objects in a set (Lamon, 1999). Children also understand that fractions can lengthen or shorten line segments (Lamon, 1999). This is related to the use of line representations.

Representing fractions

When teaching fractions, you will use a wide range of models and resources to support children's learning. It is important that you are aware of five different types of models that are available for you to use.

Activity: Resources for different types of representations

While you are reading about the different types of representations, think about resources that you could use to model each of these in your teaching.

Area/region

The area representation is the most common in textbooks and other teaching materials around the world (Alajmi, 2012; Pantziara and Philippou, 2012). It often uses figures such as a circle or rectangle with a fractional part shaded, such as fraction circles or fraction walls. In context-based problems, items such as pies, pizzas and cakes are frequently used. Paper folding is also a useful resource for representing and exploring area/region.

Number line

The number line representation involves placing fractions on a number line or identifying the fraction that is shown on a number line. Number lines, empty number lines and Cuisenaire rods can be used to provide a number line representation. Cuisenaire presents endless possibilities for exploring fractions because each rod can represent any unit fraction, or any whole number. In Figure 6.1, the brown rod could be chosen to represent 1 and children could find the value of the smaller red and white blocks. They could also see that two white blocks ($\frac{2}{8}$) is the same as one red block ($\frac{1}{4}$).

Figure 6.1 Cuisenaire rods showing 1 whole, quarters and eighths.

Sets of objects

Objects are grouped and used to represent whole sets. The fractional part is often identified as a different colour or as a subset of the whole. Objects can be as varied as toys, circles, sweets, sticks or children.

Liquid measures

In England it is commonplace to find young children sharing objects, using everyday language to talk about capacity and solving problems (DfE, 2013; STA, 2012). Liquid measures also appear in statutory tests at the end of primary school.

Symbolic

The symbolic representation of a fraction uses the notation:

$$\frac{\text{numerator}}{\text{denominator}}$$

Additionally, the numerator and denominator take on different meanings according to the type of representation. For example, as an area the denominator represents the number of parts the whole has been cut into and the numerator is the number of parts taken (Mamede et al., 2005), whereas the numerator is compared with the denominator in the ratio model. Furthermore, in the quotient representation the numerator is the number of items to be shared and the denominator is how many people the item(s) must be shared between. The line represents a division and is called the vinculum.

Bringing interpretations and representations together

As you can see from the discussion above, fractions are complex. Figure 6.2 brings together the interpretations and representations in a matrix that you can use to support your planning, ensuring that you offer your pupils a broad fractions experience.

Before reading the research focus below, think about which of the interpretations and representations you have used in your own teaching.

Research Focus: Interpretations and representations of fractions

Although there are five interpretations of fractions (Kieran, 1976; 1993), most teachers and texts around the world focus on the part-whole interpretation, which limits children's understanding of fractions (Behr et al., 1983; Charalambous et al, 2010; Panaoura et al., 2009).

Furthermore, teachers tend to use a limited number of representations in their teaching with area the most common representation (Baturo, 2004), even though there are five broad representations of fractions (Charalambous and Pitta-Pantazi, 2007; Kieran, 1976; Lamon, 2012; Pantziara and Philippou, 2012; Silver, 1983).

The understanding of one interpretation does not necessarily lead to that of another (Brousseau et al., 2004; Charalambous and Pitta-Pantazi, 2007). Therefore to have a complete understanding of fractions requires an understanding of the different representations and how they interrelate (Kieran, 1976).

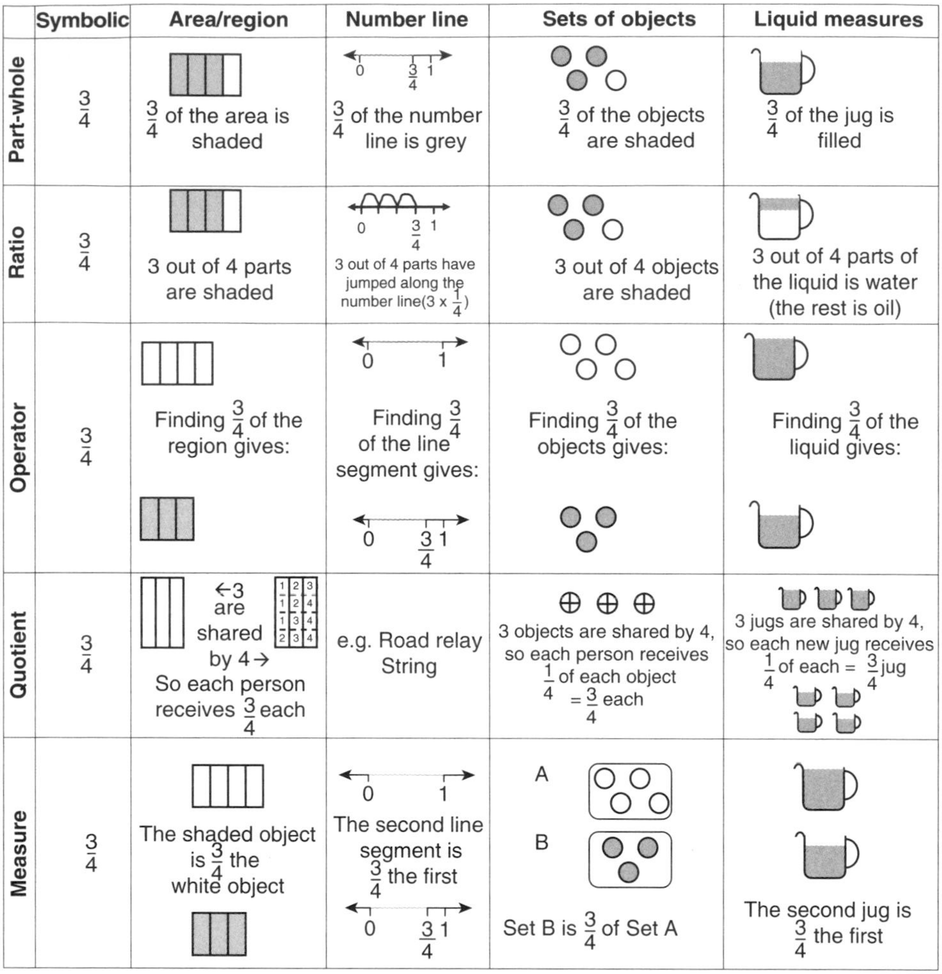

	Symbolic	Area/region	Number line	Sets of objects	Liquid measures
Part-whole	$\frac{3}{4}$	$\frac{3}{4}$ of the area is shaded	$\frac{3}{4}$ of the number line is grey	$\frac{3}{4}$ of the objects are shaded	$\frac{3}{4}$ of the jug is filled
Ratio	$\frac{3}{4}$	3 out of 4 parts are shaded	3 out of 4 parts have jumped along the number line (3 x $\frac{1}{4}$)	3 out of 4 objects are shaded	3 out of 4 parts of the liquid is water (the rest is oil)
Operator	$\frac{3}{4}$	Finding $\frac{3}{4}$ of the region gives:	Finding $\frac{3}{4}$ of the line segment gives:	Finding $\frac{3}{4}$ of the objects gives:	Finding $\frac{3}{4}$ of the liquid gives:
Quotient	$\frac{3}{4}$	3 are shared by 4 → So each person receives $\frac{3}{4}$ each	e.g. Road relay String	3 objects are shared by 4, so each person receives $\frac{1}{4}$ of each object $=\frac{3}{4}$ each	3 jugs are shared by 4, so each new jug receives $\frac{1}{4}$ of each $=\frac{3}{4}$ jug
Measure	$\frac{3}{4}$	The shaded object is $\frac{3}{4}$ the white object	The second line segment is $\frac{3}{4}$ the first	A B Set B is $\frac{3}{4}$ of Set A	The second jug is $\frac{3}{4}$ the first

Figure 6.2 The iTalk2Learn interpretations and representations matrix (Hansen et al, 2014)

Teaching fractions

Curriculum Link

Did you know that the Primary National Curriculum mentions 'fraction' 116 times? It is a significant number given that 'whole number' appears only 25 times. The document outlines clear progression in the objectives from Year 1 to Year 6, but it is essential that you read the non-statutory notes and guidance alongside the statutory requirements because these give pedagogical advice including thinking about connections and contexts.

This section provides support for putting the theoretical subject knowledge discussed earlier into practice. There are some terms that will be used throughout, and so they are defined here for you.

A *unit fraction* is the basic unit of any fraction. The numerator is always 1, for example $\frac{1}{2}, \frac{1}{6}, \frac{1}{10}$ and $\frac{1}{36}$.

A *proper fraction* is any fraction where the numerator is smaller than the denominator, for example $\frac{3}{5}, \frac{7}{8}, \frac{2}{10}$ and $\frac{13}{25}$.

An *improper fraction* is a fraction where the numerator is larger than the denominator, for example $\frac{5}{2}, \frac{8}{4}, \frac{12}{9}$ and $\frac{30}{6}$.

A *mixed number* is written as a whole number and a fraction, for example $1\frac{1}{2}, 3\frac{2}{5}, 4\frac{1}{8}$ and $11\frac{3}{5}$.

Writing fractions

Fractions are a number in their own right, and are represented by a symbol $\frac{x}{y}$. Because children have a stronger understanding of whole numbers than fractions, they will see the parts in the symbol as two whole numbers and are unlikely to see the relationship between the numbers and the role each part has in defining the fraction. This is why a careful definition of numerator and denominator is important. So a child may say two out of three or two threes for $\frac{2}{3}$. This emphasises the respective absolute magnitudes of the numerator and denominator rather than the relationship between them. It also does not generalise well to improper fractions: $\frac{4}{3}$ as 'four out of three' is not helpful (Clark and Roche, 2009). Therefore it is important to support children to begin to see the fraction symbol as one made up of a numerator and a denominator (not simply two whole numbers) by using the terms numerator and denominator to reinforce their special role in the fraction symbol.

Finding equivalent fractions and simplifying fractions

It is not possible to do much with fractions unless equivalence is used. (See discussion below on addition and subtraction of fractions.) Procedurally, to find an equivalent fraction we multiply or divide the numerator and denominator by the same amount. For example:

$$\frac{1}{2} \times \frac{5}{5} = \frac{5}{10}$$

Although this method finds the answer fluently (an aim for mathematics), it is also important for children to develop their conceptual understanding (part of the same aim). Therefore we need to know how this procedure works.

Two explanations are offered here.

Partitioning

In this example we are using a whole-part interpretation using a region, the rectangle. We can represent $\frac{1}{2}$ as:

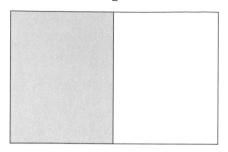

We can partition this rectangle into five:

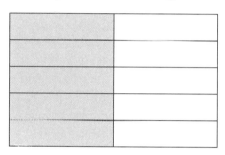

And that leaves us with a fraction $\frac{5}{10}$. We see that the fraction has not changed and that $\frac{1}{2}$ is equivalent to $\frac{5}{10}$.

Multiplying by 1

When we multiply any number by 1 the answer remains the same because 1 does not change it in any way. The same is true when we multiply a fraction by 1 and that is exactly what we are doing in the equation above: $\frac{5}{5} = 1$. So although the numerator and denominator change, the fraction itself is equivalent to the fraction we started with.

$$\frac{1}{2} \quad \times \quad \frac{5}{5} \quad = \quad \frac{5}{10}$$

= 1 whole

Simplifying fractions

When a solution is found, it can be represented in a simpler way. For example, if the solution was $\frac{4}{10}$ we could simplify this to make $\frac{2}{5}$ by finding the common factor (in this case, 2).

Activity: Comparing and ordering fractions

A group of children were asked to place unit fractions on the number line in order. This is what they produced:

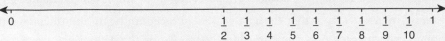

What errors have the children made?

A common error children make when comparing and ordering fractions is related to thinking about the denominator as a whole number in its own right. In the children's work above, they have correctly placed $\frac{1}{2}$ (from prior experience, knowing $\frac{1}{2}$ is in the middle of 0 and 1 on the number line), but they were unsure about placing the other fractions. They have focused on the denominators and ordered them as if they were whole numbers.

It is important for children to understand that the larger the denominator the more parts the whole has been equally divided into so the parts are smaller. Children intuitively understand this principle in practical situations, so you could include sharing in role-play situations or play games. For example, you could provide two tables (red tablecloth and blue tablecloth), each with the same desirable item on them (for example, a cake, pie or apple). Place four chairs around the red table and six chairs around the blue and ask the children which table they would prefer to sit at. Giving them a red card and blue card to hold up will involve everyone. Agree the fraction of the item the children would receive at each table (in this case $\frac{1}{4}$ and $\frac{1}{6}$) and compare the fractions with the parts of the item. Change the number of chairs and the type of items (you may even want to place undesirable items) to reinforce for children that the larger the denominator the smaller the parts become and vice versa.

The above task is straightforward when ordering unit fractions or proper fractions with the same denominator. Ordering proper fractions with different denominators, however, is more problematic. Two informal strategies (Clarke and Roche, 2009) can be particularly helpful before children begin using the formal method of finding common denominators. The first strategy, 'benchmarking', involves children comparing a group of fractions to another that acts as a 'benchmark'. So when ordering $\frac{3}{7}$ and $\frac{5}{8}$ we can compare them to $\frac{1}{2}$ and quickly deduce that the latter is the larger because the numerator is more than half of the denominator. 'Residual thinking' refers to the amount which is required to build a fraction up to a whole. So we can see that $\frac{7}{8}$ and $\frac{5}{6}$ are both one unit fraction away from being a whole, but as $\frac{1}{6}$ is larger than $\frac{1}{8}, \frac{7}{8}$ is the larger fraction. This is where children's exposure to different representations can prove so invaluable because it gives them a 'feeling' for the different sizes of fractions.

Converting mixed numbers to improper fractions and vice versa

The most common procedure for converting a mixed number to an improper fraction is to multiply the whole number by the denominator and add the product to the numerator. For example, the numerator of an equivalent improper fraction of $3\frac{1}{4}$ would be found by $3 \times 4 + 1$, so that the answer is $\frac{13}{4}$. Procedurally, to find the mixed number from an improper fraction, the numerator is divided by the denominator. For example, the numerator of $\frac{13}{4}$ (that is, 13) is divided by 4, giving 3 with a remainder of 1. So, the answer is 3 wholes with $\frac{1}{4}$ remaining.

So, how do these procedures work? Let's imagine that we are pouring liquid from a large vessel into smaller jugs:

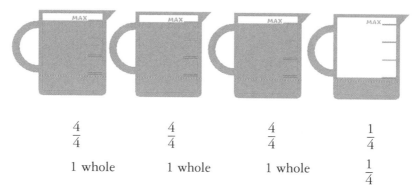

$\frac{4}{4}$	$\frac{4}{4}$	$\frac{4}{4}$	$\frac{1}{4}$
1 whole	1 whole	1 whole	$\frac{1}{4}$

If we imagine that the liquid is poured into the jugs we would pour a running total of:

$$\frac{4}{4} \qquad \frac{8}{4} \qquad \frac{12}{4} \qquad \frac{13}{4}.$$

This idea of relating one whole to the fraction equivalent to 1 (in this case 4/4) works for all fractions representations.

Adding and subtracting fractions

Adding and subtracting fractions with the same denominator

Adding and subtracting fractions is fairly straightforward when the denominators are the same, for example $\frac{5}{7} + \frac{1}{7} = \frac{6}{7}$. It may seem easiest to teach children the 'trick' that says keep the denominators the same and just add the numerators, but this procedure a) treats the numerator and denominator as discrete (something we're trying to avoid), and b) does not reinforce understanding that the unit fractions that are being added are the same (for example, five-**sevenths**, one-**seventh**, six-**sevenths**). Therefore, ensure you use the appropriate terms and that the children are adding the fractions with the same denominator together.

Adding and subtracting fractions with different denominators

Things begin to spice up when the denominators are not the same. In such cases we need to find equivalent fractions to ensure that the denominators are the same. If you are not sure how to find equivalent fractions, read pages 105–6. If two fractions have denominators that are multiples of the same number we can find an equivalent fraction of the fraction with the smallest denominator, for example $\frac{2}{3} + \frac{1}{6} = \frac{4}{6} + \frac{1}{6} = \frac{5}{6}$. If two fractions do not share a common factor, then you must find equivalent fractions of each so that they share a common denominator, for example $\frac{1}{3} + \frac{2}{5} = \frac{5}{15} + \frac{6}{15} = \frac{11}{15}$. At first this can be explored using trial and error or a computer program such as Fractions Lab (link.lkl.ac.uk/FractionsLab) to find them. As children do this, they will notice that a common denominator can also be found by multiplying together the two denominators.

Case Study: Adding fractions with unlike denominators

Jonathan, a Mathematics Specialist Teacher (MaST) uses Fractions Lab (link.lkl.ac.uk/FractionsLab) in his teaching. He explains:

'Fractions Lab is an online tool for supporting children's conceptual understanding of fractions. I like to use it with my class because it shows fractions using a wide range of representations such as regions, number lines, sets, liquid measures and the fractions symbols themselves. I also like the way it encourages children to add and subtract fractions. It isn't possible to find the answer unless the child has already made equivalent fractions so that the denominators are the same. Recently, several of my Year 5 pupils were working on computers. I gave them three addition questions:

1. $\frac{3}{7} + \frac{1}{7}$;

2. $\frac{3}{7} + \frac{3}{14}$;

3. $\frac{3}{7} + \frac{1}{3}$.

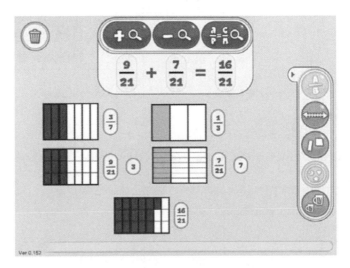

Figure 6.3   Screenshot of FractionsLab (link.lkl.ac.uk/FractionsLab)

It was straightforward for them to answer the first question. They were able to complete the second by partitioning $\frac{3}{7}$ into $\frac{6}{14}$ but the third was more challenging. They experimented by partitioning the shapes until they found fractions where the denominators were the same, in this case 21sts. It was interesting to see how the representations enabled the children to understand and how they guided the children's thinking. Without Fractions Lab most of the children would not have been able to find the answer and those that were able to use the procedure had a visual representation to show how it worked.'

Multiplying and dividing fractions

When we multiply and divide by fractions we use the interpretation of fractions as operators. The fraction changes the whole number or the fraction we are multiplying by. When we are multiplying we can use the term 'of'. For example, $\frac{1}{2}$ of 6 is the same as finding $\frac{1}{2}$ x 6.

The curriculum guidance is clear that models and representations should be used to teach children to multiply and divide fractions. Although children should not be explicitly introduced to the procedural algorithms, they can be encouraged to spot patterns as they work through tasks and identify the methods themselves.

Multiplying fractions by whole numbers

In Chapter 5 you read how 3 x 4 is three multiplied by 4 to make 3 + 3 + 3 + 3 = 12. It is possible to apply this same logic to $\frac{1}{3}$ x 4: one third multiplied by 4 is $\frac{1}{3} + \frac{1}{3} + \frac{1}{3} + \frac{1}{3} = \frac{4}{3} = 1\frac{1}{3}$. We can use the commutative law to find 4 x $\frac{1}{3}$ too.

Multiplying fractions by fractions

If we want to find the product of $\frac{1}{3}$ x $\frac{1}{4}$, we can make $\frac{1}{3}$ and $\frac{1}{4}$:

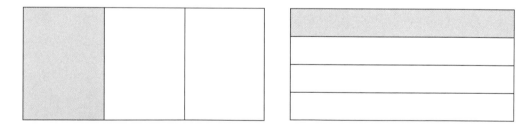

and they can be overlaid so that the intersection is identified:

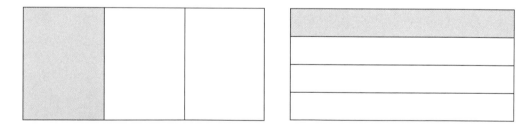

This provides the solution, in this case $\frac{1}{12}$. Once again, we can check this by using 'of': 'What is $\frac{1}{3}$ of $\frac{1}{4}$?' and use the diagram to illustrate this.

Dividing a whole number by a unit fraction

When we are dividing whole numbers, for a ÷ b we can ask, 'how many b's are there in a'? For example, for 12 ÷ 3 we can ask, 'how many 3's are in 12?' We can use the same question when we are dividing a whole number by a fraction. For example, for $1 \div \frac{1}{3}$ we can ask, 'how many thirds are there in 1 whole?'

The NCETM recommend using a bar model to represent division. For example, with $1 \div \frac{1}{3}$ it is possible to draw a bar that is 1 long:

1 whole

and find how many thirds are in it:

$\frac{1}{3}$	$\frac{1}{3}$	$\frac{1}{3}$

It is useful to give children a strip of paper that they are able to fold to find the number of fractions in the whole.

It is also possible to use this model with whole numbers greater than 1. For $3 \div \frac{1}{4}$ we can show:

1 whole				2 wholes				3 wholes			
$\frac{1}{4}$	$\frac{1}{4}$	$\frac{1}{4}$	$\frac{1}{4}$	$\frac{1}{4}$	$\frac{1}{4}$	$\frac{1}{4}$	$\frac{1}{4}$	$\frac{1}{4}$	$\frac{1}{4}$	$\frac{1}{4}$	$\frac{1}{4}$

You can insert tables and use the 'split cells' function in Word or similar to explore dividing a whole number by a unit fraction too.

Dividing a fraction by a whole number

When we are dividing a fraction by a whole number, we are starting with a part of a whole. Using the bar model again, we can demonstrate $\frac{1}{3} \div 2$.

1 whole

We can find $\frac{1}{3}$ of a whole

$\frac{1}{3}$		

and divide the part by two.

By identifying the new unit fraction, we find the solution: $\frac{1}{3} \div 2 = \frac{1}{6}$.

$\frac{1}{6}$	$\frac{1}{6}$	$\frac{1}{6}$	$\frac{1}{6}$	$\frac{1}{6}$	$\frac{1}{6}$

Solving problems using fractions

Throughout the primary curriculum children are required to solve problems using fractions. In our experience, most teachers default to using a range of food items that are shared: pizzas, cake and chocolate. However, this is a limited diet (excuse the pun) to be giving children. Be sure to use a range of interpretations and representations such as those in the Fractions Matrix (iTalk2Learn, 2014) in Figure 6.2 (see page 104) to provide a broad and balanced experience of fractions.

Research Focus: Dual representation

Symbolic objects have what Uttal et al. call *dual representation* (2009, p.156); they are seen both as representations and as objects within their own right. The danger is that children focus on the inherent properties of the tools rather than their symbolic nature. Uttal et al. suggest that *reflection and abstraction are probably facilitated by relatively simple manipulatives* (2009, p.158). Therefore, when you use pizzas and chocolate, ensure the children end up salivating over fractions and not food.

Decimals

Decimals are a natural extension of our place value system. By their very name, decimal fractions are another way of showing a part of a whole split up as tenths, hundredths, thousandths and so on.

Table 6.1 47.28 multiplied by 10 and divided by 10

	Hundreds	Tens	Ones/Units	.	tenths	hundredths	thousandths
	H	T	O/U	.	t	h	th
		4	7	.	2	8	
X10	4	7	2	.	8		
÷10			4	.	7	2	8

In Table 6.1 the number 47.28 is shown. 2 represents two tenths and 8 represents 8 hundredths.

In the next row it has been multiplied by 10. Notice how the value of each digit has increased tenfold and the 8 hundredths $\frac{8}{100}$ has become 8 tenths ($\frac{8}{10}$). In the final row

47.28 has been divided by 10. Now each digit is ten times smaller so, for example, the 8 hundredths becomes 8 thousandths ($\frac{8}{1000}$). Notice the link between the decimals and fractions. This is reinforced throughout lower Key Stage 2.

Reading and writing decimals

When we read decimals each digit after the decimal point is read out separately. So, the number 32.45 is read thirty-two point four-five and not thirty-two point forty-five. Money is the exception to this: £32.45 is typically read 'thirty-two pounds and forty-five pence' or colloquially 'thirty-two, forty-five'.

Using zero as a place holder

Just as it is not necessary to place a zero before a whole number (for example, fifty-one would not be written 051), it is not usually necessary to place a zero after a decimal (e.g. for example, 3.290 would be written as 3.29). However, there are some exceptions such as money: £78.2 should be written £78.20 and the context of a problem may also require it. For example, being asked to write an answer to three decimal places might require the use of zero as a place holder.

Comparing decimals

Using money as an introduction to decimals (and zero's use as a place holder in decimals) can be problematic for children when they compare or order decimals. For example, it is common for children to state that 3.27 is bigger than 3.3 if they read 0.27 as 'twenty-seven' and not 'two seven'. In this example the 0.27 is equivalent to $\frac{27}{100}$ (or $\frac{2}{10} + \frac{7}{100}$) and the 0.3 is equivalent to $\frac{3}{10}$ (or $\frac{30}{100}$). This can be demonstrated using a place value table such as the one in Table 6.1. By making the link between the value of the digit and its equivalent fraction, children can compare and order decimals effectively. Another resource that can be used is place value arrow cards such as those in Figure 6.4. A good context for introducing decimals is measurement. Comparing items of varying length physically can be a useful intermediate step to using abstract numbers.

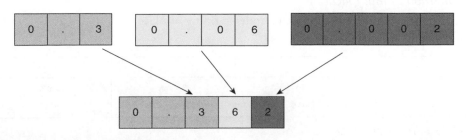

Figure 6.4 Place value arrow cards

Rounding decimals

We deal with some numbers that are rounded decimals all the time. For example, Pi is 3.1415926535898 ... but we use it rounded to 3.14 in the primary classroom. Using rounded numbers helps us to deal with numbers that are too hard to grasp or too precise for our needs. Rounding decimals in primary school provides the foundation for being able to calculate efficiently with more complex numbers later on. There are some simple rules we follow to round numbers.

1. Find the last digit that will be kept.

2. Look at the next digit. If it is 5 or more, increase the digit to be left by 1. If it is 4 or less, it stays the same.

Some examples are in Table 6.2.

Table 6.2 Examples of rounded decimal numbers

Original number	Round to	Look at	Rounded number
23.2	Nearest whole number	Digit in tenths position. Less than 5.	23
73.7	Nearest whole number	Digit in tenths position. 5 or more.	74
61.36	Nearest whole number	Digit in tenths position. Less than 5.	61
22.81	Nearest whole number	Digit in tenths position. 5 or more.	23
61.36	One decimal place	Digit in hundredths position. 5 or more.	61.4
22.81	One decimal place	Digit in hundredths position. Less than 5.	22.8
59.02	One decimal place	Digit in hundredths position. Less than 5.	59.0
18.05	One decimal place	Digit in hundredths position. 5 or more.	18.1

Multiplication and division with decimals

Towards the end of primary, children will begin to multiply numbers with decimal places by whole numbers and also perform written division methods where the answer has up to two decimal places. Multiplication and division with decimals, like decimals themselves, is a natural extension of what we do with whole numbers. It is possible to use the same multiplication and division strategies as those explained by Balbir Ahir in Chapter 5 when operating with decimals.

Grid method of multiplication

The grid method builds on children's understanding of place value and is a very useful introduction to multiplying decimals.

x	2	0.4	0.03
8	8 x 2 16	8 x 0.4 3.2	8 x 0.03 0.24

2.43 x 8 = 16 + 3.2 + 0.24
= 19.44

Formal written method for long division

In division children will progress from thinking of a quotient as having a remainder, then as a fraction and in later primary as a decimal. See page 95 for more about this progression.

$432 \div 15$ becomes

```
        2 8 .8
1 5 | 4 3 2 .0
      3 0 ↓
      1 3 2
      1 2 0 ↓
      1 2 0
      1 2 0
          0
```

Answer: 28.8

Percentages

Percentage means 'for each hundred' or 'out of one hundred'. Percentages are useful because they help us to do the following.

- Identify the proportion of sets – to do this we use proportions that are equivalent to fractions with a denominator of 100, for example 45 per cent ($\frac{45}{100}$) of the group are girls (9 out of 20 children are girls).

- Compare different-sized sets – we may compare the populations of two different countries using percentages where it would not be as easy to do so when we were looking at the raw data. For example, Ecuador's population of 15,223,680 is approximately 25 per cent of that of the UK at 63,182,000. When numbers are so large, converting them to a percentage helps us to visualise them.

- Make generalisations – a '50% off' sign can be displayed in a sale and we know how much to deduct from the original price. This is easier for the shop to display than having to reduce each individual item.

Recognising and writing percentages

At first, children will need to be able to recognise the per cent symbol (%) and show that per cent relates to parts per hundred. It is possible to use a hundreds square or a blank 10 x 10 square to reinforce this idea. It is also very helpful for children to see the link between a fraction with a denominator of 100, a decimal and its equivalent percentage.

Relating percentages to pie charts

Pie charts are used in the same way as percentages in that they help to identify the proportions of sets and compare different-sized sets. Therefore we should support children in seeing the links too. One way to do this is to create a large hand-drawn pie chart in the following way.

1. Using a strip that is one metre long, partition the strip to show the proportions being represented.

2. Join the ends of the strip together using tape to form a circle.

3. Draw around the circle then mark out the sectors by drawing from each proportion on the strip to the centre.

This easy method is a nice introduction to pie charts and helps children to see a link between percentages and how they are represented on a pie chart. To learn more about pie charts, see Chapter 8.

Bringing fractions, percentages and decimals together

Decimals are part of our base ten system, so fractions with a denominator of a power of ten are a good way to support children to develop their understanding of the relationships between our place value system, fractions, decimals and percentages.

The case study below shows how Issac, a PGCE student on final placement, encouraged children to focus on the relationships between fractions, percentages and decimals. While you are reading the case study, think about how you would carry out the task Issac asked his pupils to do.

Case Study: Bringing it all together

'I wanted to use more worthwhile formative assessment strategies in my teaching during my final placement so when it came up to a unit of work on fractions, percentages and decimals in my class I decided to start with finding out where the children were in their knowledge and understanding. They were used to using concept maps, so during the first lesson I asked them to create a map showing everything they knew about fractions, percentages and decimals and how they were connected. That really informed my planning and I also grouped most of the children according to what they wrote. As a further assessment and evaluation strategy I returned the concept maps to the children at the end of the unit and asked them to add anything else they now knew. I remember Summer was really excited about the opportunity to revisit her map. She couldn't wait to add to it.'

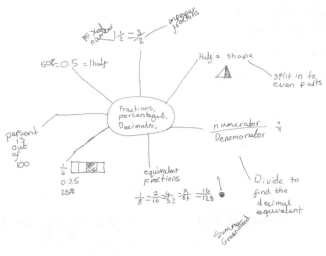

Figure 6.5 Summer's concept map

Curriculum Link

The Primary National Curriculum clearly outlines the importance of children from Year 3 onwards understanding the links between fractions, percentages, decimals, ratio and proportion. Ensure you read the non-statutory guidance that provides further detail.

Ratio and proportion

A ratio is a part to part comparison, often written with a colon (read as 'to') separating the parts, for example, 2:3 or 1:3:5. A proportion, on the other hand, is a part to whole comparison and is often written using a fraction.

An understanding of ratio and proportion is crucial because it helps children to think about the relationships between numbers and it develops their proportional reasoning. Although this area of mathematics does not appear in the Primary National Curriculum until Year 6, children have met ratio in the form of scaling (five times as big as) when they started studying multiplication. In our experience, however, children have much more exposure to the aggregation (repeated addition) structure of multiplication at the expense of the former structure.

Using counters to represent scaling/ratio and proportion

Counters can be very useful tools to help children to understand scaling/ratio and proportion. Before you read about how counters might be used, have a go at completing the following activity.

Activity: Stickers

Answer these two questions:

1. John has 6 football stickers. Elise has 4 times as many. How many does Elise have?

2. Elise has one-fifth of the stickers that John has. After John gives Elise 18 stickers they each have the same amount. How many stickers do they have in total?

We will use counters to demonstrate how you could solve these two questions.

1. John has 6 football stickers. Elise has 4 times as many. How many does Elise have?

This can be represented:

John

Elise

John has a ratio of 1:4. This representation makes it easy to understand and to calculate the answer. Double-sided counters can be used so that the colours can distinguish one part of the ratio from the other.

The question can be more complex, but it can be made accessible through the use of the representation. This time we use squares or bars.

2. Elise has one-fifth of the stickers that John has. After John gives Elise 18 stickers they each have the same amount. How many stickers do they have in total?

Elise

John

We can show:

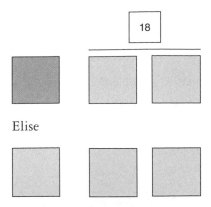

Elise

John

Therefore each square represents 9 and the total can be easily calculated. These examples show the power of representations for helping children to understand complex mathematical concepts.

Learning Outcomes Review

This chapter has only been able to scratch the surface of teaching and learning fractions, decimals, percentages, ratio and proportion (FDPRP). However, having read the chapter, you should have increased your subject knowledge of FDPRP and be more confident in teaching the aspects and their interconnected nature.

Self-assessment questions

1. Copy and complete the table.

Fraction	Decimal	Percentage
	0.1	
	0.125	
		20%
$\frac{1}{3}$		
$\frac{1}{2}$	0.5	50%
	0.6	
$\frac{7}{10}$		
1		

(Continued)

(Continued)

2. Thinking about fractions

   a) Define a fraction.

   b) Draw as many pictures/models/representations as possible to show $\frac{1}{4}$.

   c) On a scale of 1–10 (with 10 being the most), how confident are you teaching fractions?

3. Create your own mind map of fractions, percentages and decimals. Refer to the case study, *Bringing it all together*, for assistance.

References

Alajmi, A.H. (2012) How do elementary textbooks address fractions? A review of mathematics textbooks in the USA, Japan, and Kuwait. *Educational Studies in Mathematics,* 79: 239–261.

Baturo, A.R. (2004) Empowering Andrea to help year-5 students construct fraction understanding, in Høines, M.J and Fuglestad, A. (eds.) *Proceedings of the 28th PME Conference, 2.* Bergen: Bergen University College. pp.95–102.

Behr, M., Lesh, R., Post, T. and Silver, E. (1983) Rational number concepts, in Lesh, R. and Landau M. (eds) *Acquisition of Mathematics Concepts and Processes.* New York: Academic Press. pp.91–125.

Brousseau, G., Brousseau, N. and Warfield, V. (2004) Rationals and decimals as required in the school curriculum. Part 1: Rationals as measurements. *Journal of Mathematical Behavior,* 23: 1–20.

Carraher, D.W. (1996) Learning about fractions, in Steffe, L.P. and Nesher, P. (eds) *Theories of Mathematical Learning.* Mahwah, NJ: Lawrence Erlbaum Associates. pp. 241–266.

Charalambous, C., Delaney, S., Hsu, H.-Y, and Mesa, V. (2010) A comparative analysis of the addition and subtraction of fractions in textbooks from three countries. *Mathematical Thinking and Learning, 12*(2): 117–151.

Charalambous, C. and Pitta-Pantazi, D. (2007) Drawing on a theoretical model to study students' understandings of fraction. *Educational Studies in Mathematics*, 64: 293–316.

Clarke, D.M. and Roche, A. (2009) Students' fraction comparison strategies as a window into robust understanding and possible pointers for instruction. *Educational Studies in Mathematics*, 72:127–138.

DfE (2013) *National Curriculum in England: Mathematics programmes of study: key stages 1 and 2.* Available at: www.gov.uk/government/publications/national-curriculum-in-england-mathematics-programmes-of-study/national-curriculum-in-england-mathematics-programmes-of-study (accessed 25/07/14).

Hansen, A., Mavrikis, M., Grawemeyer, B., Mazziotti, C., Mubeen, J. and Koshkarbayeva, A. (2014) *Report on Learning Tasks and Cognitive Models.* Deliverable 1.2 report for the Talk,

Tutor, Explore, Learn: Intelligent Tutoring and Exploration for Robust Learning project. Available: www.italk2learn.eu/the-project/deliverables-and-publications/

Kieran, T.E. (1976) On the mathematical, cognitive, and instructional foundations of rational numbers, in Lesh, R.(ed.) *Number and Measurement: Papers from a Research Workshop*. Columbus, OH: ERIC/SMEAC. pp.101–144.

Kieran, T.E. (1993) Rational and fractional numbers: From quotient fields to recursive understanding, in Carpenter, T.P., Fennema, E. and Romberg, T.A. (eds) *Rational Numbers: An integration of research*. New Jersey: Erlbaum. pp.49–84.

Lamon, S. (1999) *Teaching Fractions and Ratios for Understanding*. London: Erlbaum.

Lamon, S.J. (2012) *Teaching Fractions and Ratios for Understanding: essential content knowledge and instructional strategies for teachers*, 3rd edition. New York: Routledge.

Leung, C.K. (2009) *A Preliminary Study on Hong Kong Students' Understanding of Fraction*. Paper presented at the 3rd Redesigning Pedagogy International Conference June 2009, Singapore.

Mamede, E., Nunes, T. and Bryant, P. (2005) *The Equivalence and Ordering of Fractions in Partwhole and Quotient Situations*. Paper presented at the Proceedings of the 29th Conference of the International Group for the Psychology of Mathematics Education, Melbourne.

Nunes, T. (2006) Fractions: difficult but crucial in mathematics learning. *Teaching and Learning Research Programme*. Available at: www.tlrp.org/pub/documents/no13_nunes. pdf (accessed 28/07/14).

Panaoura, A., Gagatsis, A., Deliyianni, E. and Elia, I. (2009) The structure of students' beliefs about the use of representations and their performance on the learning of fractions, Educational Psychology. *An International Journal of Experimental Educational Psychology*, 29(6), 713–728.

Pantziara, M. and Philippou, G. (2012) Levels of students' 'conceptions' of fractions. *Educational Studies in Mathematics*, 79: 61–83.

Siegler, R.S., Duncan, G.J., Davis-Kean, P.E., Duckworth, K., Claessens, A., Engel, M., Susperreguy, M.I. and Chen, M. (2012) Early predictors of high school mathematics achievement. *Psychological Science*, 23: 691–697.

Silver, E.A. (1983) Probing young adults' thinking about rational numbers. *Focus on Learning Problems in Mathematics*, 5: 105–117.

STA (2012) EYFS Profile exemplification for the level of learning and development expected at the end of the EYFS. Mathematics, ELG11 – Numbers. Coventry: STA.

Uttal, D.H., O'Doherty, K., Newland, R., Hand L. and DeLoache, J. (2009) Dual Representation and the Lining of Concrete Symbolic Representations. *Child Development Perspectives*, 3(3): 156–159.

7 Geometry and measurement

Diane Vaukins

Learning outcomes

In this chapter, we will explore geometry and measure. The key learning objectives for the chapter are:

- to explore the expectations and content of the National Curriculum;
- to understand what is meant by measure in terms of the National Curriculum;
- to understand what is meant by geometry in terms of the National Curriculum;
- to consider ways of developing children's reasoning through their study of shape and space.

TEACHERS' STANDARDS

1. Set high expectations which inspire, motivate and challenge pupils
2. Promote good progress and outcomes by pupils
3. Demonstrate good subject and curriculum knowledge
4. Plan and teach well-structured lessons
5. Adapt teaching to respond to the strengths and needs of all pupils
6. Make accurate and productive use of assessment

Introduction

Mathematics is often thought of as simply number. The main emphasis in the National Curriculum is on number and calculations. While this area of mathematics is of course important, it should not be forgotten that within geometry and measure there is a great deal of number and need for calculation.

It is also important to remember that having a facility with number does not automatically lead to great prowess in visual and spatial thinking and vice versa. When embarking on a sequence of lessons on geometry, it may well be worth reconsidering your classroom groupings (if you have them). Otherwise it is likely that some children will be under-challenged and others may be given work which is overly challenging. This area of mathematics is a real opportunity for some children, for whom maths is not usually their forte, to shine. If you can spot these children and acknowledge their prowess publically in this area of maths (asking them to explain their thinking, putting their work up on the walls, etc.), you may be able to encourage a more positive attitude towards the areas of mathematics that they find less easy.

Children beginning school in September 2014 will leave full-time education in 2026 and therefore the education they receive throughout their formal time in school needs to be fit for purpose and equip them with the skills they may need for jobs and a lifestyle that no one really has knowledge of today. There are a few things we can be almost sure of: life will be lived in 3-D, there will be some form of currency, there will be a form of measurement and time will pass in one form or another. So although number facts are important, shape, space and measures should not be forgotten. Indeed, children are surrounded by shape a long time before number comes into their lives.

Curriculum Link

The 2013 National Curriculum (DfE, 2013) changed emphasis from the previous curricula and used the term 'geometry'. Furthermore, it separated 'Shape, space and measure' into: 'Measurement' and 'Geometry', which is further sub-divided into 'properties of shapes' and 'position and direction'.

What is geometry? Atiyah (2001) writes:

spatial intuition or spatial perception is an enormously powerful tool and that is why geometry is actually such a powerful part of mathematics – not only for things that are obviously geometrical, but even for things that are not. We try to put them into geometrical form because that enables us to use our intuition. Our intuition is our most powerful tool …

(p.658)

The National Curriculum contains a strong injunction to create mathematical curiosity among children in primary school, to connect mathematical learning with their lived experiences and to develop their ability to reason mathematically. Therefore this chapter looks at how you might begin to do this in the context of teaching and learning geometry and measure in the primary classroom.

Below is a brief summary of the expectations for each key stage. The words in bold show a clear emphasis placed on curiosity and thought throughout the primary curriculum.

Key Stage 1 – Years 1 and 2

*At this stage, pupils should develop their ability to **recognise, describe**, draw, **compare** and sort different shapes and use the related vocabulary. Teaching should also involve using a range of measures to describe and compare different quantities such as length, mass, capacity/volume, time and money.*

(DfE, 2013, p.5)

(Continued)

(Continued)

Lower Key Stage 2 – Years 3 and 4

*Teaching should also ensure that pupils draw with increasing accuracy and develop **mathematical reasoning** so they can **analyse** shapes and their properties, and confidently **describe** the relationships between them. It should ensure that they can use measuring instruments with accuracy and **make connections** between measure and number.*

(DfE, 2013, p.17)

Upper Key Stage 2 – Years 5 and 6

*Teaching in geometry and measures should **consolidate** and **extend knowledge** developed in number. Teaching should also ensure that pupils **classify** shapes with increasingly complex geometric properties and that they learn the vocabulary they need to describe them.*

(DfE, 2013, p.30)

Activity: Measurement and geometry

Below is the National Curriculum content for one primary year group for measurement and geometry. Read through the list and try to establish which year group you think it is and why.

- **Convert** between different units of measurement (for example, kilometre to metre; hour to minute).

- **Measure and calculate** the perimeter of a rectilinear figure (including squares) in centimetres and metres.

- Find the area of rectilinear shapes by **counting squares**.

- **Estimate, compare and calculate** different measures, including money in pounds and pence.

- **Read, write and convert time** between analogue and digital 12- and 24-hour clocks.

- **Solve problems** involving converting from hours to minutes; minutes to seconds; years to months; weeks to days.

- **Compare and classify** geometric shapes, including quadrilaterals and triangles, based on their properties and sizes.

- **Identify acute and obtuse angles** and **compare and order** angles up to two right angles by size.

- Identify lines of **symmetry** in 2-D shapes presented in different orientations.

- Complete a simple symmetric figure with respect to a specific line of symmetry.

- **Describe positions** on a 2-D grid as co-ordinates in the **first quadrant**.

- **Describe movements** between positions as translations of a given unit to the left/right and up/down.

- **Plot specified points** and draw sides to complete a given polygon.

Were you correct?

If not, were you underestimating or overestimating in terms of expectations of achievement?

What were the key things that made you decide which year group you thought it was?

Research Focus: Effective teachers of geometry

Jones, Mooney and Harries (2002) reviewed what trainee teachers might need to know about geometry in order to be effective teachers of geometry in the primary classroom. Although this report was written to discuss the relevance of the required knowledge in light of the introduction of the Numeracy Strategy, many of the findings resonate with the expectations of the new curriculum.

They found that geometry was the area of mathematics where trainee teachers were the least confident and where they performed least well in baseline tests. The subject knowledge identified as being important to teach geometry included:

- co-ordinates in 2-D;

- 2-D transformations;

- congruence and similarity;

- constructions;

- area formulae;

- surface area and volume of prisms;

- properties of 3-D shapes.

Interestingly, a similar audit carried out in the USA also identified visualisation and the ability to reason with geometrical shapes as important. Exploring the properties of shapes is an excellent vehicle for developing children's mathematical reasoning skills.

One of the main conclusions in this report was the fact that it is not simply enough to have the mathematical content knowledge to be an effective teacher, but it is important for teachers and trainees to be knowledgeable about the whole mathematics curriculum and to be able to make the connections between concepts and principles from simple to complex.

Seeing mathematics everywhere

There is sometimes a distinction made between teachers who can see mathematics everywhere and those who cannot and the fact that the former group will be much better at finding ways to develop children's mathematics through activities and problems that are connected to the children's 'lived experience'.

Activity: Seeing mathematics everywhere

Think for a moment about yourself and where you fit in the description above. Are you one of the people who can just see mathematics everywhere or do you struggle to do this?

You might practise doing this now. Have a look around you and see if you can see opportunities for some work on geometry with children based on something that you can see. For example, I am looking out of my window at home at my neighbour's garden shed. It is a three-dimensional object with a sloping roof and a door that swings open. I think that it might have come as a flat-pack. I can think of quite a bit of Key Stage 2 mathematics that could be based on sheds.

Geometry – properties of shape

Encouraging reasoning

Geometry can be a very rich area for the development of reasoning and mathematical thinking alongside an understanding of geometry. Consider an activity that is commonly used in primary classrooms in geometry lessons.

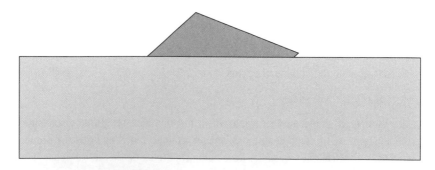

Figure 7.1   Shape Reveal Activity

The teacher has 'hidden' a shape behind the rectangular screen and slowly reveals it. Often this becomes a guessing game, as the children call out what they think the hidden shape is. A much more productive way of using this activity is to ask the children to tell you what shape it definitely cannot be and how they know this. This subtle shift in the activity opens up a lot more possibilities for mathematical reasoning. Typical responses might be as follows:

'It cannot be a square because squares only have right angles and that shape has an angle that is bigger than a right angle.'

'It cannot be a circle because it has a corner and circles have no corners.'

'It cannot be an equilateral triangle because the angle is bigger than 90 degrees and equilateral triangles have angles that are all 60 degrees.'

As more of the shape is revealed, more possibilities can be discounted using reasoning. As the children are engaging in reasoning, they are also calling on and developing a great deal of knowledge of the properties of shapes. The activity described above allows all children to participate and some of them to surprise you. Some of the possible responses cited above were more sophisticated in terms of the knowledge of geometry than others. The activity allows the children to verbalise their reasoning (see Chapter 1 for a full discussion of mathematical reasoning) and to surprise you with their knowledge of geometry, as there is no single 'right' answer that you are looking for.

Here is another example. Consider these two approaches.

1.   What is the name of this shape?

2.   What is the same and what is different about these two shapes?

Figure 7.2   Different approaches to questioning about shapes

Haylock (2010) asserts that understanding same and different is a fundamental mathematical idea. We would suggest that the second activity provides the children with a much greater opportunity to discuss (and therefore to give you an insight into their thinking) and to reason about shapes. You might like to prompt younger children to complete sentences:

'The two shapes are the same because ...'

'The two shapes are different because ...'

There are a number of common misconceptions in geometry (see Haylock, 2010, and/ or Hansen, 2014 for details). Using activities such as those suggested above is a good way of tackling some of these misconceptions. Consider this example:

What is the same and different about these shapes?

Figure 7.3 Using same and different to tackle misconceptions

Presenting the children with this might lead to a discussion about regular and irregular shapes and allow you to tackle the misconception that shapes are always presented with a side oriented horizontally. 'Same and different' discussions naturally lead children to think about the properties of shapes. Using this particular example will generate discussion about what makes a square a square and a rectangle a rectangle. If it challenges the children (or you) to investigate the properties of shapes further (to discover that a square is just a 'special' rectangle), so much the better.

A quick look online, or in any of many books, will yield dozens of geometry-based activities for children. Your challenge is to take them and adapt them and your questioning, so as to ensure that the children also have the chance to develop their mathematical reasoning as they do the activities.

Geometry – position and direction

The National Curriculum stresses the need to link what children learn to their own experience and to encourage children to enquire. Within the area of geometry, the position and direction section most readily lends itself to linking to the other subjects within the primary curriculum.

A great deal of work on movement can be incorporated into PE lessons allowing children to experience rotating clockwise and anticlockwise. Using ICT programmes children can manipulate and move objects right, left, up and down. In geography children can read maps to plot routes, and in design and technology all the areas of transformation can be used to create original designs that can be explained mathematically. There are many artists who use mathematics within their work to great effect. Much of Bridget Riley's work uses a great variety of geometric forms that produce sensations of movement or colour. M.C. Escher's artwork was inspired by mathematics and explored infinity and optical illusion. He also produced a lot of artwork which involved tessellation.

One way of enabling children to understand the mathematics involved in geometry is to allow them to explore and discover the mathematics in the world around them first and then bring this back to the classroom. A visit, either in reality or virtually, to an art gallery, wallpaper shop or fabric shop will let children experience pattern at first hand and see the results of geometry in action. A treasure hunt, orienteering or designing a scaled-down model will help them to understand grids and co-ordinates.

Activity: Repeating patterns

Take a few minutes to look around you and see how many forms of repeating patterns you can see. Look at the wallpaper, carpet or even the clothes you are wearing.

Choose an image and see when and where it occurs again. Can you explain the moves to get it from A to B?

The vocabulary of position and direction

For many children, learning the vocabulary associated with position and direction is a challenge. This is particularly the case for children whose first language is not English. Several English prepositional words (words which describe position) are small (and therefore easily missed, or misunderstood) and similar to each other. Consider the difference between 'in' and 'on'. Mastering this vocabulary will be made easier if the children can connect the words with a real and memorable experience.

You can use the day-to-day run of the classroom as a good way of helping young children to connect this vocabulary to their experiences. Tidying up is a good opportunity – asking children to put things 'in' the drawer, 'next to' the pile of books, 'on' the table, etc. is helpful. If you have a child whose first language is not English, or a child who is struggling with acquiring this vocabulary, pair the child up with a more confident child to tidy things up together. Be sure to model your own use of this vocabulary: 'I'm going to hang your coat next to Joseph's'.

You might also arrange situations where the children have to use the vocabulary of position and direction. Games where one child has to direct another to find something in the classroom, or around an obstacle course or maze set up in the hall or outside, encourage the children to be precise with their use of positional vocabulary. In 'Preposition PE' young children have to position themselves (or a bear/soft toy) along an obstacle course (for example, 'Can you put the bear *on* the bench. Now he has to jump *over* the mat and land *in* the hoop.'). A more sophisticated task to use with older children is to get them to work in pairs, sitting back to back. One child is given a picture and the other child a blank piece of paper and a pencil. The child with the picture has to describe it as accurately as possible to the other child, who is allowed to ask questions, but not to look at the picture. This child has to draw the picture as accurately as possible from the description. This activity encourages children to use positional (and other) vocabulary and is useful in highlighting to you (and to the children) any words that they are finding difficult.

Curriculum Link

Position and direction is mentioned frequently in Key Stage 1 as children are learning positional vocabulary. There is a lot of emphasis on turning, as a prerequisite to work on angles. In Year 5, children are expected to learn about reflections and translations in the context of co-ordinates and in Year 6, this is extended to include work in all four quadrants.

The National Curriculum implies that teachers will encourage their children to be curious, to reason and to ask mathematical questions (see Chapter 1). There is a lot of interesting work that can be done using shape transformations (translations, reflections and rotations – although the latter are not mentioned explicitly in the curriculum) and co-ordinates. Children should investigate what happens to the co-ordinates of a shape when it is reflected in various lines, or when it is translated. This is an excellent opportunity for the children to make their own mathematical conjectures and to test them out. Making conjectures, or predictions, and then testing them out is not only highly motivating for children, it also encourages them into real mathematical thinking rather than simply following processes or acquiring knowledge handed to them by the teacher.

Measurement

Activity: Measurement in the everyday

Think about and try to list all the everyday activities that you do that involve measuring in one form or another.

Some things may have sprung to mind straight away like:

- baking;
- shopping;
- planning a journey or holiday;

- decorating;

- gardening;

- setting the TV to record something;

- planning an obstacle course;

- reorganising the classroom.

Your everyday life is full of such activities, as are the children's lives. This presents an excellent opportunity both to capitalise on your children's experiences and to construct lessons where the use of measures is purposeful for the children. Linking mathematics with children's life experience is a key theme of the National Curriculum and something that can be achieved in the area of measure. One way to gain children's interest is to get them involved in solving problems that are meaningful to them. All children respond with more motivation to problems that require them to use the skills learned throughout the curriculum and across subject areas. This helps them to make sense of what they have been learning and why.

However, children's experiences of using measures at home may involve imperial units rather than decimal ones. The new curriculum still expects children in Year 5 to *understand and use approximate equivalences between metric units and common imperial units such as inches, pounds and pints* (DfE, 2013, p.36). However, there is no mention of imperial measure before Year 5. If some children come to school knowing how tall they are in feet and inches or how much they weigh in stones and pounds, then metres and kilogrammes are going to have to be learned.

Case Study: The secret garden

Carol is in her second year of teaching. She had been given a Year 5 class in her previous year and continued with this class into Year 6 the following year. Within the school grounds there is a waste piece of land tucked away in the corner of the playing field that had once been a small garden area but had been neglected for several years. Carol decided to give the class the task of redesigning the garden with a view to presenting their findings to the head and the governors to see if something could be done to re-establish it in the future.

Initially the children had to measure the exact area of the garden and then create a scaled-down version on squared paper. They then went to look at different gardens in the area to get some ideas as to what might work. Catalogues were used to choose items and the process of working out how much everything was going to cost and whether it would all fit in began. Each group of children was given the opportunity to work on the area that best suited their ability or interest. The cost of the project was finalised and a letter was written to the head and the governors to ask if it would be possible to reinstate the garden. Carol thought this had been a really good experience

$\longrightarrow$

for the children but was sorry that they might not ever see the result even if the governors did actually agree to having this work done.

What Carol did not know was that while the children were working on this project, one of them had told the class that his father was the manager of a local large DIY company and he was going to ask him for advice and for an idea of cost. So intrigued was the father that he spoke to the local press who were also interested in the story. The result was that the children were interviewed, they appeared in the press and the local DIY company donated the products and labour for free to see the garden come alive again.

Activity: Other curriculum subjects

Read the case study again alongside the content of the Year 6 mathematics curriculum and see how many areas are covered.

You might also like to look at the other curriculum subjects to see how much else has also been covered by allowing the children to work in this way.

Key skills in measuring

Comparing

Irrespective of what the children are measuring, an important initial skill is being able to make comparisons. Haylock (2010) highlights the fact that understanding notions of same and different is at the heart of children's mathematical learning. The vocabulary of comparison can be challenging for some children (particularly those learning English as an additional language). They have to move from 'big' to 'bigger' (and even 'biggest'). It will be important that you model the appropriate vocabulary to the children. It is also important that comparison is done in both directions, for example 'A is longer than B', but also 'B is shorter than A'.

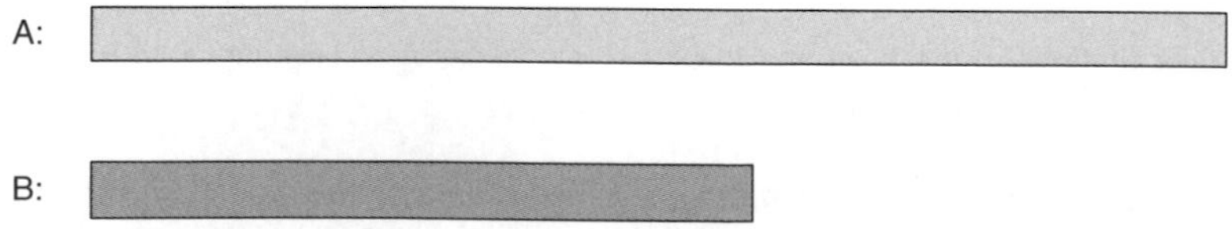

A:

B:

Figure 7.4 The language of comparison

Try to ensure that your children have plenty of opportunity to make comparisons and to use the language of comparison. This will occur naturally in their play as well as in more structured situations. Your skill will be to spot opportunities to make comparisons, model the appropriate language and to be very encouraging when you hear children doing this spontaneously.

Understanding what is being measured

Although this may seem straightforward, it can be deceptively complicated. To illustrate this, I invite you to consider the issue of 'length', which is a measure that young children encounter.

Activity: Measuring scenarios

Here are three measuring scenarios involving 'length'. Spend a couple of minutes thinking about the different words we use to describe what is being measured and the practical differences in these situations:

1. the 'length' of the table;

2. a child's 'height';

3. the 'distance' from a child's desk to the classroom door.

Although 'length', 'height' and 'distance' seem similar, their use is strictly governed (we simply would not talk about measuring a child's 'length', unless possibly they were lying down; we would not talk about the 'length' from here to the post office).

Measuring the length of the table involves measuring something tangible. A child can put a ruler or metre stick against the table, or can lay straws along its length and count them. Measuring a child's height involves measuring an imaginary vertical line from the top of the child's head to the floor – not so easy to do practically. The final example also involves imagining a line. There is a further complication with distances which cannot be covered in a straight line. The distance from our classroom to the office might be short, but involve a lot of winding corridors and a trip down some stairs. As adults we have the expression 'as the crow flies' to help explain this, but this is unlikely to be helpful to a group of children in Reception.

Estimation

When asked to estimate the length or weight of something many children and adults struggle to begin to have an idea until they compare it to something they know the length or weight of.

Activity: Estimating

Estimate the following:

1. the weight of an elephant;

2. the depth of the Atlantic Ocean;

3. the distance to the moon.

Did you struggle with this activity? Why would you need to know these sorts of things if they are not part of your everyday life? You might think the last activity was an unrealistic thing to expect anyone to be able to do. If you had been given a more everyday object it would have been easier, but would it really? Do you know the weight of an apple or how much liquid a bath can hold? These were questions that 11-year-olds were expected to be able to answer in the National Tests a few years ago. Just as you may have struggled with the last activity, the children were bewildered by these questions.

Encouraging children to estimate in the context of measure is not easy. My experience with children is that they are reluctant to estimate, for fear of being 'wrong'. I have known children to estimate and then change their estimate to the 'right' answer as soon as they have measured. This does highlight the slightly unreal nature of getting children to estimate before they measure. In reality, we would simply measure if we needed to know a particular length, weight, etc. accurately. However, estimating can be a good way to increase curiosity (see Chapter 1 for an example in the context of capacity). It should be noted here that asking children to estimate the outcome of a calculation before they carry it out is more purposeful, as it serves as a checking mechanism.

The more you model estimating (and accepting that your estimate may not have been exactly 'right'), the more likely the children are to estimate spontaneously. Having a weekly 'estimation competition' using different areas of measure can be a nice way of getting children better at estimating and excited about measuring. Becoming more accurate with estimation is largely down to having a number of 'benchmarks' that can be referred to. For example, knowing that a bag of flour has a mass of 1.5 kg (and having experience of picking up a bag of flour) combined with skills of comparison, can help children to get better at estimating. I always found it helpful to bring in packaging to help children get a feel for capacity (see Figure 7.5).

Connecting measures to children's experience

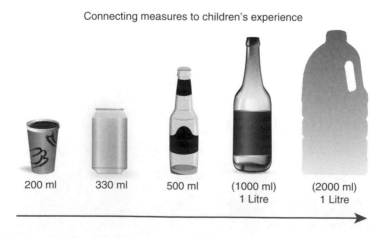

| 200 ml | 330 ml | 500 ml | (1000 ml)
1 Litre | (2000 ml)
1 Litre |

Figure 7.5 Benchmarks for estimating

Time

Although time appears in the National Curriculum under the section on measure, its very particular nature means that we give it special consideration here.

Curriculum Link

The National Curriculum has a strong emphasis on time. In Year 1, children begin to tell the time and are expected to become familiar with the vocabulary relating to time, such as units of time, days of the week, months of the year, etc. The expectations for Year 2 are that children will be able to tell the time to the nearest five minutes. As they move through Key Stage 2, children are expected to solve problems involving time with increased accuracy and sophistication and to convert between units of time.

Activity: Problems with time

Learning about time is fraught with possible misconceptions. Spend a few minutes thinking about the many possible problems children may have in learning about time.

What kinds of things did you consider? Possibly the fact that time is experienced in a relative way. The way we experience five minutes passing will vary depending on whether we are jogging up a steep hill or sitting on a perfect beach. The language of time can be very confusing. Think of a clock face for a moment and the fact that it has two scales on it. Our counting number system is base ten but the clock face is divided into twelve and each section is divided into five. Children are told that the one is sometimes a five, the two is a ten and the six is sometimes a half. Is it any wonder that they struggle? Did you consider the language we use to express time and the fact that we often tell children to 'wait a second' when we really do not mean that literally.

A lot of published lessons on time seem to involve worksheets with children drawing hands onto pre-printed clocks. While this has its place, it may be more powerful to take advantage of the fact that school days are highly structured and that we all, including the children, experience time every day.

In school, the same event often happens at the same time each day. It is relatively easy to draw the children's attention to the position of the hands on the clock at lunchtime each day or at the end of the school day. As the children get more used to this, you can start to ask them where the hands will be at lunchtime, at the end of the day, in ten minutes or in half an hour. It is only a short step from there to start thinking about how long it is until lunch or the end of the day and to refer to them using the correct mathematical vocabulary. After a while, the children will begin to notice the clock without you prompting them. Tidying up is an excellent opportunity for children to get a 'feel' for the passing of time. Using a sand timer or having a countdown timer on your interactive white board while the children are tidying up will help them to get a feel for how long two minutes or five minutes is. You might wish to have a 'tidy-up song' which lasts a precise amount of time.

In addition to noting the time at important points in the day, there are also important times during the course of a week: PE lessons, assembly, 'golden time' on a Friday. It is important to give children time cues for getting changed for PE, getting ready for lunch or getting lined up to go to assembly. It is also helpful to ask a child, or group of children, to keep an eye on the clock and remind you about something at a particular time. You may simply be contriving things to happen at a particular time ('Miss Thorne the head teacher will be coming in to tell us about the school trip at 11:30. Can someone remind me at quarter past so we can tidy up and be ready?') Many of these things would be impossible without a clock in your classroom.

Activity: The importance of time

Spend a few minutes thinking through your school day/week and list as many opportunities as you can to draw the children's attention to the clock and to the importance of time.

As a primary school teacher, one of the most useful things you can do to help your children with time, whatever their age, is to have a clock in your classroom. Have a think about the opportunities this offers as you read the following case study.

Case Study: Always have a clock in your classroom

A PGCE student was placed in a Year 1 class without a clock in the room. The children were struggling with their work on telling the time. One of the children became interested in how quickly he could eat his lunch. When asked how long he thought it would take him, he replied 'about ten minutes', but had no way to tell, as there was no clock. The student decided to put a clock up in the room. She drew the children's attention to the clock and the position of the hands at various points during the day particularly as they went to lunch and when they came back to the room to get their coats. The child in question became curious about how the hands had moved while he was away having lunch and quickly learned to work out how long it had taken him to eat. After only a few days he was able to use the clock to tell the student how long lunch had taken. As a result of looking at the clock regularly during the course of the day he and many of the other children quickly became skilled at telling the time and at reminding the teacher when it was nearly lunchtime.

Solving problems with time

In addition to being able to tell the time, it is important that children are able to solve everyday problems with time. We suggest that a timeline might be a useful visual representation of a time problem. It might also be a useful way of helping you to make a child's thinking about solving time problems visible to the other children in the class.

Consider the following problem: A man sets out for his destination at 10:45 and arrives at 12:30. How long has the journey taken?

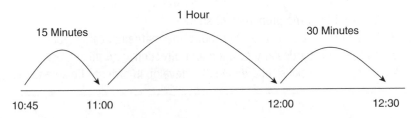

Figure 7.6 Timeline to illustrate solving time problems

By the time children come to solve time problems, they will have had experience of using number lines to solve arithmetic problems. We would suggest that the children solve this problem by counting on from 10:45 to the nearest whole hour (11:00), then to 12:00 and then to 12:30, making a note of each 'jump'. The sum of all the jumps then gives the time between 10:45 and 12:30. Children should be given opportunities to solve a variety of time problems.

- Finding the elapsed time (as illustrated above).

- Finding an end time. (For example, a man leaves his house at 07:20 and runs for 55 minutes. What time does he arrive home?)

- Finding a start time. (For example, a cake needs 48 minutes in the oven. It needs to come out of the oven by 11:25. What time should I put it in?)

Learning Outcomes Review

This chapter has explored shape, space and measure in terms of the National Curriculum and the expectations of both learning and teaching. The contents of the curriculum have been discussed in terms of how to deliver them in ways that make learning interesting and that use the prior knowledge and everyday experience of the children to enhance and improve understanding. Measure has been discussed and misconceptions highlighted, particularly where language is involved. Geometry

(Continued)

(Continued)

has been split into the two components and ideas have been provided that once again allow exploration of the real world to enhance and complement the learning and teaching in the primary classroom.

Self-assessment questions

1. What are the key areas relating to geometry and measures in the National Curriculum?
2. How might children's mathematical reasoning be developed alongside their understanding of the properties of shape?
3. How might you help children to acquire the mathematical language associated with geometry (particularly position and direction) and measures?
4. What are the key skills children need to develop in order to be able to measure?

Further Reading

Briggs, M. (2013) *Teaching and Learning Early Years Mathematics – Subject and Pedagogic Knowledge.* Northwich: Critical Publishing.

References

Atiyah, M. (2001) Mathematics in the 20th Century: Geometry versus algebra. *Mathematics Today*, 37(2): 46–53.

DfE (2013) *National Curriculum in England: Mathematics programmes of study: key stages 1 and 2*. Available at: www.gov.uk/government/publications/national-curriculum-in-england-mathematics-programmes-of-study/national-curriculum-in-england-mathematics-programmes-of-study (accessed 28/07/14).

Hansen, A. (2014) *Children's Errors in Mathematics*, 3rd edition. London: Learning Matters SAGE.

Haylock, D. (2010) *Mathematics Explained for Primary Teachers*. London: SAGE.

Jones, K., Mooney, C. and Harries, T. (2002) Trainee primary teachers' knowledge of geometry for teaching. *Proceedings of the British Society for Research into Learning Mathematics*, 22(2): 95–100.

8 Data handling

Caroline Rickard

Learning outcomes

This chapter will support you in demonstrating good subject and curriculum knowledge (Qualified Teacher Status (QTS) Standard 3) and divides the process of helping children to become good at data handling into a number of different topics. In this chapter you will:

- be reminded of the contribution of data handling to our everyday lives and learn about the data handling cycle;
- consider data of different types;
- learn about skills associated with gathering data;
- explore different formats for presenting and interpreting data;
- understand basic statistical tools, in particular averages;
- think about starting points for data handling.

TEACHERS' STANDARDS

1 **Set high expectations which inspire, motivate and challenge pupils**

   establish a safe and stimulating environment for pupils, rooted in mutual respect

2 **Promote good progress and outcomes by pupils**

   be aware of pupils' capabilities and their prior knowledge, and plan teaching to build on these

   demonstrate knowledge and understanding of how pupils learn and how this impacts on teaching

3 **Demonstrate good subject and curriculum knowledge**

   if teaching early mathematics, demonstrate a clear understanding of appropriate teaching strategies

4 **Plan and teach well-structured lessons**

   promote a love of learning and children's intellectual curiosity

5 **Adapt teaching to respond to the strengths and needs of all pupils**

   have a secure understanding of how a range of factors can inhibit pupils' ability to learn, and how best to overcome these

---

Introduction

Looking at the year group content associated with data handling one might assume that 'Statistics', as the National Curriculum refers to it from Year 2, is predominantly about mastering a series of different types of graph and chart. While we do want children to develop this understanding we need to appreciate a little more what is involved in becoming a statistically literate member of society. According to the National Curriculum, part of the purpose of studying mathematics is its contribution to understanding our world; data handling skills must surely feature prominently.

The data handling cycle

Many authors (for example, Graham, 2006) write about data handling as having several components, often describing the whole as a cyclical process:

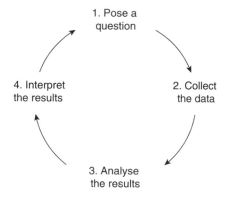

Figure 8.1   The data handling cycle

Presenting the data in a graph may play a part in this process, but is not always necessary or appropriate. Often a table lends itself to displaying specific numerical values more readily than a graph. Rickard (2013, p.204) recommends that all children should experience the full cycle from time to time but notes that teachers might at other times focus the children's attention upon a specific element of the cycle. Graham (2006) criticises some classroom projects for starting without clear questions and therefore failing to support children in deciding what to do next: *This vagueness of purpose tends to ripple through the rest of the investigation, making it hard for learners to choose an appropriate calculation or graphical representation, or to come to any conclusion about what the data reveal* (p.28). Note that while the term 'data', as used here, is the plural of 'datum', it is often now treated as a mass noun, with the associated verb being singular.

Ideally children will often have opportunities to work from their own starting points, asking their own questions rather than always investigating something someone else has contrived, however convenient this might be. It is also possible that a question can be explored using secondary data from a reliable source rather than data collected first-hand; historical lines of enquiry in particular lend themselves to exploration of secondary data. An easily accessible example of geographical data is weather station readings (www.metoffice.gov.uk).

Activity: Opportunities to engage in the data handling cycle

Thinking about sequences of data handling lessons you have taught, reflect on whether they started with a question and perhaps whose question it was. At the data collection stage did the children gather a set of data by themselves or merely make a single contribution to a class data set? Children must be given the opportunity to work sufficiently independently to develop a deep understanding of the data handling cycle. Consider whether your children experienced the cycle in full. If not, could you plan such an opportunity?

In reality, if we start with an interesting and perhaps challenging question, it may take several loops of the data handling cycle to get to the point where we feel the question has been satisfactorily answered. Presenting a claim and asking children to investigate it can be a nice way of moving through the data handling process as a class. If a certain biscuit manufacturer claims that they have the best biscuit for dunking, how do the children suggest we might investigate the claim? Defining what we mean by 'best' is clearly important with claims such as this one, and the process of trying to investigate it may raise more questions.

Reasoning, problem solving and communicating

The aims of the National Curriculum (see Chapters 1 and 2) emphasise children having opportunities to follow lines of enquiry as part of their learning to reason mathematically and the importance of using mathematics to solve real and important problems and to communicate mathematically. The data handling cycle provides a good vehicle for this. In the 'real world' children will often encounter data being used to communicate and advance an argument, or particular point of view. Encouraging children to use and present data as a way of advancing an argument both supports the development of their mathematical reasoning and communication skills, and also helps to make the mathematics more real and connected to their lived experience.

Data pervade modern life and therefore learning to interrogate data, to construct meaning and gain an accurate sense of what they might be telling us can be considered a key life skill. Anyone with access to the internet can access huge quantities of data, facts and figures pertaining to all manner of subjects and presented in different ways, each telling a story about variation, *the raison d'être for statistics* (Watson, 2007, p.5).

As adults we hopefully appreciate that statistics can emanate from a biased standpoint or be presented in a misleading way. It benefits children if they can be helped to understand that *data do not necessarily tell the whole story and do not always provide definitive answers* (Paramore, 2011, p.71). Exploring, and perhaps challenging, claims made in advertising can be a good way of developing children's understanding. According to the National Curriculum, in Year 5 children learn to access information from timetables – a nice example of a context in which we hope the information has been presented clearly and accurately.

Understanding data of different types

The data primary age children work with initially are often categorical: data collections where each result can be assigned to a category, for example asking children how they travelled to school in the morning. Each child's response can be assigned to a category (on foot, by car, by bike, by hovercraft, etc.). We can then count how many people or things belong to a certain group: children with blond hair; number of cars as opposed to other vehicles; ice cream choices. Note that where a graph is about preferences, such as favourite ice cream flavour, someone's choice does not mean that they do not also like other flavours. Categorical data does not tend to have any natural order to it and categorisation can at times be awkward due to overlaps. For example, the book I am reading at the moment is part murder mystery but there is also a heavy dose of romance; pigeon-holing data can be tricky.

Data can sometimes be numerical, for example numbers of children taking part in different races on sports day. This is an example of discrete or countable data (we can count how many people entered each race). With discrete data the values tend to be restricted; we would not expect any non-whole numbers for our competitor data, or when asking about how many people live in your house. Numbers involved in discrete data are not always integers, however; shoes, for example, are sometimes sold in half sizes.

Numerical data is, however, often continuous in nature, arising from a measurement scenario, such as room temperature or waiting time. Here a full range of results are possible. Being conscious of data type is important as it sometimes influences the type of graph which is most suitable.

In practice, while measurement is continuous, measurements are recorded to the nearest convenient unit, for example when measuring the heights of children in the class to the nearest whole centimetre, or recording the lengths of films to the nearest whole minute. The result of this is that we are able to count and graph the data in much the same way as we would if working with discrete values. However, the range of different values can prompt grouping of the data. For example, we might group the children or the films into 'bands': films between 90 and 99 minutes in length and so forth. The data could be presented in an early form of histogram with bars in order and touching (and also of equal width), indicating that we are dealing with continuous values.

At a simple level we can answer direct questions such as: 'How many children have blond hair?' from the data, but Teachers' Standard 1 expects us to have high expectations of our pupils. This suggests we might encourage children to begin to 'read between the data', i.e. to make additional observations, for example that brown hair seems to be more common than blond in our class, or that cars are more prevalent than other vehicles along the road outside our school. This requires reading the whole data set rather than looking at single elements in isolation. Even more advanced than this is the ability to 'read beyond the data', i.e. to build other ideas from the data, for example surmising that our hair colour findings might or might not be representative of a wider population, or reasoning that we might get different vehicle data at the weekend as opposed to weekdays. To a great extent, inference, or reading beyond the data, relies on being able to draw upon existing and everyday knowledge, but also upon 'intellectual curiosity', something Teachers' Standard 4 urges us to promote through planning and teaching well-structured lessons. The National Curriculum talks of children tackling comparison questions in Year 3 and then comparison, sum and difference problems from Year 4 onwards, but interpretation of graphs can begin sooner than this and is valuable with children of any age.

Research Focus: Graph sense

Research by Friel et al. (2001) explored critical factors desirable for graph comprehension, behaviours referred to as 'graph sense'.

1. Recognise key components of graphs illustrating categorical and numerical data; appreciate relationships between components.

2. Understand how specific graphs operate and possess appropriate language to talk about them.

3. Understand that the same data can be presented in different formats e.g. tables and graphs.

4. Respond to different levels of questions when interpreting graphs.

5. Recognise when one type of graph is more useful than another.

6. Be aware of personal bias.

Describing research related to behaviour 4, learners experienced few difficulties with 'read the data questions', whereas their interpretation of 'read between the data' questions was less secure, and 'read beyond the data' questions proved even more challenging.

Activity: Interpreting graphs

Select a graph you plan to interpret with children and analyse the questions you want to ask. Check you are requiring the children to do more than answer direct questions; include questions requiring reading between and beyond the data.

Data gathering skills

Ability to discriminate differences and sort information into categories is essential to data handling, remembering that categorisation can be difficult for some data. Rather than shying away from this, discussion of difficulties which are a natural part of working with real data should be welcomed. While pre-school children are not typically engaged in formal statistical activities the majority of them begin to show an interest in counting and comparing, for example to observe that their brother has more strawberries than they do and that it is not fair. Building on this, opportunities can be sought for children in Year 1 to continue to practise their counting skills while taking notice of results which are more, less or the same as other results. Early measuring and comparison of measures also underpins later graphing of measurement data.

Although statistics (data handling) is not in the Year 1 programme of study in the new curriculum, children should still spend time in Reception and in Year 1 sorting and classifying things. These may be 'natural collections' of objects such as beads, buttons and shells. These collections give the children the opportunity to find their own ways of categorising the objects (for example, big and small, ones I like and ones I don't like, by colour, etc.) Sorting and categorising activities give young children the chance to reason and to explain their reasoning (see Chapter 1) by telling a peer or a teacher why a particular object belongs in a particular group.

Structured collections such as 'Compare Bears', or Logicblocks give the children more opportunities for mathematical reasoning as they sort and categorise. The fact that there is a limited number of different attributes in the collections (for example, Logicblocks vary only by colour, shape, size and thickness) means that children can explore and articulate the reasons why a particular object should belong to a specific set or not. A game to play with Logicblocks involves each child choosing a Logicblock and then approaching the 'gatekeeper' one at a time. The 'gatekeeper' decides whether or not to let the child through the gate depending on the property of the shape (for example, only red shapes, only thin shapes, only shapes with triangular faces, shapes that are not blue, etc.) As they are waiting to approach the 'gatekeeper' the children are encouraged to work out which property or properties allow them to pass. They can then predict whether they will be allowed to pass and justify their prediction with reasoning. This not only gives children excellent opportunities to reason, but the sorting and classifying of objects based on their properties is an essential precursor to data handling.

Case study: Sampling

Where surveys take place and not everybody can be asked, the hope is that the people who are asked are fairly representative of the larger population. Consideration of sample is something I rarely come across in primary data handling lessons and yet we could easily encourage children to think about whether we might get different answers to our questions if we asked different people, as demonstrated in the case study below.

→

Emma, a student teacher, described a week of data handling in 'book week'. This included her Year 5 class interpreting given graphs and talking about factors that might have affected the data (such as whether people of different ages had been asked).

In a different school, the children were to assist the head teacher in deciding what pizza toppings to offer at a forthcoming school fête. They duly gathered data from their classmates and presented their findings. Evaluating the lesson Nick began to question whether the answers would have been the same had some adults been asked, or maybe children in other classes. While it may not have been practical to ask questions beyond the 'convenience' sample used, at least considering the possibility of getting more varied responses alerts children to this feature of data collection.

In the second case study scenario, interest in local people's tastes is implied, but other questions might require slightly different thinking, for example taking into account geographical or cultural variations in response to the question being asked. Finally, it would also be prudent to consider sample size at times – have we asked a sufficiently large sample to get a feel for the best answer to our question?

Equipping children with particular data gathering skills helps to ensure that they can gather and record the sorts of data to answer their chosen question. Tallying and tabulating are both taught in Year 2. Tallying proves particularly useful in two circumstances: when wanting to keep count of something at speed, and when numbers to be gathered are fairly large and therefore being able to total in multiples of five will prove easier than in ones. An essential part of the data handling cycle is the discussion that should come before the gathering of any data, so that the children are clear about how they will gather the data and how they will record it. Incidentally, having seen children required to turn numbers unnecessarily into tallies I am keen that we try to avoid pointless activity.

While it might sound obvious, children need opportunities to practise these skills for themselves; if children are always given a pre-prepared recording sheet they do not learn to create their own. Mistakes along the way are inevitable (not considering categories in advance; onerous recording and inability to keep up; losing track of who has been asked, etc.) but rather than being something to be avoided they are a valuable part of learning. Paramore writes that:

> unless children with their teachers are engaged in the process of designing and evaluating their own methodology they are not only reduced to the role of technician in carrying out someone else's plans, but they are unlikely to develop an understanding of the methodological difficulties associated with such an enterprise.

(2011, p.74)

Presentation of data

For children, one of the difficulties of mathematics generally and the presentation of data in particular is its highly abstract nature. To help children make the connection between data and its abstract representation (for example, as coloured bars in a bar chart), we recommend that initially *the children themselves form the representation*. In the early stages, the presentation of data can occur very naturally. We might organise the children into groups according to how they came to school that morning, essentially an early form of graph. Making human bar graphs is relatively simple by next getting the groups of children to stand in lines. A natural extension of concrete graphs involving people or objects is to draw a picture illustrating groups and quantities, recording the information in some way, perhaps involving both words and numbers. By Year 2 children are to learn about 'simple pictograms' and 'block charts', and in circumstances where children have enjoyed opportunities to communicate data in their own way, introducing the more formal ways in which data is presented tends to be fairly straightforward.

There are two interlinked reasons we might choose to create a graph of some sort from our data: because the picture created might make information or relationships within the data more obvious and open to analysis, or because we want to present the data to someone else and feel a graphical format may be more accessible or persuasive. It is not until Year 5 that the curriculum explicitly refers (in the non-statutory guidance) to children beginning to decide which representations of data are most appropriate and why. Children can, however, be encouraged to consider this right from the start – if my 'picture' does not illustrate the key information clearly, then it is not the best representation. Just as audience plays a key part in writing with purpose, so too might awareness of audience influence our graphing of data; eliciting peer feedback can be a powerful way of enhancing data presentation.

Often, once the data has been gathered in its rather messy 'raw' state it needs to be organised before it will be ready to be shared. This might be as simple as counting up the occurrences (or 'frequencies') in each category, or may require more thought to be given as to suitable categories. At a later stage children can be introduced to the idea of tabulating information in a spreadsheet and using ICT to produce a graph, noting the possible benefits of getting to grips with 'grown-up' and real world software such as Excel. Educational data handling software potentially guides the learner's input of the data to a greater extent and as the style of graph can be changed at the click of a button, this supports the idea that we might compare and contrast format prior to Year 5, perhaps deciding that one is an inappropriate choice to display the given data set. Use of ICT is not, however, a substitute for engaging in the full data handling cycle and sometimes constructing graphs by hand; children can learn a great deal about the structure of a graph when forced to think about its construction more deeply for themselves rather than letting the computer do the hard work.

Whereas counting (in ones or otherwise) is possible with block charts and pictograms, the same cannot be said for bar charts, first introduced in Year 3. When presenting information in a bar chart our audience are reliant upon having a numbered axis if they are to 'read' actual figures including estimating values between labelled points such as a scale climbing in tens with only 10, 20, 30, etc. labelled. This requires secure understanding of the number system.

Activity: Bar charts

When first working with bar charts, comparison can be a good place to start. Try this activity in a classroom.

- Show the children a bar chart like the one in Figure 8.1 explaining that it represents numbers of coloured cubes in a bag. The topic has been kept deliberately simple to establish facts, for example it seems there are more cubes of some colours than others, the same number of blue as white cubes and no green cubes.

- Children might also spot that there seem to be twice as many red cubes as yellow, with appreciation of ratio playing a useful role. Perhaps talk with the children about there being two yellow cubes, to assess whether or not they can reason that there would be four reds in this instance (double).

- But of course the numbers involved could be considerably larger. Show the children a big bag of cubes (without their knowing the numbers or seeing the colours inside) and ask for predictions as to numbers of each colour. Assess whether the children can use ratio relationships to suggest sensible numbers.

- Introducing a numbered axis could be done at the earlier stage where numbers are small and all numbers are shown, or at a later stage a scaled axis might display only certain multiples. Once either axis is in place it is possible to 'read' the graph to find out or estimate how many cubes there are of each colour, as well as how many altogether, though higher attaining mathematicians can be challenged to predict numbers of each colour from being told just the total number. So if I had about 100 cubes, how many of each colour do you estimate there are? This is an excellent way of developing the children's reasoning and problem-solving skills through data handling.

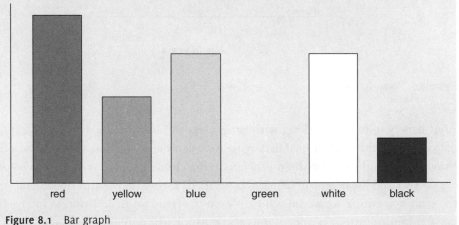

Figure 8.1 Bar graph

Note that the axis of a bar graph need not start at 0 which can be really helpful if that means a clearer display of the data, for example rather than having it all 'bunched' together making it difficult to read. This 'suppression of zero' (see, for example,

Haylock, 2010) can, however, make for misleading comparisons of data, and graphs should, as always, be produced and interpreted with care.

Time series graphs, first introduced in Year 4, allow us to illustrate data values changing over time using a line graph. A key feature of line graphs is being able to see at a glance whether something is increasing, decreasing or fluctuating.

One of the most accessible examples of change over time using continuous data (also first mentioned in Year 4) is a graph plotting a child's (or a plant's) height at various stages, as there is a clear link between the line of the graph getting higher and the child or plant growing, as we see in Figure 8.2. The changing 'slope' or gradient of the line helps to indicate whether growth is steadily gentle or more rapid (steeper) or has even plateaued.

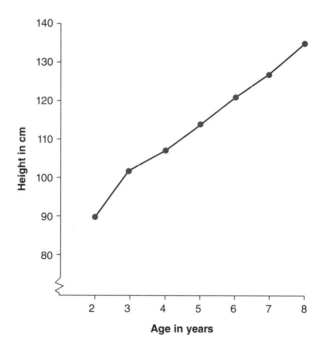

Figure 8.2 Time series graph

Another key feature of working with time series and line graphs showing continuous data is the potential additional data lying between the actual data (the plotted points through which the line has been generated); the child's height has only been recorded once a year and his height in between is implied. Estimation of additional data is therefore something we would want children to attend to. In addition to interpolation, as we might call this, extrapolation is also possible: the potential data were we to extend the line at either end. Thus we can surmise that this child was shorter than 90cm prior to the age of two and will likely get taller yet. Other line graphs are covered from Year 5 and include conversion charts in Year 6, for example showing the relationship between miles and kilometres, or dollars and euros.

The Year 6 non-statutory guidance mentions graphs relating two variables as might arise from children's own enquiries in mathematics and in other subjects, but the National Curriculum does not explicitly require learning about scatter graphs. These work in a similar way to line graphs (and link well with co-ordinates), plotting one set of ordered data against another. They are ideal for demonstrating correlation, such as noticing that time spent on homework goes down as time spent playing on the computer goes up, or that people with large hands also have large feet. Whether or not we choose to teach scatter graphs, we are able to lay good foundations by providing opportunities to spot and discuss relationships within data. The production of a scatter graph can often arise as a result of the children being curious and asking mathematical questions. In one of my classes, the children found an unnamed gym shoe and surmised that it must belong to someone tall, as the shoe was big. The explanation of scatter graphs can involve the children in a lot of mathematical reasoning.

Pie charts enable us to display data relating to proportions of a whole and are best used with only small numbers of categories, such as surveying opinions on a contentious topic and having slices of pie for 'agree', 'disagree' and 'not sure' for those like me who typically end up sitting on the fence. Children in Year 6 construct and interpret pie charts connecting this to work on angles, fractions and percentages, but prior to Year 6 children often encounter computer-generated pie charts. Friel et al. (2001) suggest that judging proportions in a pie chart can be more challenging than assessing and comparing lengths of bars in bar graphs.

Where data are presented to enable comparisons between different data sets, care should be taken where groups are of unequal size. Children should be led to appreciate that proportions should be presented and judged carefully, for example by changing the figures into fractions or percentages.

Activity: Comparing numerical data

An easy way to draw children's attention to judging numerical data carefully is to provide potentially misleading statements for discussion. You can try out the following activity in a classroom.

(Continued)

(Continued)

Following discussion about what can be gleaned from the cartoon (and children may raise questions about how many girls there are in each class) I would provide numbers. In finding out that both classes have 28 pupils, but in Steph's class only 9 girls (and so 19 boys) and in Grace's class 17 (versus 11 boys), the children may wish to revise their initial conclusions.

Statistical tools

Presenting data in appropriate graphs can facilitate the asking and answering of questions about the data and various statistical tools support this analysis. Specific statistical measures, such as 'average' and 'range', are introduced towards the end of the primary age range. While 'mode' is no longer mentioned in the National Curriculum, children are engaging in discussion of it every time they spot that a certain category is more popular or prevalent than any other. Arithmetic mean is given as the type of average to be taught, found by adding each entry in the data set and dividing the sum by the number of terms. The data has to be numerical for this to be appropriate of course, and it should be noted that any zero values in a data set should be included. In addition to teaching the mechanics of calculating mean, it is perhaps more important to support the children in developing a sense of what an average is and might be useful for. The National Curriculum suggests in the non-statutory guidance for Year 6 that pupils should know when it is appropriate to find the mean average of a data set. Averages are sometimes referred to as measures of central tendency, an answer which should feel 'typical' of the data, whereas 'range' is a simple measure of the spread of the data. For more information see 'What's Average?' by Stack et al. (2010).

Activity: Introducing averages

Here a simple activity for introducing the idea of averages is proposed. Think about why you might choose to approach the teaching of averages in this way, and the year group you feel it would be appropriate for.

- Talk with the children to see whether they have some sense of the meaning of the word 'average' from its use in everyday conversation.

- Set a scenario in which you and the children are interested in the number of raisins in little boxes from a multi-pack.

- Allow time to count, eat and compare answers with others, noting the variety of answers obtained. At this stage the full data set could be gathered and displayed as a graph.

- Initiate discussion on the average number of raisins per box. This provides an opportunity to further the children's understanding of averages, such as actual numbers of raisins ranging from more than to fewer than the average. The children may have 'invented' median or mode as opposed to mean, or have an entirely different take on how to draw a conclusion about the average number of raisins.

Measurements, for example data arising from a science or physical experiment, benefit from being taken several times. Working from an average result can then help to eliminate some of the margin of error inevitable when using measuring tools or when measuring something which itself will vary. Here the median (the result occurring in the middle of an ordered list) is often the most suitable or easiest value to use. Polly (2011), writing in the USA, describes an investigation in which the children explore the maximum width of creek they think they could jump, either with a run-up or from a standing start. Testing their jumping prowess several times they were encouraged to take the middle value rather than those at the extremes for the graphs they went on to draw. It should be noted, however, that when discussion returned to the initial question, conclusions varied as to how wide a creek someone might be able to leap across without getting their feet wet, with some optimistically choosing the maximum distance and assuming they could repeat it, and others playing it safe. This provides plenty of scope for rich discussion and a starting point I imagine many children would enjoy.

Starting points for data handling

Data handling offers many good opportunities for making cross-curricular links and in this chapter we have already met a number of different ideas for promoting statistical learning. The Smith Report (2004), writing about Key Stage 4 and beyond, argued that statistics and data handling were better suited to integration in other disciplines where genuine questions might be asked, rather than being approached through mathematics teaching. Clearly the same could be said to be true at primary level, with learning about data handling skills in the context of another curriculum area proving mutually beneficial.

Activity: Data in the wider curriculum

Peruse the subjects of the National Curriculum and list topics to which data handling might contribute. Science in particular specifies links with mathematics through 'collecting, presenting and analysing data'. For example, in the context of

(Continued)

(Continued)

learning about different materials in science Key Stage 1 children might question which of several balls is the bounciest, testing, observing and recording data to help them answer the question, whereas Key Stage 2 children could investigate the effect of temperature on different substances (chocolate, for example), perhaps using data logging equipment.

The PE curriculum encourages mastery of a range of physical activities and holding a mini-Olympics affords the class many good opportunities to put data handling (and measurement) skills into practice. Rich discussion can also be based on actual Olympic medal tables, thinking about how rankings are calculated or decided. In the London 2012 Olympics the UK was ranked third; we won fewer medals than the Russian Federation (ranked fourth) but the distribution across gold, silver and bronze was different.

Posing real-life problems can also act as the starting point for data handling activity and can emanate from various sources, for example the dinner lady who keeps having to wipe up spillages at lunchtime and wants to know which brand of kitchen roll will be best to mop up the liquid and/or yoghurt. The investigation could of course be extended, for example to include comparison of prices. Even educational policy changes offer scope for data handling to inform debate: do your Key Stage 2 class believe children would benefit from starting 'school' at the age of two (as widely reported in the press in April 2014)? Can they collect data to inform their viewpoint? No doubt you can think of other real-life or school-orientated scenarios which might lend themselves to children's engagement in data handling, for example issues raised by the school council or holding classroom elections.

The use of sorting diagrams is particularly powerful mechanism for helping children to appreciate something more about a given topic while learning about how such diagrams work at the same time, for example sorting multiples of 3 and 5 using a Venn diagram and realising that 15 is an example of both. Neither Venn nor Carroll diagrams get an explicit mention in the Primary National Curriculum 2014, but could still be used at either the data gathering or presentation stage. Venn diagrams lend themselves to finding or illustrating overlaps between categories, whereas a Carroll diagram is a specific example of a two-way table, ideal for plotting two variables against each other.

Reasoning using data handling

The National Curriculum makes it clear that teachers are expected to incorporate opportunities for their children to engage in mathematical reasoning at every step and in every area of the curriculum. Venn diagrams can provide an excellent

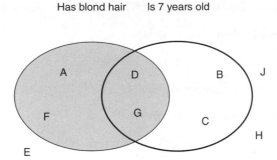

Figure 8.3   Venn diagram of children in the class

opportunity for the children to handle data and engage in mathematical reasoning at various levels of sophistication.

At its simplest, children can be asked why a particular piece of data has been put in a particular place, for example 'What do you know about Child G?' It is very important that the children verbalise their reasoning, both for the benefit of the teacher and the other children in the class. To raise the level of reasoning, children might be asked to identify two pieces of data and describe what is the same and what is different about them, for example, 'What is the same and different about Children A and G?' The introduction of true/false questions can make the reasoning more demanding, for example, 'Is it true that all blond-haired children are also seven? The inclusion of the word 'not' can make the reasoning more demanding: 'Is it true that all the seven-year-olds are not blond?'

Consider the graph (deliberately unfinished) below and the accompanying pieces of information. Consider the reasoning that the children would have to engage in to assign a particular food to each bar on the graph.

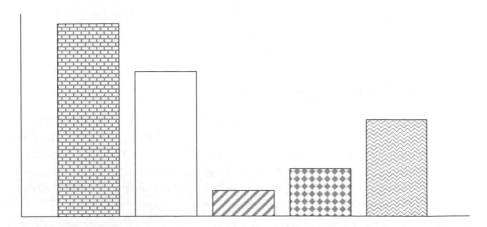

Figure 8.4   Unlabelled bar graph of favourite meals

From the information below, work out which meal belongs with which bar.

- Twice as many people liked pizza as salad.

- Half as many people liked fish and chips as liked salad.

- Only one person preferred shepherd's pie.

- More people preferred beans on toast to salad.

Finally, children's reasoning (and their skills in interpreting graphs) might be enhanced by inviting them to use graphical information to 'tell a story'.

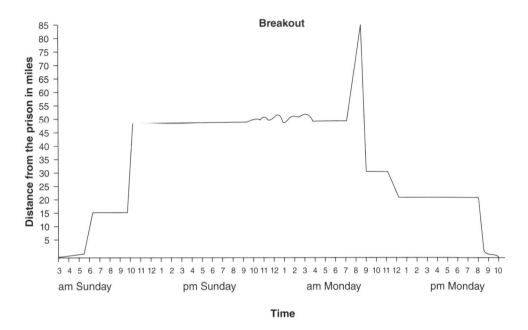

Figure 8.5   Prison Breakout

The example above gives children in Key Stage 2 a great opportunity to make up a story from the graph, explaining on the way what information from the graph they are using to determine a particular event in their story.

Case Study: Squares as rectangles

Having noticed children's reluctance to categorise squares as rectangles, David planned a series of activities to force his Year 3 class to engage in dialogue on this topic. The children were already familiar with Carroll diagrams and the one in Figure 8.6, with shapes already in it (but without the labels we see here), proved the most powerful. It provoked a great deal of debate regarding what the headings could be and the children's reasoning resulted in a far more secure understanding of shape properties and families.

$\longrightarrow$

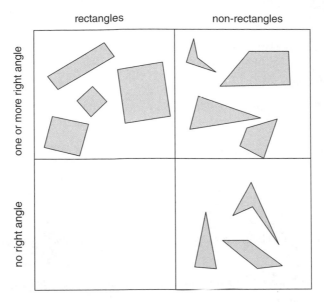

Figure 8.6 Carroll diagram involving shapes

Learning Outcomes Review

This chapter has established the role of data in our everyday lives and described data handling as a cyclic process. Make sure that you can describe this process in some detail in your own words, perhaps recording your ideas in a flow diagram.

Self-assessment questions

1. Various skills are associated with gathering data. Have the children in your class had the opportunity to be more than 'technicians' gathering data on ready-made sheets (Paramore, 2011)?
2. Having explored different formats for presenting data, reflect on the reasons we might produce a graph. What is the most powerful and purposeful graph work your class have ever done?
3. Having considered data of different types and some basic statistical tools, pick a topic you will soon teach. How will your activities really help children to get 'under the skin' of the data?
4. Rich starting points can lead to purposeful engagement in data handling. What will your next topic be and might it involve children in the full data handling cycle, gathering data themselves to answer an interesting question?
5. Given statistics' potential contribution to understanding the world we live in, consider how you might enjoy exploring some curious questions with your classes, encouraging the children to look beyond the data to draw conclusions and ask further questions.

References

Friel, S., Curcio, F. and Bright, G. (2001) Making sense of graphs: critical factors influencing comprehension and instructional implications. *Journal for Research in Mathematics Education*, 32(2):124–158.

Graham, A. (2006) *Developing Thinking in Statistics*. London: Open University Press, Paul Chapman Publishing.

Haylock, D. (2010) *Mathematics Explained for Primary Teachers*, 4th edition. London: SAGE.

Paramore, J. (2011) Data and dialogue in primary school. *Teaching Statistics,* 33(3): 71–75.

Polly, D. (2011) Best creek-jumping methods. *Teaching Children Mathematics*, 18: 136–140.

Rickard, C. (2013) *Essential Primary Mathematics*. Maidenhead: Open University Press, McGraw-Hill Education.

Smith, A. (2004) *Making Mathematics Count: an Inquiry into Post-14 Mathematics Education*. London: DfES.

Stack, S., Watson, J., Hindley, S., Samson, P. and Devlin, R. (2010) What's average? *AMT*, 66(3): 7–15.

Watson, J. (2007) The foundations of data and chance. *APMC*, 12(1): 4–7.

9 Planning with discernment

Marcus Witt

To achieve great things, two things are needed: a plan and not quite enough time.

(Leonard Bernstein)

Learning outcomes

This chapter explores the process of planning mathematics lessons. The key objectives for the chapter are:

- to explore the thought processes involved in planning mathematics lessons;
- to consider the role of discernment in lesson planning;
- to consider the particular knowledge that primary mathematics teachers need in order to plan effective lessons;
- to consider different ways to structure mathematics lessons;
- to explore ways of differentiating mathematical activities so as to make them appropriate and challenging for all learners.

TEACHERS' STANDARDS

1. Set high expectations which inspire, motivate and challenge pupils
2. Promote good progress and outcomes by pupils
3. Demonstrate good subject and curriculum knowledge
4. Plan and teach well-structured lessons
5. Adapt teaching to respond to the strengths and needs of all pupils
6. Make accurate and productive use of assessment
7. Fulfil wider professional responsibilities

Introduction

Good planning is the key to good mathematics teaching (and it is common knowledge that there is never enough time in teaching). While a good plan will not guarantee a good lesson, poor or non-existent planning will almost certainly guarantee a poor lesson.

Activity: Key questions

Think back to a mathematics lesson that you have planned recently. Spend a few minutes considering the key questions that you asked yourself before and as you were writing the lesson plan. Make a note of them before reading on.

Case Study: Louise

Louise was a trainee teacher on a PGCE course. She was working with a class of high-achieving Year 3 children in a school where parents' expectations were high. When her tutor came in to observe her lesson, Louise was visibly exhausted. The lesson was about odd and even numbers. The children spent very little time together and after chanting odd and even numbers were sent off to their tables to complete a variety of activities. There were four different activities, and the children moved round from one to the next every five minutes. All the activities involved pre-printed worksheets.

There was a good deal of enthusiasm in the room to begin with. As the lesson progressed, the noise level increased and the children became less focused on the tasks, despite Louise's efforts to engage them. Many of the tasks were very similar: circling odd and even numbers from a list, sorting odd and even numbers into groups. On another 'worksheet' the children were mapping the path of a pirate who could only pick up coins with an even value. The children were called back to the 'carpet' to talk about their answers and to compare them with others' answers.

In the discussion after the lesson, Louise admitted to having been up very late the previous evening planning the lesson for the tutor's visit. She described spending several hours each evening looking online for good activity ideas to support her teaching. She was clearly finding the school experience difficult and seemed to have no other strategies for planning lessons. When questioned about what the children had been learning, she appeared surprised and replied 'they are learning about odd and even numbers'. She was aware that there was some repetition in the work that the children had been doing, but complained that none of the activities that she had been able to find online would 'keep them busy' for very long, so she had had to find several. When asked why she had chosen particular worksheets or activities, she talked only in terms of their being easy to find.

Planning with discernment

The most important question to consider when planning mathematics lessons is *precisely what mathematics you want the children to learn.* It is important that all the activities, conceptual models and resources that you collect together are focused on this question. Louise's lesson, discussed above, was driven primarily by 'activities' about odd and even numbers that would occupy the children rather than on a clear focus about what they were learning. Without this clear focus, her planning had become a time-consuming and fruitless search online or in books to find 'good activities'.

This lack of focus on precisely what the children should learn can stem from a lack of clarity in communication, or a lack of engagement with the learning objectives outlined in the curriculum or programme of study. Whatever the reason, your first priority should be to let the learning outcomes determine what you teach and the activities that the children do (rather than allowing something as uncertain as a Google search determine what the children in the class will do).

Ensuring that learning outcomes determine activities means planning with discernment. Looking at lesson ideas that come from books, online or from your tutors and making informed decisions about how to use them with your own unique group of children ensures flexible and responsive teaching. Nobody knows the learning needs of the individual children in your class better than you do, so don't rely on a lesson idea that someone far removed from your classroom has come up with. Use your powers of discernment to adapt and modify the lesson to make it work, or if necessary, reject it outright and plan something else that is more closely matched to your children's learning needs.

As Louise discovered, planning lessons without discernment can lead to a loss of focus on the children's learning. You do not have to invent everything yourself; there are thousands of good lesson ideas (and thousands of bad ones too) in books and elsewhere. The key is to use some of the good ideas that other people have had, but to do so flexibly and thoughtfully, rather than simply because they are available and fit with the mathematical topic of your lesson.

Lesson objectives may well be given to you initially during a school practice. They may come from the National Curriculum, from the Primary Framework Document (if your school is using it) or from another scheme of work. It is worth asking your mentor or class teacher how the school determines the learning objectives for mathematics.

What the children bring to a mathematics lesson

Having identified a clear learning objective, the next step is to consider what the children will bring to the lesson. David Ausubel, psychologist and learning theorist said the following:

> *If I had to reduce all of educational psychology to just one principle, I would say this: The most important single factor influencing learning is what the learner already knows. Ascertain this and teach him accordingly.*

(1968, p.18)

Although this sounds simple, in reality it is not. It is particularly difficult for you as a trainee teacher having to get to know an unfamiliar class quickly. It is more difficult with mathematics, which is broken down into more distinct topics than a subject like English, where it might be possible to get a feel for a child's facility with writing or reading fairly quickly. In mathematics, it may have been some time since the children last looked at the topic you are preparing to teach. Their understanding may have been incomplete at the time and they may have forgotten things since then. Therefore, before planning a mathematics lesson or lessons, you should try to find out as much as you can about what the children already know.

- Check the National Curriculum programmes of study to see what children of a particular age should know about the given topic.

- Talk to the class teacher and teaching assistant (TA) about what the children understood when they last looked at the topic.

- Ask to see the class teacher's records of the children's attainment in the given topic area.

- Look at the children's books.

- If possible, talk to one or two of the children about the topic before you teach it, or try to find five minutes to do a short elicitation activity with them.

Unlike some other subjects, mathematics has inherent internal connections, which make it possible to approach one topic using understanding that the children have in another. For example, children learning about decimals for the first time should have a good understanding of place value. They will also have had practical experiences of dividing whole things up into fractional parts (often food) and sharing things. Considering what the children can bring to the learning should involve thinking about these internal connections in mathematics and how they can be exploited.

Children's mathematical education continues outside and beyond school. Activities undertaken at home or with friends may help to foster the children's sense of mathematical curiosity (see Chapter 1). However, children's mathematical experiences outside the classroom are unlikely to be obviously mathematical, so it is up to you to

Title of Activity: *Finding the difference*	Date and time: *25.12.13 9:00 -10:00* Class/Year: *Y1*
What have the children learned before this session? **Review previous information from planning/evaluations.** **Why has this activity been chosen? Why is this the next step in the children's learning?** **Be aware of differences in the children's previous learning.** *The children have never looked at this.*	

Title of Activity: *Finding the difference.*	Date and time: *25.12.13 9:00-10:00* Class/Year: *YI*
What have the children learned before this session? **Review previous information from planning/evaluations.** **Why has this activity been chosen? Why is this the next step in the children's learning?** **Be aware of differences in the children's previous learning.** *The children have done some work on addition. Most of the children are able to solve simple addition problems by counting along a number line. The 'octagons' group have needed a lot of support as they were counting on from the wrong number (e.g. for 7 + 4 they would count 'seven, eight, nine, ten'). This activity will extend these skills in the context of counting on to find the difference. SP and NK will work with the 'squares' (see yesterday's evaluation).*	

Figure 9.1 Lesson plans – prior knowledge

consider things that the children have done that might contribute to the mathematics that you are going to teach them.

Opposite are sections of two lesson plans. The first illustrates a level of detail that is commonly seen; the second is an example of a sufficient level of detail.

Activity: Using other experience

Choose a mathematical topic that you are likely to teach in the near future. Spend a few moments thinking about how it relates to other areas of mathematics that the children have already encountered. Think too about any experiences that the children may have had outside school that could help with their understanding. How might you 'exploit' this to help children's understanding of the mathematics?

Assessment for Learning (AfL)

Knowing the children's current level of understanding and planning from that underpins the idea of AfL, or formative assessment. Black and Wiliam, in a paper entitled *Inside the Black Box* (1998) argued strongly that planning lessons based on a clear understanding of what the children already know and where gaps in their understanding lie can have dramatic effects on the progress they make.

They and other authors (see Clarke, 2005 and Swaffield, 2008 for accessible texts) have explored the techniques that classroom teachers can use to elicit this valuable information and therefore help them to plan subsequent lessons more effectively. There is not sufficient space in this chapter to have a detailed discussion of all AfL techniques and strategies that are discussed in the literature; some further reading is suggested at the end of the chapter. I will consider briefly how AfL might be distinctive when planning mathematics.

- Setting clear learning objectives – it is important to distinguish between mathematical concepts, skills and activities. I recently saw a lesson where the learning objective was 'To learn how to find the area of the classroom using newspaper'. This describes what the children were doing, but the conceptual learning goes beyond this description. Children learn a lot of other, more generic skills in the course of learning mathematics and reflecting them in learning objectives (for example, to be able to solve complex problems by working systematically), alongside more mathematically specific learning objectives (for example, to find the area of rectangles), might help children to see the point of some of the mathematics they are doing.

- Success criteria – Clarke (2005) defines success criteria as *a reminder of steps (as in a mathematical procedure) or ingredients which either must be used (as in instructional writing) or could help the child achieve the learning objective.'* (p.37). While success criteria work well in subjects such as English, it is more difficult to do this in all areas of mathematical learning. There is a danger that success criteria can simply become a list of procedures that the children follow rather blindly. It may be helpful to think of success criteria as features of a good piece of work. They enable the children to compare the features of their own work with those that have been identified as being indicative of 'success'. If their own work does not contain some of the identified features, there is clear direction about how to improve.

- Open questioning – due to the assumption that mathematical answers are either right or wrong, the range of mathematical questions that children are asked can become narrow. It is relatively easy to come up with closed questions ('What is 7 multiplied by 6?'). In Chapter 1 I considered ways in which children's mathematical reasoning can be developed and encouraged through questions which invite the children to explain and justify their thinking. These kinds of questions should be planned into mathematics lessons (see Chapter 10 for more on mathematical questions).

- Clear teacher feedback – again, the 'right and wrong' nature of mathematics can mean that children largely receive quantitative feedback, i.e. a mark out of ten. Feedback, both written and verbal, should concentrate on the children's mathematical thought processes. Research by Butler (1998) has suggested that children are highly sensitive to feedback that is given in the form of marks and will focus on these rather than comments. However, children in the study who were given feedback that contained only comments (i.e. no explicit grade or mark) made significantly more progress than children who were given a mark, even if it was accompanied by formative written feedback.

- Self- and peer-assessment – this needs to go beyond children marking their own or each other's work. Children can be encouraged to comment on each other's thought processes and the extent to which they have been able to explain or justify their mathematical thinking (see Chapter 1).

The principles of AfL outlined above should form part of the planning process.

Activity: Success criteria

Some aspects of mathematics, such as constructing a bar graph, lend themselves easily to the establishment of success criteria; others, such as carrying out a calculation, less so. Consider what the success criteria might be for a long multiplication calculation.

Again, sections of the two example lesson plans are included below to illustrate differing levels of detail.

Assessment for learning:

What are you looking for? How will you know what the children have learnt? How will you record these assessments?
Who else is involved?
Ask the children if they have understood.

Assessment for learning:

What are you looking for?
How will you know what the children have learnt?
How will you record these assessments?
Who else is involved?
TA and teacher to work with specific groups and note down the children's responses to the game. Children to record their answers on a pro forma, which can be used as a record and for assessment. AfL – children to explain to each other how to find the difference between two numbers.

Activity: Mathematics lesson structure

Think about the mathematics lessons that you have taught or seen.

- What elements did the lessons have?

- What were the factors that led to the lessons being structured in the way that they were?

- Could the lessons have been structured differently, and if so, how?

When planning lessons, it is important to consider how you will structure the learning. There is now more freedom to move away from the three-part structure first suggested in the National Numeracy Strategy (DfEE, 1999). However, the structure has many merits.

There is some debate about whether the mental and oral starter should be connected to the rest of the lesson. When planning your starter, connect it to the main part of the lesson unless there is a good reason that it should stand alone. In some circumstances (for example, a class whose knowledge of multiplication tables is particularly poor and therefore who need regular practice with tables), there may be good reasons to keep the mental and oral part of the lesson separate. Plan this part of the lesson *after* you have considered the main part, so that you know which skills the children will need to practise.

As the teacher, your time with the children is at a premium. You should aim to be interacting with the children for as much of the lesson as possible. This may mean that you make yourself available to the children during the main part of the lesson and move around the room checking the children's understanding (gathering formative assessment evidence) and offering support. It may mean that you decide to focus your

Table 9.1 Purposes of the elements of a three-part mathematics lesson

Part of lesson	Purpose
Mental and oral starter	To get the children 'warmed up' and receptive to new learning To practise skills needed for the main part of the lesson
Main part	Direct input, i.e. teaching the children something Sustained engagement in some mathematics Opportunity for the children to develop both skills and conceptual understanding Continued monitoring and gathering of assessment information
Plenary	Several possible purposes: • To celebrate the children's learning; children present their work and thinking to the rest of the class • To address a widespread misconception; gathering on-the-spot evidence in a lesson may lead to this conclusion • To set homework or an out-of-school activity • To consolidate the children's learning • To excite the children about the next step in their mathematical learning

attention on a particular group or groups, working with the children in a guided way. You may choose to rotate your attention over the course of a week or a sequence of lessons to ensure that each child benefits from your intervention. In deciding where to focus your support for the main part of the lesson, it is important that all the children benefit and particularly that those children who are labelled as 'higher attainers' and who may be able to work more independently are challenged through your direct intervention. It is equally important that children labelled as 'lower attainers' do not become overly dependent on adult support.

The plenary is potentially the most difficult part of the planning process, as it should be flexible and responsive to the needs of the children and will vary depending on what happens in the lesson. This means that you might need to have a loose plan for several different possible plenary sessions. Threlfall (2005) discusses the notion of 'contingent planning', i.e. of having several possible scenarios in mind, so that you are responsive to the way that the lesson unfolds.

Activity: Purpose of a plenary

Before continuing, think back to some mathematics lessons that you have taught or seen and consider the purpose(s) of the plenary in those lessons.

A further question to consider is when the plenary should occur. The original guidance from the NNS suggested that the plenary session should occur at the end of the lesson, usually in the final 10 or 15 minutes. However, there may well be lessons where it is necessary to have a plenary session before the end of the lesson. Consider a situation where there is a widespread mathematical misconception in the classroom. Addressing this misconception in a plenary session at the end of the lesson may be too late. By that time, the children may have spent several minutes inadvertently reinforcing their misconception. If you realise that there is a widespread misconception, it is best to step in, hold an impromptu plenary session and address it immediately. For some trainee teachers, particularly those at the beginning of their training or those who are being observed, it is difficult to have the confidence to deviate from the lesson plan. Have the confidence to respond flexibly and imaginatively to the learning that is unfolding in front of you, rather than sticking rigidly to a plan that may be redundant.

Research Focus: Traditional lesson structure

Adhami (2003) challenges the notion that we should stick rigidly to the 'traditional' three-part lesson structure and proposes several reasons why it may not fit mathematics lessons. He discusses a lesson where the learning progresses in small steps, which build on each other, leading the children to greater mathematical insight. The traditional three-part structure does not allow for this kind of gradual building of understanding and often relies on children understanding an initial mathematical input and then being able to work independently for a sustained period.

It is debatable whether young children are able to concentrate for the 30 to 40 minutes of the main part of the lesson. This could mean that some of this time is not used as effectively as it might be with greater teacher–pupil interaction. Mathematics lessons in other countries (such as Hungary) follow a structure more like that described by Adhami, where small bursts of teacher input are followed by focused activity by the children, which is then followed by further teacher input responding to the children's learning that has just taken place.

Adhami also challenges the idea that the plenary session should always and only happen at the end of a lesson. The lesson structure described in his chapter really contains a number of small plenary sessions in which the learners' understanding is checked (both by the teacher and through a process of self-assessment) before some additional thoughts and questions are offered by the teacher.

Planning for differentiation in mathematics

One of the biggest difficulties when planning mathematics lessons is ensuring that the content of the lesson is challenging but not unattainable for all the children. This is especially difficult when there is a very wide range of mathematical attainment in your class. This is a particular problem in mathematics, where giving the children the same task and accepting that there will be variations in outcome (as when writing a poem or painting a picture) is often not possible.

A common way of differentiating mathematical learning is by task, i.e. different children are given different tasks, which are deemed appropriate. In order to facilitate this kind of differentiation, the children are often grouped by 'ability' (either within a particular class or sometimes across two or more classes) so that children in the same group receive the same task. In this next section, other approaches to differentiation and some of the implications this may have for the planning process, as well as for the children concerned, are considered.

While there is not scope in this chapter for a full discussion about grouping or setting, it is worth considering the criteria you might use to determine how the children are organised. Children are often grouped by 'ability'. However, there are several problems with this simple notion of mathematical 'ability'. Mathematics is a broad subject and there is no guarantee that a child who finds work with numbers more of a challenge will find the same challenges when engaging in spatial thinking. If children are always in a particular group for mathematics, it is likely that some will be under-challenged in some lessons. When planning mathematics lessons, give careful consideration to the way that your children are grouped. Boaler (2010) is clear in her view that grouping children by 'ability' does considerable harm in conveying messages to them about their mathematical future.

If simply putting children into groups of similar 'ability' and giving them more or less demanding tasks (differentiation by task) has its drawbacks, you may wish to consider alternatives.

Activity: Alternatives to differentiation by task

What alternatives to differentiation by task can you think of? This could be ways of differentiation that you have observed in lessons, or have used in your own lessons. Be imaginative here and try to consider other ways of differentiation that are outside your experience.

Here are some possibilities:

- differentiation by resources;
- differentiation by adult support;
- differentiation by peer support;
- differentiation by outcome;
- differentiation by choice.

How might these affect your planning of mathematics lessons?

Many children find the move from concrete representations of mathematical ideas to more symbolic or abstract representations difficult (Hughes, 1986). Providing children with concrete materials to support their mathematical thinking is common practice.

As children's competence and understanding develop, they become better able to use and manipulate abstract symbols. One way of differentiating mathematical tasks is to provide more resources for children who are not yet ready to make the move to more abstract ways of thinking. This form of differentiation enables all the children in the class to work on the same mathematics, but with different resources.

Consider the possibility of giving the children a choice about the nature of the resources that they might use to tackle a particular mathematical task. Clearly you should retain a degree of control and you may well want to encourage certain children (who are possibly a little over-optimistic) to use resources and others (who are possibly less confident, or who just enjoy an easy life) to try tasks without the help of particular resources. Nobody knows the class as well as you do, so you are in a good position to make those decisions. More importantly, by giving an element of choice to the children, you are conveying important messages about autonomy and independence and about taking the children seriously as learners who have valid opinions and views about their own learning.

There are several ways of differentiating work by the level of support. You may choose to ask your TA, if you are lucky enough to have one, to work with a particular group or groups. Differentiation is about making the mathematics challenging and appropriate for all the children in the class. The TA could equally work with any group of children in the class. You may choose to work with a particular group of children to provide some additional support or challenge.

Case Study: Maths commandos

A trainee teacher had a system of 'maths commandos' in her class. These were children who had a good understanding of a particular mathematical topic and were available to help their peers whose understanding was not as strong. The teacher was careful that different children were selected as maths commandos throughout the term and was always looking to give the children who usually found maths more demanding the chance whenever possible (for example, in sessions on shape and space).

The teacher was also careful that the learning of the maths commandos was not hampered by their being in constant demand. She did find a beneficial effect for both the commandos and those they were supporting. The practice gave her additional time to spend with some children, gave the children a source of support when she was busy and gave an opportunity for the commandos to think through their own understanding of a topic and articulate it very carefully. Most importantly, it gave all the children in the class more of a sense of ownership and independence in their learning.

There is considerable evidence (Boaler, 2010) that children derive a great benefit from working together in 'mixed ability' groups. It is possible in this situation that the children could all be given the same task or activity and that the differentiation comes through the outcomes that the children produce. Planning mathematics lessons in this way requires a different kind of mathematical task, one that can be characterised by the phrase 'low threshold, high ceiling'. Such tasks are simple enough for all the children to be able to make a start and to contribute something, but are not limiting, so that some children can make them mathematically more demanding. Planning such tasks is more demanding than giving children closed tasks where there are specific answers, but arguably leads to much richer mathematical learning. Planning and teaching in this way requires a shift in focus away from answers to the children's mathematical thinking and reasoning (see Chapter 1).

As before, consider the two examples of planning given below.

Mental/Oral Starter:

What skills/knowledge are you hoping to review?
How will you ensure sufficient pace?
How will you ensure that all the children are involved all the time?
Counting with the number stick.

Introducing the activity:

How are you going to motivate and inspire all the children?
How will the lesson help them grow as a learner?
How are you going to inform the children of the learning intentions? How will you do this?
What language/examples/questions/demonstration will you use?
How will you involve the children and other adults?
Introduce the activity to the children. Hand out the worksheets.

The Activity:

Which children? Where? Resources? Timing?
What are the children going to do?
What are you going to do?
Are any other adults involved? Who? What?
All children to do the activity. Children will use the number lines on the worksheet to find the difference between two numbers and write the answer in the box provided. I will work with the low ability. The TA will work with the high ability children.

Equality and Diversity/Differentiation:

How will you make personalised provision for all learners?
How are you promoting equality and inclusion in your teaching?
How are potential barriers to learning to be overcome?
How will you differentiate your activity so that all the children can take part?
Different numbers on the cards

Concluding the Activity/session:

How will you celebrate/consolidate/continue the learning?
Children show the rest of the class what they have been doing.

This plan lacks detail. It is unclear whether the teacher has thought the activity through or not. It would certainly be difficult for another teacher to teach from this plan.

Contrast this with the plan given below, where the teacher has explicitly addressed misconceptions and has given considerable thought to the way that the concept is to be modelled to the children.

Mental/Oral Starter:

What skills/knowledge are you hoping to review?
How will you ensure sufficient pace?
How will you ensure that all the children are involved all the time?
Counting along the number stick, clapping where there are missing numbers.
Forwards and backwards. Could extend to counting in 5s and 10s.

Introducing the activity:
How are you going to motivate and inspire all the children?
How will the lesson help them grow as a learner?
How are you going to inform the children of the learning intentions? How will you do this?
What language/ examples/ questions/ demonstration will you use?
How will you involve the children and other adults?
Introduce the idea of using addition to find the difference between two numbers.
Model the activity, one child picks a number – another child picks a second number. Decide which
of the two numbers is bigger. Model writing the two number, in the right place on the pro forma
(flipchart). One child comes up and puts the lily pad (green cushion) on the bigger number line (on the
big number line on the floor). Another child comes up and is the 'frog'. Whole class counts together as
the frog jumps to the lily pad. Model the recording of the number of jumps on the proforma (flipchart).
Ensure that the children don't count the start number and that they do count the number of jumps.

The Activity:
Which children? Where? Resources? Timing?
What are the children going to do?
What are you going to do?
Are any other adults involved? Who? What?
Children to work in pairs. They each pick a card from the pile and write the lower and higher number
in the correct place on the pro forma. Put the frog on the smaller number and a green counter (lily
pad) on the higher number. Count the number of jumps the frog has to make to land on his lily pad.
Resources — laminated number lines, frogs, lily pads, pro forma, number cards (0–30)

Equality and Diversity/Differentiation:
How will you make personalised provision for all learners?
How are you promoting equality and inclusion in your teaching?
How are potential barriers to learning to be overcome?
How will you differentiate your activity so that all the children can take part?
The 'octagons' group (lower attainers) will work with me to ensure that they start on the correct
number and count the jumps. Numbers will be under 10. The 'circles' (high attainers) will work with
Miss Trentham (TA) and will be bridging through 10 (frogs always jump to 10 and then on to the lily
pad).

Concluding the Activity/session:
How will you celebrate/ consolidate/ continue the learning?
Children to explain to each other how to find the difference between two numbers. (Look out for
children who are finding ways to speed the process up i.e. whose frogs are making jumps bigger
than 1) 'Give me a pair of numbers with a difference of 3'.
Use skills to work out how much the beans have grown over night (tell the children the height of the
beans now and compare with yesterday's measurement to work out how much they have grown).

Planning sequences of lessons

When planning sequences of lessons, it is especially important that information from
one lesson is used to inform the planning of subsequent lessons. This means that you
cannot plan all the lessons in detail in advance. You may go into the sequence with
the first lesson or two planned in detail and an idea of the content of the sequence, but
then use AfL as a way of determining the details of subsequent lessons.

While you will not be able to plan each individual lesson in a sequence in detail, it is important to have a clear idea about the order in which the mathematical concepts are introduced to the children. Mathematical knowledge is cumulative; new concepts often rest on a good understanding of prior concepts. This is true on a big scale (understanding decimals is impossible without a good understanding of place value) and on a smaller scale during a sequence of two or three weeks of lessons, for example that finding the area of a triangle is not possible without understanding how to find the area of a rectangle. As you plan, you will need to consider carefully how the different concepts build on each other and therefore the order in which they are introduced.

Subject-specific pedagogical knowledge that informs planning

Activity

The most competent mathematicians make the best primary mathematics teachers. Spend a few minutes reflecting on this statement. Try to decide why it might be true and why it might not be true. What arguments can you find in support of and to contradict it?

There is research evidence (Hill and Ball, 2009) to suggest that, beyond a certain minimum level of competence, being more qualified in mathematics does not result in better primary mathematics teaching. Therefore you need to consider the precise nature of the knowledge that makes a difference to the quality of primary teachers' lesson planning and teaching. What particular mathematical knowledge do effective teachers of primary mathematics have?

Research Focus: Four kinds of mathematical knowledge

Rowland et al. (2009) identified four kinds of mathematical knowledge that are not prevalent in the general population, but which are specific to teachers. They called these four kinds of knowledge the 'Knowledge Quartet' and suggest that all four are important for good mathematics planning and teaching. The four kinds of knowledge are as follows.

1. **Foundation Knowledge** – basic knowledge of and beliefs about mathematics and mathematics teaching, acquired either at school or through teacher training.

2. **Transformation Knowledge** – knowledge about how to transform an understanding of the mathematics into a form that will be understandable to children (see also Hill and

→

Ball, 2009) This enables teachers to break new mathematical ideas down into mean-ingful pieces and to have a range of models, illustrations, explanations and activities to develop children's understanding.

3. **Connection Knowledge** – knowledge about how different elements of mathematics connect and about the inherent, internal structure of mathematics. This helps teach-ers to sequence learning episodes and to draw on children's understanding of other areas of mathematics to develop understanding of new concepts.

4. **Contingent Knowledge** – knowledge about possible mathematical misconceptions or errors. This enables teachers to respond flexibly to children's questions and answers, and to adapt and change a lesson in response to the learning that is taking place.

Planning good mathematics lessons involves considering all these different types of knowledge and incorporating them into your planning. Rather than considering each different 'type' of knowledge in turn, I will discuss some of the key questions and thought processes that contribute to a good lesson plan.

Mathematics is full of problematic vocabulary. There are several words, which have a precise mathematical meaning, which children need to use in order to be able to express their mathematical thinking. This not only helps you, as the teacher, to understand and assess their mathematical thinking (Lee, 2006), but it also helps the children to develop their mathematical understanding, as language is more than simply a means of giving voice to existing thought processes (Vygotsky, 1980). Mathematical vocabulary can be particularly problematic, as there are words which have a particular mathematical meaning but which also have an everyday meaning. Consider the following exchange, which I still remember well from early in my teaching career.

Me: So, what's the difference between three and seven?

Child: Well, ... one's all round and the other is kind of pointy.

Some consideration of the word 'difference' and explanation of that to my children would have helped that particular lesson to proceed more smoothly.

What are the common misconceptions that children might have in this particular mathematical topic? There are a number of books which explore children's mathematical misconceptions in detail (for example, Hansen, 2014). Consult them as you plan a new sequence of lessons and add to them as the sequence progresses. In addition to reading about children's misconceptions, explore the mathematics for yourself and try, as part of your planning process, to put yourself into the shoes of the children you are going to teach. Try to imagine how they might misunderstand a particular mathematical idea or a particular mathematical word. This is harder to do than it sounds and is particularly difficult if you are teaching very young children, as the distance that you have to travel to get into the mind of a three- or four-year-old is considerably further than that needed to get into that of an 11-year-old.

Activity: Difference by counting on

Imagine a lesson in which the teacher is encouraging the children to find the difference by counting on from the smaller number to the greater on a number line. They are putting a blue counter on the smaller number and a red counter on the higher number and counting on to find the difference.

The teacher asks the children, 'What is the difference between 3 and 5?'

Figure 9.2 'What is the difference between 3 and 5?'

What possible answers do you think the children could give to this problem? There are at least four in addition to the correct answer.

The most common possible answers are 1, 2 (the correct answer), 3, 4 and 8.

One: Some children might focus on the word 'between' in the question, look at the number line and conclude that there is only one number between 3 and 5.

Three: Many children in this situation make the mistake of beginning to count on by counting the number where they begin. This leads them to arrive at a final total that is one greater than the correct answer (i.e. they will count 3, 4, 5 raising one finger for each count, arriving at a total of 3).

Four: Some children may focus on the word 'between' and see that the number '4' is between 3 and 5 and so give that as the answer.

Eight: Some children will simply add the three and the five together, possibly because they see 'three and five' in the question, or possibly because they are most used to adding and do this as a default if they are uncertain about what to do.

Children's experience of number lines with addition might lead them to think that the number you end up on is the answer, so may give the answer 5.

Having considered the ways in which the children might misunderstand the mathematics, it is possible to alert the children to the pitfalls. Given that it is impossible to protect children from all misunderstandings, this kind of thinking will help you to respond appropriately to a child who has a misunderstanding.

Case Study: Number bonds

Patrick is teaching his Reception class about number bonds up to ten. He is playing a simple game with the children where he indicates a number between zero and ten and the children have to hold up the number of fingers that make the total up to ten. The game proceeds as follows.

Patrick: I'm going to hold up some fingers. You will need to count how many fingers I am holding up and then think about how many more I would need to hold up to make ten altogether. Does everyone understand?

Class: Yes. (There is general agreement from the children, although one or two look slightly bemused).

Patrick: (Holds up five fingers.) Now then, how many am I holding up?

Class: (Several children are now holding up five fingers.)

Patrick: Good, I'm holding up five fingers, so I need five more to make ten. Excellent. Let's try another one. (He now holds up seven fingers.)

Class: (Most of the children are now holding up seven fingers.)

Patrick: OK, let's try this again. Put your fingers away for a minute. Let's count how many fingers I'm holding up. Let's do it together.

Class: (Everyone counts to seven together.)

Patrick: Now, how many more would I need to make ten altogether. Have a think and when you think you know the answer, hold up that many fingers.

Class: (Some of the children are holding up four fingers, some are holding up three and some seven.)

Patrick: Suzie, how many fingers are you holding up?

Suzie: Three.

Patrick: Good girl. Can you tell everyone else how you knew the answer was three?

Suzie: Seven ... eight, nine, ten. (Counts on using her fingers to end up with three fingers raised.)

Patrick: Fantastic. Let's try another one. (Holds up eight fingers)

Class: (Several of the children hold up three fingers, several hold up two.)

Patrick: Wonderful. Lots of people with the right answer. Let's try some more. (Holds up four fingers).

The lesson proceeds in this way for several minutes. The examples that Patrick uses in the lesson were as follows:

5; 7; 8; 4; 9; 6; 4; 6; 9; 1; 10; 0

Activity: Number bonds

Consider the excerpt from the lesson above.

What do you think of Patrick's choice of examples?

(Continued)

(Continued)

Why do you think he began with five?

Would you have chosen a different example to begin with, and why?

Why do you think he chose the numbers he did at the end; were they random choices, or were they planned?

Would you have chosen different numbers, or chosen to give the examples in a different order?

The examples that you choose to help illustrate or consolidate a particular mathematical concept or process are key to the planning process. In the case study above, Patrick's choice of five as his first example initially seems like a good one; it is an easy question and familiar to the children. However, in choosing this example, he has created a misunderstanding that takes a while to be resolved. In that instance, the question is the same as the answer. While this certainly can happen in mathematics, it is often confusing to begin with such examples.

Later in the lesson, Patrick used his examples carefully to get the children to think about an interesting mathematical idea. By choosing six and then four and then going back to six, he is emphasising the commutative property of addition. This is reinforced with subsequent examples, beginning with nine (which is a much easier question than one for children who are counting on) and then one. He then introduces the idea of zero through his choice of examples. Choosing the best examples to use can be a powerful tool in your teaching, but requires careful planning. Conversely, a careless choice of example can unwittingly cause problems.

Finally, it is important to give explicit consideration to the different models and representations that you intend to use to illustrate a particular concept. These images can have a profound effect on the way that a child comes to understand mathematics. When planning mathematics lessons, you might want to consider the depth of your own understanding and the images that you use to make sense of the mathematics, and to consider that some of the children may need different models to help them understand concepts.

The following is a checklist of the key elements of pedagogical subject knowledge:

- key mathematical vocabulary;
- prerequisite knowledge: the mathematical knowledge and experiences the children bring to the lessons;
- possible misconceptions;
- ways of modelling and representing the concepts;
- choice of examples.

Activity: Concept mapping

This is the most important activity in this chapter. If you do no others, do this one.

Select a mathematical topic that you are going to teach in the future. This should be a broad enough topic to cover a sequence of lessons over a week or maybe more.

Create a diagram/concept map or a short piece of prose, based on the reading of a book such as Haylock (2010) and a book on misconceptions such as Hansen (2014), which details some of the specific mathematical understanding that you will need to plan effectively for that topic. Be sure to cover the areas mentioned above. Ideally do this task with a fellow trainee teacher and then compare your thoughts, each adding to the other's 'map'. Keep this as a resource for the next time you teach that topic and add to it as your mathematical pedagogical knowledge increases.

Learning Outcomes Review

In this chapter, some of the key ideas and questions that you should consider when planning both individual mathematics lessons and sequences of lessons have been reviewed. The notion of discernment has been explored in the hope that you will be able to free yourself from endless searching online for lessons. Importantly, the process of identifying key ideas prior to teaching a sequence of lessons has been identified.

Self-assessment questions

1. How could Ausubel's ideas about children's prior knowledge help you to plan mathematics lessons?
2. How might mathematics lessons be differentiated to ensure that all children are suitably challenged?
3. What are the key elements to consider when planning a sequence of maths lessons?

References

Adhami, M. (2003) From lesson objectives to lesson agenda: flexibility in whole-class lesson structure, in Thompson, I. (ed.) *Enhancing Primary Mathematics Teaching*. Maidenhead: Open University Press.

Ausubel, David P. (1968) *Educational Psychology: A cognitive view*. London: Holt, Reinhart, and Winston.

Black, P. and Wiliam, D. (1998) *Inside the Black Box: Raising standards through classroom assessment*. London: Granada Learning.

Boaler, J. (2010) *The Elephant in the Classroom. Helping children learn and love maths*. London: Souvenir Press.

Butler, R. (1998) Enhancing and undermining intrinsic motivation: the effects of task-involving and ego-involving evaluation on interest and performance. *British Journal of Educational Psychology*, 58: 1–14.

Clarke, S. (2005) *Formative Assessment in Action: weaving the elements together*. Abingdon: Hodder Education.

DfEE (1999) *The National Numeracy Strategy*. Suffolk: DfEE.

Hansen, A. (2014) *Children's Errors in Mathematics*, 3rd edition. London: Learning Matters SAGE.

Haylock, D. (2010) *Mathematics Explained for Primary Teachers*. London: SAGE.

Hill, H. and Ball, D.L. (2009) The curious – and crucial – case of mathematical knowledge for teaching. *Phi Delta Kappan*, 91(2): 68–71.

Hughes, M. (1986) *Children and Number*. Oxford: Blackwell.

Lee, C. (2006) *Language for Learning Mathematics*. Maidenhead: Open University Press.

Rowland, T., Turner, F., Thwaites, A. and Huckstep, P. (2009) *Developing Primary Mathematics Teaching*. London: SAGE.

Swaffield, S. (2008) *Unlocking Assessment. Understanding for reflection and application*. Abingdon: Routledge.

Threlfall, J. (2005) The formative use of assessment information in planning – the notion of contingent planning. *British Journal of Educational Studies*, 53(1): 54–65.

Vygotsky, L.S. (1980) *Mind in Society: The development of higher psychological processes*. Cambridge MA: Harvard University Press.

10 Communicating mathematically

Balbir Ahir

Learning outcomes

By reading this chapter you will develop:

- an understanding of why communicating mathematically is challenging;
- an awareness of the different strategies to encourage children to communicate mathematics through use of discourse;
- an awareness of the different strategies to encourage children to communicate mathematics through writing.

TEACHERS' STANDARDS

2. Promote good progress and outcomes by pupils
3. Demonstrate good subject and curriculum knowledge
8. Fulfil wider professional responsibilities

Introduction

Mathematics is a linguistic activity; its ultimate area is preciseness of communication.

(Schaff, W.L., cited in A Learning Place)

Primary mathematics is often not thought of as a 'linguistic activity', yet the subject provides a wealth of opportunities to communicate meanings in creative, expressive and diverse ways. These opportunities need to be planned for in maths lessons to allow children to gain a deeper understanding of the subject, which Biggs (2003) defines as learning for meaning, understanding and application for life.

To communicate mathematically is to be able to articulate conceptual understanding of mathematics, its structures and relationships through a variety of forms and make it visible to the outside world. Children should be taught how to communicate mathematically, and teaching should provide opportunities for children to communicate their ideas through:

- discussion, listening, describing and talking about concepts using concise mathematical vocabulary with the teacher and/or with peers;

- reading, recording, interpreting and representing mathematics through pictures, diagrams, illustrations, signs, charts and symbols.

The ability to see the relationship between vocabulary, signs, symbols and concepts is *integral to our learning of mathematics*, and should be instigated through an iterative process of carefully planned tasks, activities and discussion to refine children's understanding of the subject (Barmby et al., 2009, p.7). Derek Haylock and Anne Cockburn propose a *connections model of understanding* and emphasise the importance of children making connections between language, symbols, pictures and practical real-life experiences (2008, p.10). The National Curriculum also describes mathematics as being *an interconnected subject* allowing children to move *between representations of mathematical ideas* (DFE, 2013, p.3).

The use of concrete experiences (often using everyday materials) allows children to understand and communicate mathematical concepts, which can otherwise be abstract. Using language to describe a number problem can make connections to the concrete experience. A further connection is made when the child draws the picture or diagram to show the number problem. The use of pictures can also progress to the use of a number track or number line and tallies which can support mental imagery. The final connection is communicating the mathematics in an abstract way using the signs and symbols (Haylock and Cockburn, 2008). Although this model is explained in the context of number, the four components can be applied to all areas of mathematics as a process of *building up cognitive connections* and as a means of communicating (Haylock, 2010, pp.26–27).

The aim of this chapter is to address some of the challenges that children may face when communicating their understanding of mathematical concepts. It will identify and explore classroom strategies that encourage children to become better communicators of mathematics through use of discourse and writing and by exploring some of the connections between the four components of the Haylock and Cockburn model discussed above. The approaches will assist you to develop your practice and

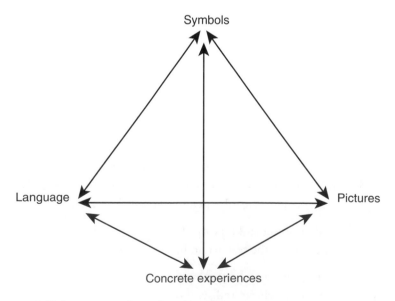

Figure 10.1 Multiple representations of mathematics

benefit children by providing opportunities to engage in activities that support their mathematical communication and therefore their mathematical learning.

Mathematical communication through the use of discourse

Mathematical 'discourse' as discussed in this chapter, refers to:

- use of concise vocabulary;

- ascribing meaning to mathematical words and phrases;

- sharing mathematical instructions;

- talk and discussion of ideas and strategies between peers and between children and adults;

- listening and reflecting on ideas shared by peers and relating it to one's own understanding;

- developing mathematical reasoning, justifying findings and solving problems;

- questioning and challenging mathematical ideas (Kieran et al., 2005).

The above behaviours support thinking and contribute to an understanding of mathematical ideas and concepts. Lee (2006) further extends her understanding of mathematical discourse to include *the full range of language required to learn mathematics* (2006 p.1). However, the use of mathematical language in itself can be a challenge. Mathematical language can be likened to the learning of a second language as it involves the acquisition of a new specialised vocabulary to interpret, understand and communicate the mathematics, which can make the subject harder to understand (Barmby et al., 2009; Haylock and Thangata, 2007). In the context of your classroom this would mean that children need to acquire appropriate vocabulary so that they are not just *talking about maths* but they are also *talking mathematically* to develop thinking (Askew, 2011, p.5; Lee, 2006).

Encouraging mathematical discourse and being an active participant in talk can foster mathematical communities in classrooms, where children's explanation of ideas, enables them to gain greater ownership of these ideas so that they are able to transfer them to other situations (Lee, 2006). There has been a lot of research and discussion on the importance of mathematical discourse in constructing meaning and understanding and what this may look like in classroom practice (Wickham, 2008; Evans, 2002; Houssart and Mason, 2009; University of Cambridge, 2013; Kieran et al., 2005).

Research Focus: Dialogue in mathematics

Evidence for Policy and Practice Information and Co-ordinating Centre (EPPI-Centre) examined 15 research case studies concerning the quality of teacher–pupil dialogue in mathematics for children in Key Stages 2 and 3. This review focused on research evidence that represented *effective teacher-initiated teacher–pupil dialogue* which developed children's conceptual understanding in mathematics as opposed to 'procedural fluency' during lessons. The findings from the review identified eight characteristics of effective teacher-initiated teacher–pupil dialogue.

1. Going beyond 'Initiate, Response, Feedback' – traditional initiation-response-feedback (IRF) discourse, which included the use of mostly closed questions, dominated teacher-initiated teacher–pupil dialogue in mathematics lessons. It was recommended that using words such as 'why', 'if' and 'because' through 'open questions' encouraged the notion of exploratory talk and mathematical reasoning and extended pupils' thinking to assimilate new understanding.

2. Focusing attention on the mathematics involved rather than on 'getting the answer right'.

3. Creating a learning environment where pupil and teacher work collaboratively together to explore mathematical problems.

4. Transformative listening – listening to pupils' contributions and responses and being guided by pupils to explore ideas and suggestions.

5. Scaffolding.

6. Encouraging children to appreciate how using talk and listening to teachers and other pupils talking is a learning experience.

7. Encouraging high quality pupil dialogue using concise mathematical vocabulary.

8. Inclusive teaching – valuing contributions and engaging all pupils, especially the less able or less confident pupil (Kyriacou and Issitt, 2008).

Ofsted identified the importance of developing mathematical language to support thinking as 'good practice' (Ofsted, 2011; 2008; DCSF, 2008). In the independent review of mathematics teaching by Sir Peter Williams, the following point was made on effective pedagogy of primary mathematics.

Talking mathematics should not be seen simply as a rehearsal in class of the vocabulary of mathematics, novel and important though that may be for the young learner. It should extend to high-quality discussion that develops children's logic, reasoning and deduction skills, and underpins all mathematical learning activity. The ultimate goal is to develop mathematical understanding – comprehension of mathematical ideas and applications.

(DCSF, 2008)

The independent review explored the nature of meaningful and high-quality talk during lessons as a process of developing children's thinking so that they were learning with a relational understanding – knowing what to do and why (Skemp, 1972) and empowering children to apply their knowledge flexibly to new situations and contexts.

However, this was all preceded by the outcomes of *The Cockcroft Report* (*Mathematics Counts*) which emphasised the importance of language as *an essential part in the formulation and expression of mathematical ideas* for all children (HMSO, 1982, p.89), but specifically indicated the benefits for those children for whom English was not their first language.

The National Curriculum emphasises the centrality of spoken language to children's cognitive, social and linguistic development (DfE, 2013). Part of your role as a teacher is to provide a structured approach to the learning and teaching of mathematical language and implementation through mathematical discourse. Your teaching should include planned opportunities for the development of mathematical vocabulary. Assuming that children will know the meaning of words in a mathematical context can be misleading and can lead to misunderstandings. An example of this is when a PGCE student recently asked the children in her class to 'draw a table' in their books and was surprised when several of them asked whether they should also draw the children sitting round it.

All teachers should have a clear understanding of the key vocabulary related to the maths topic that is to be taught, which is relevant to the key stage and year group (see Chapter 9 on planning). They should also be aware of the progression of the mathematical language in that topic across the year groups. The National Numeracy Strategy (DfEE, 1999) emphasised the importance of maths vocabulary through its publication of the Mathematical Vocabulary Book (DfEE, 2000), which corresponded to the strategy. The booklet provided details of the progression of the language that should be used during teaching, but could also be used by children when talking mathematically. The above booklet is still a valuable guidance document for all teachers but particularly trainee teachers. It can be downloaded (see the URL at the end of this chapter). You may also like to have the following in your classroom: published child-friendly primary mathematics dictionaries to define key words; vocabulary cards which are visible and accessible for all children to use during lessons; class-made dictionaries personal to the children. You may like to use key websites such as the Jenny Eater Maths dictionary for kids (Eater, 2014) aimed at the primary phase which provides definitions and illustrations of many mathematical words.

Activity

The table below includes some maths vocabulary that may cause children to have misconceptions or misunderstanding.

Use the online dictionary (http://amathsdictionaryforkids.com/dictionary.html) to find out the mathematical definition. In the final column write down the definition or understanding of that word in everyday language. Add other key maths vocabulary to the list that you feel children may misunderstand.

(Continued)

(*Continued*)

	Maths vocabulary	Alternative words used in everyday language and other misconceptions
Number	Sum – the result of adding	Some – unknown or unspecified Sometimes the word sum is used to mean all number operations (which is incorrect)
	Operation – four basic operations in mathematics: subtraction, addition, multiplication and division	Operation – surgery performed on a patient
	Sequence Array Mixed number Score Difference	
Measure	Balance Division Yard	
Data	Mean Table	
Shape	Face Surface Net Translation	

Social interaction and particularly language is central to Vygotsky's theory of intellectual and cognitive development. He proposed that children's initial understanding results from interaction with others and is then internalised (Keenan, 2002). This can be encouraged through carefully planned opportunities for discussion, allowing children to talk about the work they are engaged in. Your role is to create and manage opportunities for discussion, listening and oral work across whole-class work, group work and with the use of talk partners so that accurate mathematical language can be scaffolded and modelled. The teacher is *crucial in bringing about an inquiry based approach through maths talk* (Kieran et al., 2005, p.793). The following points would need to be considered when planning for talk partners to generate productive mathematical learning.

- Opportunities for talk between partners should be identified at the planning stage. At what stages during a maths lesson will children be required to talk about the mathematics? What will be the aim/focus of this talk and how will it contribute to learning? What opportunities will children have to record or share some of the conversations?

- Think about how children will be paired and arranged for partner talk. It might be useful to have different pairings for different occasions during lessons.

- Ensure that children are aware of the 'ground rules' for partner talk.

- Build up the partner talk skills in small steps through sessions, led by an adult with a clear focus on the development of spoken language, the modelling of vocabulary to be used, and on questioning. This can be done during whole-class direct teaching sessions as well as during small group work directed by the teacher/adult.

- Identify key questions to scaffold the talk.

- Pre-empt and consider your response to misconceptions/misunderstandings when they arise during partner talk (see Chapter 9 for more detail).

The use of talk partners can provide opportunities to practise and rehearse language, allow a quick interchange of ideas and allow partially formed ideas to evolve, whereas group discussion may provide opportunities for mathematical ideas to be shared, considered and new ideas to be developed and constructed (Hansen and Ahir, 2014). Vygotsky relates this to a *more knowledgeable other* (not necessarily the teacher) who scaffolds and moves learning on (Pritchard, 2005, p.30).

Case Study: Use of geometric language to describe quadrilaterals

James teaches Year 4. As part of his lessons on geometry he investigated the properties of quadrilaterals and encouraged children to use the correct mathematical language. Key words such as parallel, symmetry and perpendicular were displayed on each table.

Children worked in groups of four and each group was given a different quadrilateral to describe. The children were given a few minutes to discuss the properties of their shape (rhombus, parallelogram, rectangle, trapezium, kite). One person was selected to speak for a minute (using a timer) on the properties of their shape to the other groups in the class using correct mathematical language and full sentences. Some children in the group were ticking off the words used correctly, engaging in peer assessment. The class was brought together for a discussion on the properties of shape and use of correct language and to address any misunderstandings that may have arisen. The activity was repeated throughout the week; shapes and the key spokesperson were changed so that all children had a chance to practise their use of language.

Introducing new vocabulary in context is important. For example, when naming 3-D shapes, you could provide real-life examples of these shapes to develop understanding of the terminology and to assist children to see the maths in the world around them. The use of specialised mathematical apparatus such as place value resources (Dienes apparatus, arrow cards) can also aid the use of precise language. Concrete materials provide a visual image to support and scaffold children's understanding that can be translated into verbal explanations.

Displaying the vocabulary in symbols, pictures, words or diagrams, such as = equal, > greater than, < less than, can become an important scaffold. It is strongly recommended that you have 'maths learning walls' where the key language associated with the topics taught or valuable prompts to promote discourse are displayed. It should also be a shared space for children to interact with. Part of your summary and reflection points in a maths lesson could include identifying valuable prompts that could come from children's mathematical discourse for display on the maths learning wall (Hansen and Ahir, 2014).

The art of questioning in mathematics

Mason (2002) suggests that asking questions is so embedded in our educational culture that most adults ask questions when interacting with children and children ask questions when playing 'schools'. As a teacher, it is probably embedded as part of your practice. However, Mason suggests that teachers almost always know the answer to the questions they are asking and that the children know they know. Questioning has been reduced to a game of 'guess what's in my head'. Communication of mathematical ideas is very often prompted by a question, usually, but not always, from a teacher. In the following section we will consider ways to improve the quality of mathematical questioning and suggest that responses to the children's answers are as important as the questions themselves.

The purpose of mathematical questions

The NCETM suggests that mathematical questions have several possible purposes and that the questions you ask will depend, in part at least, on that purpose. You may ask questions as a form of assessment to establish what the children already know, so that you can make appropriate adjustments to your lessons. If this is the case, you are perfectly justified in asking a question to which you already know the answer. In this instance a closed question (i.e. a question with a single, specific answer) may be entirely appropriate: 'What is 7 x 8?'

However, questions may have a number of other purposes. They should be used to encourage thinking and therefore the communication of mathematical ideas. Consider these two examples.

1. What is the name of this shape?

2. Is it always, sometimes or never true that a shape with four equal sides is a rhombus?

In the second example, the question has been used to prompt the children's mathematical thinking and discussion. Although there is a 'right answer', we are much more interested in the discussion that the children will have than the 'answer'. The NCETM suggests that questioning should promote children's mathematical reasoning (a key feature of the new National Curriculum). Children answering the second question above are more likely to use the language of reasoning (see Chapter 1) in explaining their answer. The question invites reasoning. Questions might also be used to excite and motivate children. Beginning a lesson with a suitable question that requires mathematical thinking should prompt dialogue and interest. Questions such as these are more powerful if they are 'real'; 'Where would be the best place to site the new climbing frame?', or 'How much will it cost to have new carpet tiles in the book corner?' are potentially motivating questions if the children will be genuinely involved in their outcome. Finally, the NCETM suggests that questions should encourage children to think about their own thinking and to consider how they have learned something.

Possible question stems

A quick look online will yield a number of different question openings. The 'art' of questioning lies in choosing the right question and in our reactions to the children's answers. Jenni Way writing on the NRICH website (http://nrich.maths.org/2473) suggests that questions can be divided into starter questions, questions to promote mathematical thinking, assessment questions and final discussion questions. Here are a few suggested question openings. You can decide how you would use them in your classroom.

1. What is the same and what is different about …?

2. Can you find me an example to show …?

3. Is it always, sometimes, or never true that …?

4. Of these numbers/shapes/graphs/measures of average/calculation which is the odd one out and why?

5. Do you agree or disagree that …? Why?

6. What would need to be changed so that …?

7. What happens if you change …?

Whether you are asking assessment questions where there is a 'right answer', or more open questions such as those suggested above, there is a lot of research to suggest that giving children time to think has a beneficial effect on the quality of their responses and on the range of pupils who are likely to contribute (Maroni, 2011). You should consider ways of eliciting responses that do not (always) involve children putting their hands up. This can be hugely demotivating for children who are not first to raise their hands, or who feel intimidated into doing so. Others may simply realise that answering mathematical questions is a game they cannot win and withdraw. Clarke (2005) offers a detailed explanation of ways of asking questions without the children putting their hands up to respond. Assuring the children that you are more interested in the quality of their discussion than their final answer and giving them time to collect their thoughts before offering a response means children are more likely to participate.

Children asking mathematical questions

We want our classrooms to be places where the children's curiosity about mathematics prompts them to ask mathematical questions. They will be more motivated to answer their own questions than other people's. Wong (2012) suggests that there are two key reasons why it is important for children to feel free to ask mathematical questions. Firstly, they need to have the confidence to ask for clarification if they do not understand something. Secondly, asking mathematical questions (and making conjectures – see Chapter 1) is an essential part of thinking like a mathematician.

It is therefore important that you foster an environment in your classroom where children are happy to ask questions. Your response to the children's requests for clarification will determine how likely they are to continue to ask. If your response suggests that the child is at fault for not having understood, or not having listened, the children will quickly pick up that asking for clarification leads to admonishment and trouble. If, however, you not only answer the question, but make it clear that you are really pleased that the child needed to ask a question as a result of thinking about the maths so much, the rest of the children will note that asking for clarification is a desirable behaviour.

Wong (2012) also suggests that asking mathematical questions is an essential part of thinking like a mathematician. Conveying the desirability of this is essential. Give the child who has asked a question a reward from the system that you usually use. You might like to consider having a particular award for 'best maths question of the day/week', or put the name of all the children who ask a mathematical question into a draw for the 'mathematician of the week' award. You might also consider asking yourself mathematical questions out loud. This is particularly powerful if you genuinely are not sure of the answer to the question. Musing to the children 'I wonder what would happen here if we began the sequence with an even number' conveys the message that asking mathematical questions is a desirable mathematical behaviour.

Communicating mathematically through writing

Communicating mathematics through writing, whether informal or formal, is an important stage in understanding mathematical concepts (Taylor and Harris, 2014; Briggs, 2013; Haylock and Cockburn, 2008). Goldin and Shteingold (2001 cited in Barmby et al., 2009) suggest that representations are important for learning mathematics. Different representations emphasise different aspects of a concept, and so the development of an understanding of a particular concept comes from having a range of representations (2009, p.6). Writing mathematics shares many of the qualities of talking mathematically, but it has some unique characteristics of its own, such as creating a record of our thinking that we can analyse, reflect upon and modify. Writing in mathematics can include any or all of the following:

- pictures;

- diagrams;

- graphs and charts;

- use of abbreviations and symbols;

- patterns;

- informal jottings or hieroglyphs (invented symbols that are meaningful to the child (Briggs, 2013);

- maths stories;

- formal mathematical recording such as standard algorithms for the four number operations.

As well as having a distinct richness of vocabulary particular to the subject, mathematics has its own set of abbreviations, symbols and conventions which are also commonly used to communicate ideas. It is the symbolic nature of mathematical communication which can quickly make it more abstract (Taylor and Harris, 2014; Briggs, 2013; Worthington and Carruthers, 2003). The abstractness can lead to some children being challenged with reading, verbalisation and spelling as well as the semantics of mathematics which *refers to the underlying meaning of these symbols or abbreviations* (Quinnell and Carter, 2013, p.8).

Sometimes spoken mathematics can be difficult to interpret in a symbolic form as many words or phrases can be used to represent a single symbol. For the symbol of subtraction – the language that is introduced to children in Key Stage 1 can include words and phrases such as take away; minus; leave; how many left?; how many left over?; difference between; how much less is? However, some of these words and phrases can be difficult to interpret, i.e. what is the difference between 12 and 20? The difficulty here is that children can interpret this problem symbolically as being represented as $12 - 20$. As an informal representation it can be shown using a number track; start at 12 and count the number of steps to 20, or start at 20 and count the number of steps to 12. Either way you are finding the difference between 12 and 20. The phrases 'how many left?' or 'how many left over?' can also be used to discuss remainders in a division calculation.

The bridge from the verbal to the written is quite a complex move and it is often at this stage that children begin to show difficulties, misconceptions and misunderstandings. Interpreting written word problems or spoken mathematics as symbolic representation can be even more problematic for children who have EAL or for those children who have learning difficulties. As a teacher you will need to identify points of transition or steps that direct children to transfer from their own informal way of recording mathematics towards a more formal approach so that children develop 'mathematical literacy', which Munn describes as being *essential for their continued mathematical development* (Munn, 1997 cited in Briggs, 2013, p.107). Some suggestions about how precisely to do this are made after the research focus.

Research Focus: Children's understanding of written mathematics

Worthington and Carruthers (2003) carried out research into young children's understanding of written mathematics. The problems they encountered with early 'written' mathematics were that it did not have a real purpose and was therefore not contributing to the understanding of their subject. This research led to an extensive study of children's formal and informal understanding of mathematical graphics. Worthington and Carruthers (2012) refer to mathematical graphics as a 'powerful means for exploring and communicating thoughts, ideas and feelings and for solving problems in all aspects of life. For young children it offers valuable and significant means to explore the 'written' language of mathematics, helping them to come to understand the abstract written language of mathematics in personally meaningful ways.'

The research involved 700 examples of mathematical graphics from children aged between three and eight years. The early stages of communicating an understanding of written mathematics were often based on a personal use of pictures, models and apparatus, allowing children to *translate between their home mathematics and the abstract mathematics of school* (p.2) and gain a better understanding of the symbols and conventions used to communicate mathematics later on. The recommendations from the study emphasised that effective teaching should encourage children to:

- be creative in how they record their mathematics so that it has purpose and meaning for them rather than being an early introduction to an abstract and formal way of recording;

- be provided with as many opportunities as possible to use their own ways of recording before they begin to record more formally;

- talk and write about their work in their own way, as an early introduction of symbols without meaning can lead to misconceptions and gaps in understanding.

From their research Worthington and Carruthers developed a taxonomy that focused on the mathematical functions and meanings of children's mathematical graphics (Worthington and Carruthers, 2013).

Their taxonomy built on the work previously carried out by Hughes (1986) and provided a global view of young children's developing understanding of mathematical signs and

→

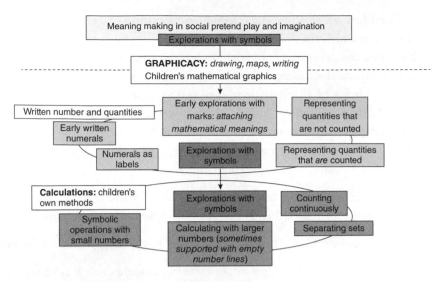

Figure 10.2 (Worthington and Carruthers, 2013)

symbols. The importance of mathematical 'mark making' and the work carried out by Worthington and Carruthers was also highlighted in the Williams Review and was identified as effective mathematical pedagogy in the Early Years. A similar 'taxonomy tracing the development of children's mathematical graphics from birth to 8 years' was also shared in the Williams Review (DCSF, 2008, p.35).

Below are some suggestions to promote and support children's representation of mathematics during lessons and bridge the transition between informal and formal representations of mathematics.

A 'maths jotter' or journal allows children to organise, record, select and represent mathematical ideas using models and written language in an informal manner. You might give the children two maths books – one for doing informal calculations 'in rough' where they could make mistakes, jottings and express their mathematics 'freely' and a 'best' book where they can write about some of their maths. Children might use a page to write about 'equivalent fractions' using their own examples and diagrams to explain what they know about the topic. Such a resource is valuable in gaining insights into what the child has understood, as it reveals the process of thinking and how the child approaches ideas, highlights any misconceptions and can be used as a means of assessment. As it is informal and personal to the child it removes the obstacle of having to represent maths in a particular way for an audience, thus supporting the pedagogy recommended in the Early Years (DCSF, 2008) being transferred into the primary phase. Our thanks to the great Bob Davies for this suggestion.

With the development of ICT, formal and informal mathematical jottings can take on a completely new meaning. Some schools have allocated children their own iPads™ or tablets which allow the freedom and flexibility to represent learning in both written and verbal forms concurrently. Writing mathematical ideas on the tablet/iPad and recordings of verbal understanding to go with it can easily be saved and stored for discussion and assessment at a later stage, shared with the teacher and made visible for small group or whole-class analysis. Maths journals, of any nature, can build a portfolio of 'mathematical jottings' to demonstrate progression of understanding towards a more formal approach. By dating entries the journal provides a chronological record of the development of a child's mathematical thinking and communication throughout the year.

Give children the opportunity to publish their mathematical writing, in a comprehensible manner, for different audiences and for different purposes.

- You may ask older children to write a maths trail for younger children to follow.

- Children might share their experience of solving a mathematical investigation.

- Share interesting facts about geometric shapes that are being explored during a maths lesson.

- Create a whole-class working maths vocabulary booklet that includes both teacher and pupil annotations.

- Engineer opportunities to discuss and evaluate different methods of presenting the solution to a problem.

- Write story problems to number sentences.

Writing for an audience and the opportunity to publish work can provide a purpose and a need to present the maths in a more uniform way.

Case Study: Using a story to support visualisation of multiplication arrays

Incorporating mathematics into a story can make it more meaningful for children. Miya, the Year 3 class teacher, was exploring multiplication through arrays. She started off with a story called *One Hundred Hungry Ants*. As Miya read the story she emphasised the language of rows, questioned children's understanding (What would 100 ants marching in 10 rows look like? How many ants in each row, or in each column? How can we work this out?) and asked them to visualise what they could see and then modelled their thoughts as a whole class, leading to the arrangements of arrays.

The independent task involved children working in pairs to illustrate the arrays for a given target number. The activity was differentiated with the target numbers 12, 24 and 48. Resources such as dots, number lines, interactive whiteboard and counters were available. Part of this activity required children to use visualisation to see the

$\longrightarrow$

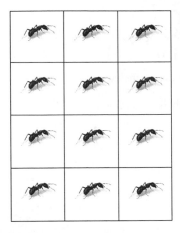

arrangements. They had to record their work as an illustration but also write a number sentence such as 12 hungry ants = marching in 4 rows of 3; 12 = 4 x 3. During the reflection part of the lesson Miya explicitly made the connection that 4 x 3 was equal to 3 x 4 and that multiplication is commutative.

The above example demonstrates a socially structured and organised activity whereby children are encouraged to internalise and communicate mathematics using resources, signs and symbols.

Try to provide your children with opportunities to read and write symbolic statements as well as interpret them. The activity below can be used with children to make connections between the diagrams, pictures and symbols. This could be developed further by asking children to explore and take pictures of examples of multiplication in the classroom environment but then to express it in a symbolic form.

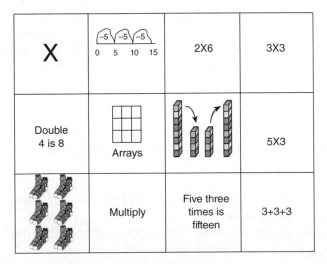

Figure 10.3 Different visual representations of multiplication

Activity: Add missing symbols to make the statements true

Find out what each symbol means <, >, +, =, -, X, ≤, ≥, ÷, ≠

Use some of these symbols to complete the following number sentences. (More than one symbol can be used in some number sentences).

1.   69 Δ 56 = 25 Δ 5

2.   144 ÷ 12 Δ 165 − 134

3.   128 Δ 8 = 54 − 32

Learning Outcomes Review

Suggate et al. (2006) state that teachers new to the profession often have the 'wrong kind of understanding' of mathematics and what is required is a greater understanding of how the different components of mathematics link together. Some of the challenges to communicating effectively in this subject have been highlighted, such as knowing and using subject-specific vocabulary and the relationship between written mathematics and an understanding of the language of mathematics. The challenge for many children, as well as teachers, is the acquisition of a 'new language' while at the same time assimilating understanding of mathematical concepts.

When representing mathematics children are yet again faced with another challenge to their learning and understanding which involves the use of symbolic and other subject-specific notations. Sometimes symbols and mathematical notations are introduced to children with little meaning and understanding which limits children's understanding to the context in which they have seen them being used. For example the = sign is mostly seen after a number sentence to denote an answer, when in fact it represents more than that; it is equal and can be placed at the beginning of a number sentence not necessarily at the end, for example: $? = 4 + 7$ or $5 + 6 = 8 + 3$.

As stated in the National Curriculum: *The quality and variety of language that pupils hear and speak are key factors in developing their mathematical vocabulary and presenting a mathematical justification* (DfE, 2013, p.4).

Self-assessment questions

1. Think about how you plan for and present key vocabulary, related to the mathematics lesson, to children?
2. What opportunities are provided for children to communicate their mathematics during guided sessions and/or independent group work?

> 3. What strategies are used to further support acquisition of mathematical language and representation of mathematics for different learning styles and for learners who have EAL?
> 4. Identify two key points that you wish to develop in your practice.

Further Reading

Mason, J. (1980) When is a symbol symbolic? *For the Learning of Mathematics,* 1(2): 8–12.

Way, J. and Berdon, T. (2003) *ICT and Primary Mathematics*. Maidenhead: Open University Press.

References

A Learning Place (n.d.) *Pedagogy*. Available at: http://alearningplace.com.au/pedagogy/ (accessed 28/07/14).

Askew, M. (2011) *Private Talk, Public Conversation*. Available at: www.mikeaskew.net/page3/page5/page5.html (accessed 28/07/14).

Barmby, P., Bilsborough, L., Harries, T. and Higgins, S. (2009) *Primary Mathematics: Teaching for Understanding*. Maidenhead: Open University McGraw Hill.

Biggs, J. (2003) *Teaching for Quality Learning at University*, 2nd edition. Maidenhead: Open University.

Briggs, M. (2013) *Teaching and Learning Early Years Mathematic: Subject and Pedagogic Knowledge*. Northwich: Critical Publishing.

Clarke, S. (2005) *Formative Assessment in Action: weaving the elements together*. London: Hodder Murray.

DCSF (2008) *Independent Review of Mathematics Teaching in Early Years Settings and Primary Schools*. Nottingham: DCSF.

DfE (2013) *The National Curriculum in England: Key stages 1 and 2 framework document*. Available at: www.gov.uk/government/uploads/system/uploads/attachment_data/file/260481/PRIMARY_national_curriculum_11-9-13_2.pdf (accessed 28/07/14).

DfE (2013) *National Curriculum in England: Mathematics programmes of study: key stages 1 and 2*. Available at: www.gov.uk/government/publications/national-curriculum-in-england-mathematics-programmes-of-study/national-curriculum-in-england-mathematics-programmes-of-study (accessed 25/07/14).

DfEE (1999) *The National Numeracy Strategy*. Suffolk: DfEE.

DfEE (2000) *Mathematical Vocabulary Book*. Available at: http://webarchive.nationalarchives.gov.uk/20110202093118/http:/nationalstrategies.standards.dcsf.gov.uk/node/84996 (accessed 28/07/14).

Eater, J. (2014) *A Maths Dictionary for Kids*. Available at http://amathsdictionaryforkids.com/dictionary.html (accessed 28/07/14).

Evans, J. (2002) Talking about maths. *Education 3–13: International Journal of Primary, Elementary and Early Years Education*, 30(1): 66–71.

Hansen, A. and Ahir, B. (2014) Mathematics, in Smith, P. and Dawes, L. (eds) *Subject Teaching in Primary Education*. London: SAGE.

Haylock, D. (2010) *Mathematics Explained for Primary Teachers*, 4th edition. London: SAGE.

Haylock, D. and Cockburn, A. (2008) *Understanding Mathematics for Young Children: a Guide for Foundation Stage and Lower Primary Teachers*. London: SAGE.

Haylock, D. and Thangata, F. (2007) *Key Concepts in Teaching Primary Mathematics*. London: SAGE.

HMSO (1982) *Mathematics Counts: The Cockcroft Report*. Available at: www.educationengland.org.uk/documents/cockcroft/cockcroft1982.html#06 (accessed 28/07/14).

Houssart, J. and Mason, J. (eds) (2009) *Listening Counts! Listening to Young Learners of Mathematics*. Staffordshire: Trentham Books.

Hughes, M. (1986) *Children and Number*. Oxford: Blackwell.

Keenan, T. (2002) *An Introduction to Child Development*. California: SAGE.

Kieran, C. Forman, E. and Sfard, A. (2005) Mathematics, discourse and democracy. *British Educational Research Journal*, 31(6): 787–798.

Kyriacou, C. and Issitt, J. (2008) What characterises effective teacher-initiated teacher–pupil dialogue to promote conceptual understanding in mathematics lessons in England in Key Stages 2 and 3: a systematic review. Report. In: *Research Evidence in Education Library*. London: EPPI-Centre, Social Science Research Unit, Institute of Education, University of London.

Lee, C. (2006) *Language for Learning Mathematics*. Berkshire: Open University Press.

Maroni, B. (2011) Pauses, gaps and wait time in classroom interaction in primary schools. *Journal of Pragmatics*, 43(7): 2081–2093.

Mason, J. (2002) Minding Your Qs and Rs: effective questioning and responding in the mathematics classroom, in Haggerty, L. (ed.) *Aspects of Teaching Secondary Mathematics: perspectives on practice*. London: RoutledgeFalmer. pp.248–258.

Ofsted (2008) *Mathematics: understanding the score*. London: Ofsted.

Ofsted (2011) *Good Practice in Primary Mathematics: evidence from 20 successful schools*. London: Ofsted.

Pritchard, A. (2005) *Ways of Learning: Learning Theories and Learning Styles in the Classroom*. London: David Fulton Publishers.

Quinnell, L. and Carter, M. (2013) Gibberish or what? Use of symbolic language in primary mathematics. *Australian Primary Mathematics Classroom*, 18(1): 8–14.

Skemp, R.R (1972) *Relational Understanding and Instrumental Understanding*. Department of Education: University of Warwick.

Suggate, J., Davis, A. and Golding, M. (2006) *Mathematical Knowledge for Primary Teachers*, 4th edition. Abingdon: Routledge.

Taylor, H. and Harris, A. (2014) *Learning and Teaching Mathematics 0–8*. London: SAGE.

University of Cambridge (2014) *Thinking Together Project*. Available at: http://thinkingtogether.educ.cam.ac.uk/ (accessed 28/07/14).

Way, J. and Berdon, T. (2003) *ICT and Primary Mathematics*. Maidenhead: Open University Press.

Wickham, L. (2008) Generating mathematical talk in the Key Stage 2 classroom. *Proceedings of the British Society for Research into Learning Mathematics*, 28(2). Available at: bsrlm.org.uk (accessed 28/07/14).

Wong, K,Y. (2012) Use of student mathematics questioning to promote active learning and metacognition. *12th International Congress on Mathematical Education*. 8–15 July, 2012, COEX, Seoul, Korea. Available at: www.icme12.org/upload/submission/1879_F.pdf (accessed 28/07/14).

Worthington, M. and Carruthers, E. (2003) *Children's Mathematics: Making Marks, Making Meaning*. London: Paul Chapman Publishers.

Worthington, M. and Carruthers, E. (2012) *Children's Mathematics Network*. Available at: www.childrens-mathematics.net/cmgraphics.htm (accessed 28/07/14).

Worthington, M. and Carruthers, E. (2013) Taxonomy: charting children's mathematical graphics, (birth – 8 years) Available at: www.childrens-mathematics.org.uk/taxonomy.pdf (accessed 28/07/14).

11 Problems in learning mathematics

Ronit Bird

Learning outcomes

In this chapter we will explore what might lie behind a child's difficulty in acquiring basic mathematics skills and what kind of classroom support can help such pupils. The key learning objectives for the chapter are:

- to consider maths anxiety;
- to appreciate the role of working memory in learning maths;
- to increase your understanding of dyscalculia and its effect on learners;
- to recognise some of the indicators that could help you spot children with dyscalculia;
- to explore ways of supporting dyscalculic pupils at school.

TEACHERS' STANDARDS

2. Promote good progress and outcomes by pupils
5. Adapt teaching to respond to the strengths and needs of all pupils
6. Make accurate and productive use of assessment
8. Fulfil wider professional responsibilities

Introduction

All children are individuals who learn and develop at their own pace. Teachers can expect to come across a wide range of aptitude and performance among their pupils, much of which can be accounted for by differing levels of intelligence (note here that 'intelligence' is a hugely contested idea) as well as varying degrees of interest in the subject, or by different personal histories that might include poor teaching, long or frequent absences from school and medical issues. But some children stand out as having particularly marked and persistent problems in learning mathematics that cannot be attributed to any obvious cause. Some pupils' difficulties are especially surprising in view of their general level of intelligence and the abilities they demonstrate in other subjects. What are we to make of pupils who struggle with maths for no obvious reason? In fact, some of these children may be underperforming as a result of maths anxiety. Others – perhaps 5 per cent or more – may have dyscalculia, a specific learning difficulty that affects a person's ability to acquire basic arithmetic skills. What this means in practice is that, in any average class, teachers can expect to find at least one or two pupils with significant problems in learning mathematics.

Maths anxiety

We can all recognise that sinking feeling associated with a fear of exposing our ignorance or ineptitude in front of others. As we get older and gain more control over our lives, we are much less likely to find ourselves in such a position, and yet many people admit to having nightmares well into adulthood that are about taking exams for which they are unprepared. We wake from such nightmares with a thumping heart and a sense of dread, followed by a wave of relief on realising that it was only a dream. The situation may have been imaginary, but the physical symptoms are all too real. Anxiety is a powerful emotion. Knowing that anxiety is 'all in the mind' does not lessen its effect on our feelings or behaviour.

Maths anxiety is usually described as fear or panic that interferes with maths performance. But maths anxiety, which can be found in school and college populations all over the world, has repercussions far beyond its effect on individuals. In particular, when maths anxiety leads to maths avoidance, causing those affected – consciously or unconsciously – to avoid further study of certain subjects or steer away from certain career paths, the result is a loss of opportunity both for the individuals themselves and the societies in which they live. It is worth noting that many teachers admit to a high level of maths anxiety, with some primary teachers having deliberately chosen to teach younger children in order to avoid having to teach higher level maths.

Working memory and maths anxiety

Maths anxiety has been recognised for at least sixty years, but it is only more recently that an increasing number of studies have sought to investigate the phenomenon in more detail. There is still some debate about whether maths anxiety is triggered by, or whether it is a cause of, low ability or performance in maths. The current thinking is that maths anxiety disrupts the normal functioning of the central processing ability of the brain and, in particular, that maths anxiety interferes with the availability of working memory resources. It is as if the anxiety consumes some of the learner's attention, thereby leaving fewer resources available for the task at hand.

Preoccupation impairs our memory as well as our performance. Working memory is what is needed for storing information while manipulating it. In the context of mathematics, working memory is what allows us to hold onto the numbers within a calculation while we keep track of the various stages and processes of the calculation itself. Therefore, anything that impacts negatively on our working memory is bound to supress our mathematical perfomance.

Research Focus: Working memory and maths anxiety

A study by Ashcraft and Kirk in 2001 into the relationship between working memory and maths anxiety explored the idea that *individuals with high maths anxiety demonstrated*

→

smaller working memory spans (p.224). It concluded that *maths anxiety disrupts the on-going, task-relevant activities of working memory, slowing down performance and degrading its accuracy* (p.236).

The Ashcraft and Kirk study built on previous work by Ashcraft in collaboration with other colleagues (with Faust in 1994; with Faust and Fleck in 1996) showing that participants with a high level of maths anxiety had particular difficulties with questions involving carrying in two-digit addition problems, difficulties that were not observed for basic whole number facts of simple addition and multiplication. It also found that, if the more difficult problems were answered correctly, the participants took nearly three times as long to manage the embedded carry operation as participants with low levels of anxiety. A 1992 study by Michael Eysenck and Manuel Calvo is important as a background to these findings because it was Eysenck and Calvo who established the Processing Efficiency Theory, which postulated that anxiety impairs children's performance particularly in those tasks that involve using the limited capacity of working memory.

How to help learners with maths anxiety

What can you, as a teacher, do about maths anxiety? You could start by recognising that there is a link betweeen anxiety and performance and that anyone who feels anxious about doing something less well than they would like is responding in a perfectly normal and rational manner. This applies as much to teachers who are worried that their own maths anxiety will damage their ability to teach children maths as it does to their pupils' anxiety about learning maths. Anxiety is beyond a person's conscious control, although it can be alleviated by relaxation and breathing exercises. Secondly, you should maintain high expectations for all your pupils and communicate to both pupils and parents your belief that everyone can become numerate, not only those born with a special talent for mathematics. It is striking that so many adults cheerfully admit to being 'hopeless at maths' while a similar admission about reading would be unthinkable. We need to challenge the idea that being innumerate is a bit of a joke, or a situation that does not deserve to be taken as seriously as being illiterate. Thirdly, you can do your very best to establish a stress-free learning environment in your classroom. It is this third idea that gives you the most scope to make a difference by thinking carefully about the culture, behaviour and expectations you would like to establish in your classroom.

Activity: Thinking about the learning environment

Before reading on, discuss with others or write down any ideas you have about how teachers could foster a classroom atmosphere in which anxiety and stress are minimised.

Fostering a stress-free learning environment in the classroom

My own contributions to the discussion suggested in the activity above would include the following ideas. Add your own ideas to the list and ask your pupils for suggestions, too. Note that all these suggestions to improve conditions for anxious pupils would also benefit all the others in the class.

- Establish very firmly, right from the start, that mistakes are not only normal and inescapable but can be a very valuable part of the learning process.

- Never respond to a child's mistake with laughter, impatience or sarcasm. Insist on all pupils treating eath other's comments and suggestions with respect.

- Try to avoid saying 'No' or 'That's wrong' too often. But don't let your attempts to be tactful obscure whether a child's answer is, or is not, correct. Be especially careful with the term 'OK'. If you say 'OK, let's think about your answer,' you might believe that you are giving a clear signal that something is not right, while the child might stop listening at 'OK'.

- Praise effort, concentration and a determination not to give up at least as often, and as warmly, as you praise achievement.

- Give pupils their homework marks or test results privately, not in front of the whole class.

- Rather than calling a pupil up to the board to answer a question in front of others, ask for volunteers.

- Provide pupils with a small whiteboard on which to record their answers in class. This gives pupils the freedom to make mistakes, secure in the knowledge that there will be no permanent record.

- Avoid imposing any unnecessary time pressures.

Dyscalculia

Dyscalculia is a developmental condition affecting approximately 5 per cent of the population. It is a difficulty that affects a person's ability to deal with numbers and quantities and to acquire arithmetic skills. People who have never heard of dyscalculia before might find it helpful to think of it as the mathematical equivalent of dyslexia, with dyslexia affecting the acquisition of literacy while dyscalculia affects the acquisition of numeracy.

Dyscalculia is classed as a Specific Learning Difficulty (SpLD), an umbrella term that encompasses dyslexia, dyscalculia and dyspraxia as well as other frequently co-occurring disorders such as dysgraphia and attention disorders. The word 'specific' indicates that we are talking about children within the normal range of intelligence. Despite average or even above-average cognitive abilities, learners with an SpLD have a difficulty that is specific to numeracy (dyscalculia) or literacy (dyslexia) or motor skills (dyspraxia) or handwriting (dysgraphia) or attention (attention deficit disorder or attention deficit hyperactivity disorder).

A certain amount of overlap between the different conditions is common. In addition, every affected individual lies somewhere along a spectrum that ranges from those most affected to those least affected, for each condition. This means that people with a specific learning difficulty will all be different, with their own individual patterns of strengths and weaknesses. Nevertheless, the labels can be a useful shorthand and can serve as headings under which we can group certain common symptoms and indicators. There is an ongoing debate about how useful educational labels are and to what extent children are helped or hindered by being categorised according to their learning abilities or difficulties, not to mention the problematic issue of self-fulfilling expectations. However, many individuals report that a diagnosis of SpLD is enormously liberating, particularly for those children who were previousy labelled as lazy or stupid, or scolded by their parents or teachers for simply not trying hard enough.

Dyscalculia is not synonymous with maths anxiety. Many people have maths anxiety without being dyscalculic. It would be much rarer to find someone who has dyscalculia without exhibiting any maths anxiety. Dyscalculia cannot be cured. It is the result of differences in brain architecture or brain function that are observable in those areas of the brain that deal with numeracy. Dyscalculic learners cannot expect to 'grow out of' their problems. What they can do, however, is to learn how best to manage and work around their specific difficulties by developing appropriate strategies.

In the UK, the term 'dyscalculia' made its first appearance in official government literature in 2001. The Department for Education and Skills (as it was known at the time) defined dyscalculia as:

> *a condition that affects the ability to acquire arithmetical skills. Dyscalculic learners may have difficulty understanding simple number concepts, lack an intuitive grasp of numbers, and have problems learning number facts and procedures. Even if they produce a correct answer or use a correct method, they may do so mechanically and without confidence.*

(DfES, 2001, p.2)

One of the most striking aspects of this definition is its date – 2001 – compared to the first government reference to 'dyslexia' that appeared thirty years earlier, in 1970.

Within the DfES definition, I consider these the three most important points:

- Dyscalculia affects 'arithmetic skills'. We need to remember that arithmetic is just one small part of the larger subject we call mathematics. People with dyscalculia do not necessarily have any problem with other mathematical topics or with mathematical concepts. It is perfectly possible for someone with dyscalculia to study science subjects to degree level, despite a continuing difficulty with basic arithmetic.

- The definition includes both number facts and procedures. An example of number facts might be all the times tables facts up to 10 × 10. An example of procedures might be all the sequential steps needed to work through the standard algorithm for long division. The salient point is that both aspects, number facts and mathematical procedures, can be affected by dyscalculia.

- The final sentence in the definition implies that teachers must aim higher than just teaching children to 'produce a correct answer or use a correct method'. Most maths educationalists strongly agree that teaching children to find answers mechanically is simply not good enough. A child who just goes through a series of prescribed and memorised steps has only learned how to follow a recipe, not how to really understand, or undertake, the maths.

Symptoms and indicators for dyscalculia

The list below (first published in *The Dyscalculia Toolkit*) is provided as a convenient reference. Indicators for dyscalculia are:

- no 'feel' for numbers and relative quantities;

- an inability to subitise (see without counting) even very small quantities;

- an inability to estimate whether a numerical answer is reasonable;

- weaknesses in both short-term and long-term memory;

- an inability to count backwards reliably;

- a weakness in visual and spatial orientation;

- directional (left/right) confusion;

- slow processing speeds when engaged in maths activities;

- trouble with sequencing;

- a tendency not to notice patterns;

- a problem with all aspects of money;

- a marked delay in learning to read an analogue clock to tell the time;

- An inability to manage time in daily life.

Activity: Identifying the indicators for dyscalculia

Read the list above. Have you come across any learners who exhibited some of these indicators? Share with others some details of the behaviours you observed. Then read the case studies below.

Case Study

The following descriptions and quotations (from two different children on two different occasions in 2012) exemplify what it means to have very little sensitivity to magnitude or sense of the relationships between numbers. Both children are of above average intelligence. As you read the case study, consider how you might help Mia and Charlie if they were in your class.

Mia aged 7 years and 11 months

In order to assess Mia's sense of quantity, I put out a small group of glass nuggets, asked her to estimate how many there were but prevented her from counting them. I first put out 3 nuggets, then 7 nuggets and Mia guessed both quantities correctly. For the third challenge, ostentatiously filling my hands with as many as they could hold, I put out 26 nuggets. Mia estimated there were 9. I had her check the quantity by lining up rows of 10, deliberately preventing her from keeping a running total. With two rows of 10 and a shorter row of 6 in front of her on the table I asked, 'So, how many are there?' Mia could not say. She had to count all 26 again, starting from 1.

I asked her to count aloud, abstractly, starting at various different points. She struggled when I asked her to start at 86 and hesitated for a long time between 89 and 90. Finally, she got to 100 and stopped. 'I can't do any more.'

I asked Mia if she knew any doubles. 'No, I learned them at school,' she replied, 'but I forgot.'

'What about double 2?' I asked. ' I know that's 2 times 2. But I don't know what that is.'

Charlie aged 9 years and 4 months

Asked about doubles facts, Charlie proved confident about all the doubles from 1 + 1 to 5 + 5, which I asked in a random order. 'Now,' I said, 'can you use a doubles fact, but no counting, to answer this question: What must we add to 4 to make 9?' I asked the question orally, while simultaneously writing 4 + ? = 9. Charlie said, 'Could it be 5? No, because, well, 4 plus 4 is 8, and 5 is much bigger than 4. So, 4 + 5 would be much more than 9.'

What is striking about these case studies is how little connection there appears to be in both children's minds between the words they use to name numbers and the quantities or magnitudes that the numbers actually represent. When Mia looked at 26 items while estimating that there were 9, she revealed how little concept she has of 9, let alone 26, as a numerical quantity. Mia has learned how to recite the counting numbers in order, but the words seem to carry no more meaning than the words to a song learned by heart as a string of sounds. Similarly, Charlie, who told me that '5 is much bigger than 4', is probably imagining that the word 'five' is positioned much further along a memorised sequence of numbers than the word 'four', thereby revealing no sense of what 4 or 5 represent as numerical quantities. Despite this, Charlie demonstrated good logical thinking skills when trying to derive a new fact from a related fact. An ability to reason intelligently does not preclude a specific difficulty in learning basic numeracy.

→

We can see from Mia's responses that mathematical vocabulary can cause problems for learners with specific maths difficulties. Mia recognised 'times' as a word having some connection to doubling. But both 'double two' and 'two times two' were empty phrases from which Mia was unable to extract any meaning.

One final point to notice is that Mia, one week short of her eighth birthday, was unable to count beyond 100. To put this into context, one of the requirements of the National Curriculum's Year 1 mathematics programme of study is 'to count to and across 100, forwards and backwards'. Mia's counting ceiling of 100 indicates that she is oblivious to the regular number patterns produced by the repeating decade structure of our counting system. This observation is confirmed by Mia's inability to combine two groups of ten plus another six items and read the total as 26.

Research Focus: Mapping numerical magnitudes onto symbols

In 2009 Holloway and Ansari set out to explore whether *the understanding and processing of numerical quantity is crucial for success in education and employment* (p.17). Eighty-seven children in the north-eastern USA, aged between six and nine years, were tested. Holloway and Ansari were able to demonstrate *the existence of a relationship between individual difference in the NDE* [numerical distance effect] *and mathematical competence* (p.28) and also that *individual differences in the distance effect were related to mathematics achievement but not to reading achievevement* (p.17). They conclude that the *finding highlights the importance of efficient mappings between numerical symbols and their quantitative meaning for the development of mathematical abilities* (p.28).

A 1967 study by Robert S. Moyer and Thomas K. Landauer is important as a background to the findings of the 2009 study by Holloway and Ansari because Moyer and Landauer provided the first strong evidence for the 'distance effect', the name given to the phenomenon by which it takes longer to identify which of two numbers is greater when the distance between them is small. For example, the reaction time when deciding that 9 is larger than 2 is much shorter than when deciding that 3 is larger than 2, which in turn takes less time than deciding that 9 is larger than 8.

Evidence of the 'distance effect' fed into numerous later studies by various researchers, some of whom explored the idea that the numbers along our mental number lines are not evenly spaced and that in fact mental number lines may be logarithmic rather than linear. Stanislas Dehaene suggested in 1997 that numbers are not mapped onto precise points along a mental number line, but rather onto small ranges that round up or down to an approximation of each number, which results in overlapping ranges for numbers that are close to each other.

How to help dyscalculic learners

The following is not a comprehensive list of suggestions about how to help learners with dyscalculia but will, I hope, serve as a useful set of pointers. Some suggestions can be implemented by individual teachers in their own classrooms. Much more can be done for pupils who struggle with maths if there is a school-wide policy and committed support from the Senior Management/Leadership Team. Note that all these suggestions to support dyscalculic learners would also benefit other pupils in the class.

- Allow plenty of time and focus on what is most important. True understanding of a very few topics is more valuable than superficially covering many topics. Good foundation skills are essential as a preparation for teaching higher level skills at a later stage. The implication of this advice is that some children may need one-to-one teaching in order to master essential numeracy skills.

- Introduce children to activities that draw attention to quantity, i.e. the total number within a set irrespective of what kind of items make up the set. Sensitivity to quantity, and the ability to compare two different magnitudes, are critical skills for the development of number sense.

- Use concrete materials, chosen with care. The materials should be capable of modelling many different topics at different levels. Apparatus should not be used only by the teacher for demonstrations, but should be available to pupils to use freely as a way of exploring quantities, number relationships and mathematical operations. In my own teaching, the one resource I could not do without is the versatile combination of Cuisenaire rods and base ten materials.

- Focus on practical activities, not on drill and repetition. Remember that children with weak memories will be unable to learn facts by heart reliably and will therefore need to be taught to find solutions from first principles. After plenty of hands-on exploration, show how concrete work can be recorded diagrammatically. Diagrams help pupils to visualise maths, which in turn helps to underpin a whole variety of mental calculation strategies.

- Aim to move pupils' understanding forward in very small stages. Break down new learning into the tiniest of incremental steps and address only one step at a time. Aim to pitch the level of difficulty at whatever level you expect each pupil to manage so that you are setting up the pupil to experience success as frequently as possible.

- Encourage pupils to talk and reason aloud about what they are doing. Spend more time on 'how' an answer is found than on 'what' the answer is.

- Target children who are using counting as their only calculation strategy. Many children who struggle with maths get stuck at this stage and will be unable to make progress until they have learned more efficient calculation strategies. Children stuck in 'the counting trap' will need to engage in a lot of component work, i.e. partitioning, splitting and recombining quantities, with the focus on larger numbers being built from smaller numbers, or chunks, and not just from a string of ones.

- Dyscalculic children find it much harder to count backwards than most children. Therefore, when using number lines to support mental calculation strategies, encourage the child to work in the forward direction (but in chunks or jumps along an empty number line, not in ones along a labelled line). For the same reason, teach complementary addition as a way of solving some subtraction problems.

- Make explicit connections between different maths topics. For example, teach subtraction at the same time as addition, reinforcing the relationship between the two operations and showing how hidden quantity activities and missing number formulations relate to both addition and subtraction.

- Do not expect dyscalculic or dyslexic pupils to memorise multiplication tables. Teach the area model of multiplication and division, because it is a highly visual method that can be easily modelled with concrete equipment as well as by diagrams. It is also a good method for supporting the idea that any tables facts can be found by logic, starting from a very few key tables facts. Provide tables squares where appropriate, i.e. whenever the focus of the activity is not on learning the tables facts themselves.

- Minimise the number of facts and procedures that pupils must know by heart. Focus only on those facts and strategies that have the widest application, so as to reduce the burden on the child's memory. When there are several good methods from which to choose, allow the child to choose and practise only one.

- Teach reasoning strategies explicitly. Show pupils how to use logic and reasoning to extend their knowledge of facts and calculation procedures.

- Spell out to your pupils that making a mistake is not synonymous with failure. On the contrary, mistakes can be extremely valuable in revealing a person's thinking process and in uncovering misconceptions. Use your pupils' mistakes to diagnose what topics or issues need further work (more on this below). To avoid too much focus on what is right or wrong, try providing the answer along with the question. For example, rather than asking, 'What is 6 x 8?' ask, 'How can we work out that 6 x 8 is 48 by using another tables fact as a starting point? Would you prefer to work from 6 x 2 and then 6 x 4, or from 5 x 8? Why?'

- The transition between concrete and abstract work is an extremely important stage for children with dyscalculia. Do not be tempted to rush this stage. Diagrams can provide a valuable bridge between concrete and abstract work, especially when the child is given practice in visualisation techniques at the same time. Allow diagrams to lead to informal jottings and only later to the more widely accepted standard methods of recording.

- Beware of making assumptions about what your pupils already know. It is always worth working out which pre-skills are necessary before starting to teach a new topic and making sure these foundation skills are secure before proceeding.

Children's errors and misconceptions

Many children with specific maths difficulties are well practised in hiding their confusion and many have gaps in their knowledge at a very basic level. Working with pupils individually and asking them to think aloud as they work is a valuable way of gaining some insight into any misconceptions or gaps in their understanding. Another useful tool is to analyse their mistakes. Here, for example, are a few common errors in written column arithmetic.

(a)	(b)	(c)	(d)
$\begin{array}{r} 2\ 4 \\ +\ 3\ 5 \\ \hline 48 \end{array}$	$\begin{array}{r} 5\ 4 \\ +\ 2\ 7 \\ \hline 71 \end{array}$	$\begin{array}{r} 5\ 4 \\ +\ 2\ 7 \\ \hline 531 \end{array}$	$\begin{array}{r} 5\ 4 \\ -\ 2\ 7 \\ \hline 33 \end{array}$

Activity: Identifying and addressing mathematical misconceptions

Before reading on, look at the written problems above, all of which have been answered incorrectly. Can you work out what the pupil was thinking to make these particular mistakes? What will the pupils need to work on to prevent future mistakes of the same sort?

Read the following only after you have studied the incorrect answers above.

The child answering question (a) was probably counting using fingers but was including the starting number as part of the count. In other words, he said '4' while putting up one finger and continued putting up one finger at a time while saying '5, 6, 7, 8', stopping at 8 because he saw 5 raised fingers. The same error occurs in the tens column.

The answers to (b) and (c) show carrying errors. One child simply ignores or forgets the carried ten; the other probably records it as a large digit between the digits in the top row, making the 5 look as if it is in the hundreds column.

The child answering question (d) sees that '4 minus 7 can't be done' and flips the digits to read them as '7 minus 3'. It is possible that this child was once told that subtraction means taking a smaller number away from a larger number. It is equally possible that the child thinks that the minus sign indicates the gap between two numbers and has not actually realised that subtraction is not commutative.

All four children would benefit from working with manipulative equipment such as Cuisenaire rods and base ten blocks on a place value mat, practising building and partitioning two-digit and three-digit numbers and exploring the idea of carrying and decomposition at the concrete level.

Learning Outcomes Review

....

You will now be aware that children can struggle with maths for a variety of reasons and that poor numeracy skills can have an adverse effect on a person's life well beyond the school years. You will realise that maths anxiety can impact on performance and can affect both teachers and children. You will appreciate that many factors contribute to a person's ability to acquire basic numeracy, including circumstances beyond the control of the individual, such as their working memory capacity or sensitivity to magnitude. You will have a better understanding of dyscalculia and how to identify children who may be affected. You will have considered many suggestions for supporting children with specific maths difficulties, the chief of which are:

- fostering a stress-free learning environment;
- teaching children for understanding and not by rote learning;
- giving children practical experience with concrete materials and making sure not to move them on to abstract work too soon;
- using children's errors to identify misconceptions and gaps in their knowledge;
- breaking the learning down into small sequential steps in order to build sound foundations.

Self-assessment questions

1. How can children with maths anxiety or dyscalculia be identified?
2. What is your attitude to using concrete materials in class? Has your opinion changed at all as the result of reading this chapter?
3. Which of the suggestions for supporting dyscalculic learners at school are you planning to try?

Further Reading

Ashcraft, M.H. (2002) Math anxiety: Personal, educational, and cognitive consequences. *Directions in Psychological Science*, 11(5): 181–185.

Ashcraft, M.H. and Krause, J.A. (2007) Working memory, math performance, and math anxiety. *Psychonomic Bulletin & Review*, 14(2): 243–248.

Bird, R. (2009) *Overcoming Difficulties with Number: Supporting Dyscalculia and Students Who Struggle With Maths*. London: SAGE.

Bird, R. (2013) *The Dyscalculia Toolkit*. London: SAGE.

Butterworth, B. (1999) *The Mathematical Brain*. Basingstoke: Macmillan.

Bynner, J. and Parsons, S. (1997) *Does Numeracy Matter?* London: The Basic Skills Agency.

Gathercole, S. and Alloway, T.P. (2008) *Working Memory and Learning: A Practical Guide for Teachers*. London: SAGE.

Sheffield, D. and Hunt, T.E. (2006) 'How does anxiety influence maths performance and what can we do about it?'. *MSOR Connections*, 6(4): 19–23.

Witt, M. (2012) The impact of mathematics anxiety on primary school children's working memory. *Europe's Journal of Psychology*, 8(2): 263–274.

References

Ashcraft, M.H. and Faust, M.W. (1994) Mathematics anxiety and mental arithmetic performance: An exploratory investigation. *Cognition & Emotion,* 8(2): 97–125.

Ashcraft, M.H. and Kirk, E.P. (2001) The relationships among working memory, math anxiety, and performance. *Journal of Experimental Psychology*, 13 (2): 224–237.

Dehaene, S. (1997) *The Number Sense*. London: Penguin.

DfES (2001) *The National Numeracy Strategy: Guidance to Support Pupils with Dyslexia and Dyscalculia*. DfES 0512/2001.

Eysenck, M.W. and Calvo, M.G. (1992) Anxiety and performance: the processing efficiency theory. *Cognition and Emotion*, 6(6): 409–434.

Faust, M.W., Ashcraft, M.H. and Fleck, D.E. (1996) Mathematics anxiety effects in simple and complex addition. *Mathematical Cognition*, 2: 25–62.

Holloway, I.D. and Ansari, D. (2009) Mapping numerical magnitudes onto symbols: The numerical distance effect and individual differences in children's mathematics achievement. *Journal of Experimental Child Psychology*, 103(1): 17–29.

Moyer, R.S. and Landauer, T.K. (1967) Time required for judgements of numerical inequality. *Nature*, 215: 1519–1520.

12 What kind of primary mathematics teacher do you want to be?

Marcus Witt

Learning outcomes

The key learning objectives for the chapter are:

- To explore our values and beliefs about mathematics and mathematics teaching;
- To consider the role of mathematics in children's learning and in the wider world;
- To explore why we teach mathematics at all;
- To consider the kind of primary mathematics teacher that you are and are becoming and the factors that determine the kind of primary mathematics teacher you will be.

TEACHERS' STANDARDS

1 **Set high expectations which inspire, motivate and challenge pupils**

establish a safe and stimulating environment for pupils, rooted in mutual respect

2 **Promote good progress and outcomes by pupils**

be aware of pupils' capabilities and their prior knowledge, and plan teaching to build on these

demonstrate knowledge and understanding of how pupils learn and how this impacts on teaching

3 **Demonstrate good subject and curriculum knowledge**

if teaching early mathematics, demonstrate a clear understanding of appropriate teaching strategies

4 **Plan and teach well-structured lessons**

promote a love of learning and children's intellectual curiosity

5 **Adapt teaching to respond to the strengths and needs of all pupils**

have a secure understanding of how a range of factors can inhibit pupils' ability to learn, and how best to overcome these

---

Introduction
Why do we need to know this?

There can be few teachers of mathematics at any level in the UK who have not, at some time or another, had one of their pupils ask them, 'Why do we need to know this?' I imagine that many of you asked that question. When I put this to my cohorts of trainee teachers, the vast majority admit (or claim) that they have asked that question. Maybe you were one of them? The vast majority were also given answers that were usually variations on the theme that the maths was in the exam, that being good at maths is essential for getting a good job, or that they were learning it because it was on the curriculum. I firmly believe that we have to have better answers for the children who ask us the fundamental question of why we have to learn maths.

This concluding chapter aims to look at some bigger issues and questions about the teaching of primary mathematics. This chapter will explore why we bother to teach maths at all in an age where almost everyone carries around a mobile device with a built-in calculator. I will then go on to consider some of the ways in which mathematics and mathematically literate people might be a force for social change. The chapter will consider what values and beliefs we bring to our mathematics teaching and how our teacher behaviours in maths lessons convey some of those values and beliefs to the children we teach. I believe that considering these questions is important, as your views about them will have a profound impact on the kind of primary maths teacher that you become.

Curriculum Link

The National Curriculum is clearly driven by the mathematical values and beliefs of the people who have written it. These values are made clear in the opening section, which is discussed in Chapter 1.

> *A high-quality mathematics education therefore provides a foundation for understanding the world, the ability to reason mathematically, an appreciation of the beauty and power of mathematics, and a sense of enjoyment and curiosity about the subject.*

> (DfE, 2013, p.3)

The writers of the curriculum document have clear ideas about the power and beauty of mathematics, and about its key role in solving problems and illuminating important issues. They also have definite ideas about how mathematics should be taught and about the importance of fluency in calculation. There is an implication in the curriculum that understanding comes with fluency, rather than the other way round. They are clear about the importance of reasoning.

There are other, less explicit, but nonetheless powerful messages in the curriculum: particular methods of calculation are clearly favoured over others; there is an implication that introducing children to particular concepts earlier than they were before the introduction of the curriculum will improve their mathematical outcomes; calculation and the ability to manipulate numbers is even more prominent than in earlier versions of the curriculum, whereas the handling and understanding of data has less emphasis and probability has gone altogether. The challenge for you as an aspiring (or practising) primary school teacher is to teach to this curriculum with all its inherent values and beliefs, while keeping true to your own. Let us now consider one of the important questions that a curriculum such as this inevitably asks.

Why teach calculation?

Today it is possible to buy a 99p calculator, which will calculate more quickly and more accurately than any person possibly can. When they become adults, almost every child in school today will own and carry a mobile communication device that has a calculator built in, almost as an incidental application. We need therefore to have good reasons why we spend so much of children's time in mathematics lessons teaching them to do something (i.e. calculate) that they are unlikely to have to do for themselves when they leave school.

Activity: Why teach calculation?

What would your answer be to someone who asked why we spend so long teaching children to calculate when they own or will own a mobile device that will do it for them? Mentally prepare your argument, or write down some ideas if it helps.

Case Study: Maths may not save your life, but it can certainly save you money

As an illustration, consider the following true story relating to acquiring a mortgage a few years ago. During the negotiation process it became apparent that although Steve was borrowing about £50,000, he would be paying back over £88,000 over the course of the 25 years of the mortgage. This struck him as being quite a poor deal, so he enquired about increasing the monthly payment slightly (from about £290 to £330) and therefore paying the mortgage off in 20 years rather than 25. The total repayment fell to about £78,000. Spurred on by the thought of making a £10,000 saving, he enquired what the situation would be if the mortgage were repaid over 15 years rather than 20. Again a relatively modest and affordable increase in the monthly repayment led to a considerable overall saving of several thousand pounds over the course of the mortgage. Steve weighed up his options, calculated that he could afford the monthly repayments over 15 years and saved himself tens of thousands of pounds overall.

The important thing here is that the discussion would not have taken place if Steve had not had a 'feel' for the numbers involved and had not enquired about and understood the interaction between the monthly repayments, the term of the mortgage and the overall repayment figure. All the actual calculation involved was done automatically, accurately and in seconds by the mortgage company's dedicated software. The results of the calculations needed human interpretation and were prompted by an understanding of how changing one variable affected the others.

While this example might help to make a case for teaching mathematics, it suggests that certain kinds of mathematics teaching might be of more use than others. Consider again the injunction in the curriculum that mathematics be a vehicle to develop curiosity and mathematical reasoning. Had Steve's mathematics education consisted solely of carrying out calculations without any real understanding of the answers, or of what was happening when he multiplied or divided, he may not have been able to see the connections that led to the important conversation that saved him tens of thousands of pounds. Had he never been encouraged to ask mathematical questions, or to be mathematically curious, he may not have thought to question the figures and seek to explore ways of getting a better deal. Our responsibility as primary mathematics teachers working within the National Curriculum is to see opportunities to develop curiosity and reasoning in *all* the mathematics that we teach.

Activity: Teaching calculations

Consider your own approach to teaching calculations. To what extent does it enable the children to understand the fundamental nature of the operation that they are carrying out?

How might you be able to refine or develop your practice to enable your children to see this more clearly? You may wish to refer back to the two chapters on calculation (Chapters 4 and 5) for some inspiration.

Why teach mathematics at all?

Conrad Wolfram in his article in the *Observer* (February 2014) argues that mathematics education is focusing on the wrong things. Calculation is the one area of mathematics that can be done better by machines than it can by human beings. However, the key mathematical skills of interpreting problems mathematically and making sense of the results of the calculations so as to solve a real problem cannot be done by machine. He contends that mathematics education should focus far more on those skills and less on calculation.

Wolfram's views align with those expressed in the National Curriculum that mathematics is a powerful way of understanding the world (but align less with its emphasis on calculation). I hope that many of the ideas in the book will help you to plan and teach mathematics lessons that enable children to understand and make sense of their world. However, Wolfram argues that this goal is not attainable unless we make deliberate efforts to connect mathematics teaching to solving real problems that are meaningful to the children.

Activity: Real-life contexts

Choose an area of the curriculum that you have recently taught, or are about to teach. Think of ways that this particular area of the curriculum might be used in 'real life'. This will be easier for some areas of the curriculum than for others. Can you plan a mathematical activity or problem for the children that makes the connection between the curriculum and the real-life context more explicit and therefore might make the lesson more motivating for the children?

Mathematics as a force for social change

Activity: Birth month

Before looking at this piece of research, consider whether you think that the month in which you were born would make a difference to your level of 'intelligence'? Do you think that it would make a difference to your educational outcomes, and if so, why?

Research Focus: Summer-born children

A study produced by the Institute for Fiscal Studies (Crawford et al., 2007) explored differences in academic attainment between children born in August and children born in September. The findings of the study were unequivocal: the month in which you were born can have a significant impact on your educational outcomes. The study found that children born in the summer had, on average, significantly poorer academic outcomes at all stages during their primary education than those children born in the autumn. Although less pronounced, these differences were still visible at the end of secondary schooling. A later study (Crawford et al., 2011), also by the IFS, found that summer-born children were less likely to go to university than their autumn-born counterparts and had poorer labour market outcomes.

While there is an interesting discussion to be conducted (beyond the scope of this chapter) about the reasons for these differences, the important thing to note is that it is the power of mathematics that has alerted us to the problems summer-born children face in school and therefore helps us to devise solutions. Mathematics can therefore be a very powerful vehicle for revealing injustice, inequality and disadvantage. Mathematics helps us to measure the effects of climate change, to know how well women are represented on the boards of major companies or in government; it helps us to see the relationship between poverty and health outcomes, or the effects of low income on educational outcomes. (See Hans Rosling's website – Gapminder at www.gapminder. org/ – for some graphic illustrations of the relationship between income and many life outcomes in different countries around the world).

The pace of technological change and the increasingly complex nature of the world mean that mathematics is becoming an essential tool for understanding the world. Mathematics and a mathematics education is important, not only due to its role in understanding the world so that we can make better decisions for ourselves, but also because mathematics prepares children to be better citizens and to be a force for change and improvement in the world. Mathematics is a way to open up children's eyes to some of the things in their world that need to be tackled, challenged and changed.

Mathematical values and beliefs

When we teach mathematics, our beliefs and values about mathematics and about the world more generally become clear to the children we teach.

Activity: Too pretty to do maths?

Consider the scenarios outlined below and what your response to the children would be:

1. On non-uniform day, a child comes into your classroom wearing a t-shirt stating 'I'm too pretty to do maths'. What would you say to the child, or to the child's parent at the end of the day?

2. In a whole-school assembly, the local vicar comes in to talk to the children and makes several thinly veiled references to the fact that mathematics is not fun and that you have to get it over with in the morning before you can do something more interesting in the afternoon.

3. During a discussion in the classroom about how maths is used in different situations, a child expresses a view that market traders in the developing world who have not been to school cannot possibly do maths.

Our mathematical values become very apparent in the way that we behave mathematically in our classrooms: by the way we talk about mathematics, by the activities we give the children to do and by the way we respond to them. Our values about the world more generally are also conveyed in the way that we connect mathematics to the world we seek to understand and in the examples that we choose to illustrate mathematics and to set mathematical problems.

Cotton (2013) provides an excellent example in the context of data handling. A lot of data handling done in schools relates to food (favourite crisp flavours, pizza toppings, sweets, etc.) However, Cotton gives an example of some children in Year 5 looking at attitudes to prejudice as a context for some interesting data handling. The children in Cotton's example are not only connecting the mathematics to their own experiences of the world, they are beginning to see the power of mathematics to illuminate inequality and therefore to be a force to challenge it. I am not suggesting that data handling about crisp flavours is inappropriate or bad. I am suggesting that there are opportunities to connect children's mathematics not only to things that are interesting to them, but also to things that matter both to them and in the context of the wider world.

Activity: Examining data

Look at the graph below (taken from Hans Rosling's website www.gapminder.org/; click on the 'Gapminder World' tab at the top). What kind of mathematical activities could the children engage in from looking at the data? What else might they do? This is better viewed on the website, where the graph is both in colour and dynamic, i.e. the data can be tracked over time.

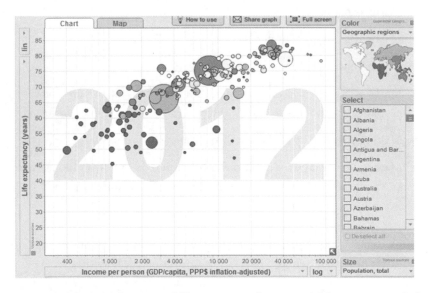

Figure 12.1   The link between income and life expectancy (Free material from www.gapminder.org)

Choosing examples

The National Curriculum emphasises the importance of connecting mathematics to the children's 'lived experiences', whether these be 'real' experiences, or books and stories that have captured their interest and imagination. The examples that we choose to illustrate mathematical ideas and concepts will convey messages to the children about our beliefs about mathematics and about the world more widely.

How many of your examples to illustrate calculation involve children and sweets? While I am not suggesting that we never use sweets as a way of introducing or modelling calculation, surely we can be a little more 'creative' in our choice of example? Could we simply use apples, or strawberries with younger children? As the children get older, can we use our mathematical examples sometimes as a way of getting them not only to think about and question the world, but also to see that mathematics can be and is used to solve non-trivial problems?

As you think further about your values and beliefs about mathematics, it may be worth considering some views about mathematics that are highly prevalent in society.

Activity: Common beliefs about mathematics

Here are some highly prevalent beliefs about maths. As honestly as you can, go through the list and consider the extent to which you think that there is some truth in them.

Pick one or two and think about how your own teaching of maths conveys your beliefs and values about the statement.

- Maths is really for boys.

- Maths is really just for nerds.

- You are either good at maths or you aren't.

- Maths is a good measure of general intelligence – if you are not very good at maths, you are just not very clever.

- Making mistakes is the worst thing you can do in maths.

- Maths is not a creative subject (and therefore people who like, or are good at, maths are not creative and are therefore dull people).

While a discussion of the substance of each belief is beyond the scope of the book, consider a little how your beliefs will have an impact on the way that you teach maths.

Reacting to mistakes

It is well established in the research literature (see Boaler, 2013, for example) that making mistakes is an important part of the learning process, and that this is just as true for mathematics as it is for any other subject. However, our beliefs about mistakes in maths and therefore the way that we respond to them (and to children's mathematical successes) may have a substantial impact on how the children come to view themselves as mathematical learners.

Activity: Reacting to mistakes

Think back to the last maths lesson you taught. What happened when a child gave you a 'wrong' answer? How did you respond? What did you say? What did your body language say?

Now think back to a maths lesson where you had reason to praise a child's mathematics. Can you remember precisely what you said?

Research Focus: Effects of beliefs

Carol Dweck has spent the last twenty years exploring the effect that learners' and teachers' implicit beliefs about the nature of intelligence can have on learning. In a recent study (Rattan et al., 2012) she and her colleagues explored the extent to which teachers' views about the nature of mathematical ability had an impact on their practice. These researchers identified two broad beliefs about mathematical 'intelligence'. Some teachers believe that mathematical 'intelligence' is essentially fixed. The researchers call this an 'entity theory' of intelligence. Other teachers have an 'incremental' theory of mathematical intelligence and believe that it is possible to get better at mathematics with hard work.

Dweck and her colleagues found that these, often implicit, teacher beliefs affected their responses to children. Those holding an 'entity theory' of intelligence were more likely to describe children as having low ability in maths and to use 'kind' strategies such as giving the children less homework. Interestingly, the same study found that children taught by 'entity-theory' teachers perceived this lack of expectation and reported lower motivation for and engagement with mathematics as a result.

This study, and many others like it, should alert us to the fact that what we, as teachers, think about mathematics will have a profound impact on the kind of mathematics teacher we are. It might now be worth going back to the list of beliefs about maths that were highlighted above and consider how your own view about them might affect the way that you respond to the children you teach.

Dweck and her colleagues (Dweck, 2007) also discovered that the way we praise children has a profound effect on the way that children perceive themselves as learners, particularly in mathematics. Dweck found that praising children's intelligence ('Well, done. You are clever.') leads them to view their mathematical 'ability' as fixed, whereas praising children for their effort ('Well done. I can see that you worked really hard to solve that problem.') leads children to view their mathematical 'ability' as malleable. Not surprisingly, these beliefs can cause children's learning behaviours to change markedly, particularly in the face of challenges or new learning. Interestingly, the way that we (possibly unconsciously) think about children's mathematical intelligence may well determine how we praise the children and therefore perpetuate our own views.

One of the great strengths of our education system is the fact that not all teachers are the same. Each person reading this book will bring different experiences, interests, thoughts and beliefs to the classroom and to their mathematics teaching.

Activity: What kind of mathematics teacher would you like to be?

As a final activity, it might be worth spending a few minutes thinking, or ideally talking with other trainee teachers, about the kind of primary mathematics teacher you are, or you would like to become. Consider these questions for a minute:

If someone were to walk into one of your maths lessons, what would they see? What would be going on in your maths classroom?

If your visitor were to talk to the children about your maths lessons, what would the children say about them? About you? About mathematics?

Would the visitor to your classroom see (and hear) children talking? Would the visitor see children asking mathematical questions and making mathematical suggestions, or would you be doing all the talking and asking all the questions? How would the visitor see mathematical ideas and concepts being explained and modelled? Would there be scope for different children, or groups of children, to take mathematical ideas in different directions and explore them, or would all the children be engaged in identical activity? How much control would the children have over their mathematical learning?

Would the children talk about mathematics as something that helps them to make sense of and question their world, or would they talk about it as something that they 'get through' at school with no connection to their lives. Will the children's eyes shine with excitement and curiosity as they talk about mathematics and their mathematical learning? Will they be children who go on to jobs and careers that involve mathematics? Or will a dull sheen come over their eyes and a flatness enter their voices as they talk about mathematics?

There is really only one person who can determine the answers to these questions and that person is you.

Learning Outcomes Review

The truth is that not all primary maths teachers are the same. There are teachers who 'see' mathematical opportunities everywhere and who continually make connections between mathematics in school and the children's lives. And there are teachers who do not. There are teachers whose understanding of mathematics and the curriculum is so deep that they find opportunities for their children to engage in mathematical reasoning at every stage of the curriculum. And there are those who do not. There are teachers who teach children to understand the mathematics they are doing at a deep level. And there are those who do not.

You will now have a clear(er) idea about the kind of mathematical experiences you want for the children you teach and the kind of maths teacher you want to be. The chapter offers some practical ideas about how to work with the National Curriculum while preserving the children's mathematical understanding. I hope that you have found a renewed enthusiasm for teaching primary mathematics and that you will step into your classroom ready to open the children's eyes to the challenges and the beauty of mathematics as well as its usefulness and connection with their lives.

Self-Assessment questions

1. How might your values about mathematics and about the world be conveyed in your teaching of maths?
2. How does the way that we praise children for their mathematics affect their view of themselves as mathematical learners?
3. How might mathematics act as a force for social change?
4. What kind of primary mathematics teacher are you?

Further Reading

Dweck, C. (2006) *Mindset: how we can fulfil our potential'.* New York: Random House. Carol Dweck has published a host of papers about mindsets and their impact on children's (and adults') learning. This book is very accessible and has a section about education.

Boaler, J. (2010) *The Elephant in the Classroom.* London: Souvenir Press. Jo Boaler's book is essential reading for any prospective, or practising primary mathematics teacher.

Useful websites

www.youcubed.org/ – Jo Boaler's website is an excellent source of resources and ideas about mathematics teaching.

www.gapminder.org/ – Hans Rosling's website is a great source of data, which might provoke discussion about the role of mathematics in illuminating the need for social change.

References

Boaler, J. (2013) Ability and mindset: the revolution that is reshaping education. *Forum* 55, 1: 143–152.

Cotton, T. (2013) *Understanding and Teaching Primary Mathematics.* Harlow: Pearson.

Crawford, C., Dearden, L.C. and Meghir, C. (2007) *When You Are Born Matters: the Impact of Date of Birth on Child Cognitive Outcomes in England*. London: Institute for Fiscal Studies.

Crawford, C., Dearden, L. and Greaves, E. (2011) *Does When You are Born Matter? The impact of month of birth on children's cognitive and non-cognitive skills*. London: Institute for Fiscal Studies, 2.

DfE (2013) *National Curriculum in England: Mathematics programmes of study: key stages 1 and 2*. Available at: www.gov.uk/government/publications/national-curriculum-in-england-mathematics-programmes-of-study/national-curriculum-in-england-mathematics-programmes-of-study (accessed 28/07/14).

Dweck, C.S. (2007) The perils and promises of praise. *Educational Leadership*, 65(2): 34–39.

Rattan, A., Good, C. and Dweck, C.S. (2012) 'It's ok – Not everyone can be good at math': Instructors with an entity theory comfort (and demotivate) students. *Journal of Experimental Social Psychology*, 48(3): 731–737.

Wolfram, C. (2014) The UK needs a revolution in the way maths is taught. Here's why … The *Observer*, 22 February 2014.

Appendix 1: Model answers to self-assessment questions

Chapter 1

1. Identify three things that you could incorporate into your next mathematics lesson which will encourage the children to engage in mathematical reasoning.

Answers to this will vary. However, suggestions could include some of the following.

- Use questions which explicitly draw out children's reasoning.

- Include a learning objective about reasoning.

- Spend time before the lesson identifying opportunities for reasoning.

- Ask the children to explain to each other how they reached a particular answer.

- Include a part of the lesson where you model your own reasoning to the children.

- Discuss with the children what they understand by the term 'mathematical reasoning'.

- Try to notice moments in the lesson where children are engaged in mathematical reasoning and draw the attention of the class to it.

2. How might children's reasoning lead to a deeper understanding of the mathematics that they are engaged in?

Again, answers to this will vary. You could have discussed the fact that reasoning makes it impossible to following processes or procedures without really considering why or how they work. Encouraging children to explain and justify their own mathematical processes will help them to move beyond the convenient but potentially unthinking application of processes.

3. What are the barriers to reasoning and curiosity that exist among your class of children? What could you do to try to reduce these?

Some of the barriers to reasoning are related to the teacher feeling the pressure of time and therefore not giving sufficient time for children to explain their reasoning. Teachers might also be jumping in too quickly and not allowing the children to complete the reasoning process. Other barriers are a lack of vocabulary to express reasoning, or a lack of understanding and/or expectation on the part of the teacher, which could cause the teacher to shut down the child's reasoning.

4. How might you develop your own curiosity about mathematics and convey this to your children?

Curiosity could be developed by engaging in some mathematics of your own, either connected to the mathematics that you are going to teach the children, or independent of it (depending on the age of the children you are teaching). Exploring the mathematics that you will be teaching (see Chapter 9 on planning later in the book) is a really good way of understanding some of the logical connections inherent in the mathematics and of developing your own curiosity about it.

Developing curiosity might involve asking yourself some questions about the mathematics that you are teaching: Why do the numbers/shapes, etc. behave in certain ways? What would happen if ...? What stays the same and what changes? etc. As you are simply exploring the mathematics, there is no reason not to ask yourself some of these questions. There is no imperative to come up with an answer, but exploring some of the possibilities might increase your curiosity about the maths. Once your curiosity has been piqued, you will not be able to help yourself from communicating this to the children.

Chapter 2

1.   What are the implications of the key changes to the National Curriculum?

Answers will vary here, but there are a few key changes. Some of the content of the curriculum is now taught at an earlier age than before. There is an increased emphasis on fluency and a renewed focus on mathematical reasoning. Problem solving is also highlighted along with the interconnected nature of mathematics and its connections to the wider world.

2.   Jot down key words from the three aims of the National Curriculum. How can you ensure that these aims underpin all of your planning and children's learning?

Answers will vary. Along with all teachers, you will be thinking about how to help your children become fluent with calculations while preserving their understanding of what they are doing. You will also consider the opportunities for reasoning presented by each area of maths you teach.

3.   What messages are given in the introductory text to the mathematics programme of study? How will you use these ideas (for example, moving between representations, making connections) to meet the higher expectations embedded in the curriculum?

Answers will vary depending on the messages you have identified as important. However, you may want to consider how to connect the mathematics you are teaching to the wider world, paying particular attention to the children's own experiences.

4.   Where do the main challenges lie for your subject knowledge in its widest sense? Identify three key areas.

Answers will vary.

Chapter 3

1. How might you ensure that children understand all five of Gelman and Galistel's counting principles?

You will think of particular answers depending on your children. However, it will be important to find as many opportunities for your children to engage in meaningful counting as you can, particularly counting things in different orders and counting abstract things. Be sure to emphasise the cardinal principle, by modelling the fact that the final word in the count represents the value of the set you are counting.

2. What are some of the barriers to children understanding place value.

The English language can be deeply unhelpful (four-teen written 14; confusions between forty and fourteen, etc.). The numbers are not written as they are said, for example 'one hundred and four' is not written 1004. Place value can be quite counter-intuitive: 99 with all its 9s seems that it should be 'worth' more than 100.

3. What could you do to help children to overcome these barriers?

The use of physical representations of place value, such as Dienes blocks or bundles of straws, can be hugely helpful. Arrow cards (also called place value cards) can be really useful in helping children to move from written numbers to their constituent parts and back again.

Chapter 4

1. Reflecting on your own practice, what are the key areas for you to develop in your teaching of addition and subtraction?

Answers will vary. However, you may wish to think about the language you use, the examples you choose, your own understanding of progression in methods, your understanding of possible misconceptions and your skill in modelling calculations.

2. What strategies could you use to help incorporate opportunities for reasoning into your teaching of addition and subtraction?

Again, answers will vary. You may wish to consider how you encourage children to estimate the reasonableness of their answers and how they justify these estimates.

Chapter 5

1. Look at the National Curriculum 'Mathematics Appendix 1: Examples of formal written methods for addition, subtraction, multiplication and division' (DfE, 2013, p.46). Note the errors, misconceptions and difficulties that some children may have with the suggested formal written methods. What strategies could you put in place to address these?

Answers will vary depending on the specific calculations chosen. This process is an important one to go through as part of your planning (see Chapter 9).

2. Access the school's calculation policy and note down the progression of teaching multiplication and division across Key Stages 1 and 2.

Your thoughts should pay close attention to the development of both skills and conceptual understanding as the children move through the curriculum.

3. What opportunities are provided for children to develop informal methods of multiplication and division during guided sessions and/or independent work?

Your answers should lead you to think about and explore possible ways of representing and recording calculations as the children work towards the standard algorithms.

4. Identify two key points that you wish to develop in your practice.

Answers will vary.

Chapter 6

1. Copy and complete the table.

Fraction	Decimal	Percentage
$\frac{1}{10}$	0.1	10%
$\frac{1}{8}$	0.125	12.5%
$\frac{1}{5}$	0.2	20%
$\frac{1}{3}$	0.333	33.3%
$\frac{1}{2}$	0.5	50%
$\frac{3}{5}$	0.6	60%
$\frac{7}{10}$	0.7	70%
1	1	100%

2. Thinking about fractions

    a) Define a fraction.

    b) Draw as many pictures/models/representations as possible to show $\frac{1}{4}$.

    c) On a scale of 1–10 (with 10 being the most), how confident are you teaching fractions?

Answers will vary.

3. Create your own mind map of fractions, percentages and decimals. Refer to the case study, Bringing it all together, for assistance.

Answers will vary.

Chapter 7

1. What are the key areas relating to geometry and measures in the National Curriculum?

Geometry is broadly divided into the study of shapes and their properties (2-D and 3-D shapes), and position and direction. While there are several underlying skills relating to measure, children are expected to encounter length (and later perimeter and area), money, weight/mass, capacity and time.

2. How might children's mathematical reasoning be developed alongside their understanding of the properties of shape?

Answers will vary. However, you should consider ways of getting children to do more than simply recognise shapes. Activities should allow children to explore the reasoning inherent in their understanding of the properties, i.e. what makes a square a square and does that mean that it is also a rhombus?

3. How might you help children to acquire the mathematical language associated with geometry (particularly position and direction) and measures?

It is important to provide children with the key terms, so that they can use them in their own explanations. Model the language in your teaching and give children the opportunity to use the language in their own explanations. When they do, draw the other children's attention to the fact and be effusive about the children who are doing so.

4. What are the key skills children need to develop in order to be able to measure?

Comparison, estimation, an understanding of units (both non-standard and then standard) and, importantly, a really good understanding of precisely what it is that they are measuring.

Chapter 8

1. Various skills are associated with gathering data. Have the children in your class had the opportunity to be more than 'technicians' gathering data on ready-made sheets (Paramore, 2011)?

You may wish to consider ways of helping your children to design their own surveys and to be involved in designing the data collection.

2. Having explored different formats for presenting data, reflect on the reasons we might produce a graph. What is the most powerful and purposeful graph work your class have ever done?

Answers will vary. Try to give some thought to the reasons for using a particular graph and the purpose for presenting the information in that way.

3. Having considered data of different types and some basic statistical tools, pick a topic you will soon teach. How will your activities really help children to get 'under the skin' of the data?

Answers will vary depending on the particular topic.

4. Rich starting points can lead to purposeful engagement in data handling. What will your next topic be and might it involve children in the full data handling cycle, gathering data themselves to answer an interesting question?

Answers will vary depending on the topic.

5. Given statistics' potential contribution to understanding the world we live in, consider how you might enjoy exploring some curious questions with your classes, encouraging the children to look beyond the data to draw conclusions and ask further questions.

Answers will vary. If you are short of inspiration, read Chapter 12 for some suggestions.

Chapter 9

1. How could Ausubel's ideas about children's prior knowledge help you to plan mathematics lessons?

Your thinking here should be about what the children have already met mathematically that may help them to understand the new concepts that you are intending to teach. Importantly, you should also think about other experiences they will have had, which you could build on to help them make sense of new concepts.

2. How might mathematics lessons be differentiated to ensure that all children are suitably challenged?

Again, answers will vary. Try to move beyond thinking about differentiation simply as making the task easier for the lower attaining children and more difficult for the higher attainers. Try to think about other ways (the amount of support, the resources available, etc.) that you could make the concept accessible to every child.

3. What are the key elements to consider when planning a sequence of maths lessons?

Your thinking should focus on progression and how you will ensure that the concepts connect in a logical and structured way. You may also wish to consider what you want the children to understand at the end of a sequence and work backwards, breaking the overall learning up into smaller, lesson-sized steps.

Chapter 10

1. Think about how you plan for and present key vocabulary, related to the mathematics lesson, to children.

Answers will vary. You may want to consider how you prompt yourself to consider vocabulary (for example, having a space on your lesson plan, pro forma, etc.). See Chapter 9 for further thoughts about planning for vocabulary.

2. What opportunities are provided for children to communicate their mathematics during guided sessions and/or independent group work?

Again, answers will vary. Consider the opportunities you provide for children to talk to each other about their maths and to communicate meaningfully in writing.

3. What strategies are used to further support acquisition of mathematical language and representation of mathematics for different learning styles and for learners who have EAL?

Children learning English as an additional language may require particular help with mathematical vocabulary, possibly in the form of a crib sheet with key terms in both English and their mother tongue and diagrammatic explanations. They may need to be physically involved in learning vocabulary so as to connect an experience with the word (for example, walking round the playground saying the word perimeter).

4. Identify two key points that you wish to develop in your practice.

Answers will vary.

Chapter 11

1. How can children with maths anxiety or dyscalculia be identified?

Some of these children will be easy to spot. Children with extreme cases of maths anxiety may become visibly anxious. Others may simply try to avoid maths as much as possible, may withdraw and/or not offer contributions during lessons. Others may seek to disguise their anxiety by relying heavily on other children for help.

2. What is your attitude to using concrete materials in class? Has your opinion changed at all as the result of reading this chapter?

Answers will vary.

3. Which of the suggestions for supporting dyscalculic learners at school are you planning to try?

Answers will vary.

Chapter 12

1. How might your values about mathematics and about the world be conveyed in
    your teaching of maths?

They are conveyed through responses to children's answers and other contributions
to your maths lessons. Values about the world can be conveyed through our choice of
examples and the ways in which we connect school maths with the 'real world'.

2. How does the way that we praise children for their mathematics affect their view
    of themselves as mathematical learners?

The nature of our praise may have an effect on whether children perceive their
mathematical competence as inherent, or as something that can be altered with hard
work. This view will have a profound bearing on children's attitude to mathematical
learning and their responses to the challenges in that learning.

3. How might mathematics act as a force for social change?

Connecting mathematics teaching to the wider world offers the chance for the children
to see that mathematics helps to illuminate and therefore address issues of injustice and
inequality in the world.

4. What kind of primary mathematics teacher are you?

Answers will vary. Try to consider what features an observer would note in one of your
maths lessons.

Mathematics programmes of study: key stages 1 and 2

National curriculum in England

September 2013

Contents

Purpose of study

Mathematics is a creative and highly inter-connected discipline that has been developed over centuries, providing the solution to some of history's most intriguing problems. It is essential to everyday life, critical to science, technology and engineering, and necessary for financial literacy and most forms of employment. A high-quality mathematics education therefore provides a foundation for understanding the world, the ability to reason mathematically, an appreciation of the beauty and power of mathematics, and a sense of enjoyment and curiosity about the subject.

Aims

The national curriculum for mathematics aims to ensure that all pupils:

- become **fluent** in the fundamentals of mathematics, including through varied and frequent practice with increasingly complex problems over time, so that pupils develop conceptual understanding and the ability to recall and apply knowledge rapidly and accurately.

- **reason mathematically** by following a line of enquiry, conjecturing relationships and generalisations, and developing an argument, justification or proof using mathematical language.

- can **solve problems** by applying their mathematics to a variety of routine and non-routine problems with increasing sophistication, including breaking down problems into a series of simpler steps and persevering in seeking solutions.

Mathematics is an interconnected subject in which pupils need to be able to move fluently between representations of mathematical ideas. The programmes of study are, by necessity, organised into apparently distinct domains, but pupils should make rich connections across mathematical ideas to develop fluency, mathematical reasoning and competence in solving increasingly sophisticated problems. They should also apply their mathematical knowledge to science and other subjects.

The expectation is that the majority of pupils will move through the programmes of study at broadly the same pace. However, decisions about when to progress should always be based on the security of pupils' understanding and their readiness to progress to the next stage. Pupils who grasp concepts rapidly should be challenged through being offered rich and sophisticated problems before any acceleration through new content. Those who are not sufficiently fluent with earlier material should consolidate their understanding, including through additional practice, before moving on.

Information and communication technology (ICT)

Calculators should not be used as a substitute for good written and mental arithmetic. They should therefore only be introduced near the end of key stage 2 to support pupils' conceptual understanding and exploration of more complex number problems, if written and mental arithmetic are secure. In both primary and secondary schools, teachers should use their judgement about when ICT tools should be used.

Spoken language

The national curriculum for mathematics reflects the importance of spoken language in pupils' development across the whole curriculum – cognitively, socially and linguistically. The quality and variety of language that pupils hear and speak are key factors in developing their mathematical vocabulary and presenting a mathematical justification, argument or proof. They must be assisted in making their thinking clear to themselves as well as others and teachers should ensure that pupils build secure foundations by using discussion to probe and remedy their misconceptions.

School curriculum

The programmes of study for mathematics are set out year-by-year for key stages 1 and 2. Schools are, however, only required to teach the relevant programme of study by the end of the key stage. Within each key stage, schools therefore have the flexibility to introduce content earlier or later than set out in the programme of study. In addition, schools can introduce key stage content during an earlier key stage, if appropriate. All schools are also required to set out their school curriculum for mathematics on a year-by-year basis and make this information available online.

Attainment targets

By the end of each key stage, pupils are expected to know, apply and understand the matters, skills and processes specified in the relevant programme of study.

Schools are not required by law to teach the example content in [square brackets] or the content indicated as being 'non-statutory'.

Key stage 1 – years 1 and 2

The principal focus of mathematics teaching in key stage 1 is to ensure that pupils develop confidence and mental fluency with whole numbers, counting and place value. This should involve working with numerals, words and the four operations, including with practical resources [for example, concrete objects and measuring tools].

At this stage, pupils should develop their ability to recognise, describe, draw, compare and sort different shapes and use the related vocabulary. Teaching should also involve using a range of measures to describe and compare different quantities such as length, mass, capacity/volume, time and money.

By the end of year 2, pupils should know the number bonds to 20 and be precise in using and understanding place value. An emphasis on practice at this early stage will aid fluency.

Pupils should read and spell mathematical vocabulary, at a level consistent with their increasing word reading and spelling knowledge at key stage 1.

Year 1 programme of study

Number – number and place value

Statutory requirements

Pupils should be taught to:

- count to and across 100, forwards and backwards, beginning with 0 or 1, or from any given number

- count, read and write numbers to 100 in numerals; count in multiples of twos, fives and tens

- given a number, identify one more and one less

- identify and represent numbers using objects and pictorial representations including the number line, and use the language of: equal to, more than, less than (fewer), most, least

- read and write numbers from 1 to 20 in numerals and words.

Notes and guidance (non-statutory)

Pupils practise counting (1, 2, 3…), ordering (for example, first, second, third…), and to indicate a quantity (for example, 3 apples, 2 centimetres), including solving simple concrete problems, until they are fluent.

Pupils begin to recognise place value in numbers beyond 20 by reading, writing, counting and comparing numbers up to 100, supported by objects and pictorial representations.

They practise counting as reciting numbers and counting as enumerating objects, and counting in twos, fives and tens from different multiples to develop their recognition of patterns in the number system (for example, odd and even numbers), including varied and frequent practice through increasingly complex questions.

They recognise and create repeating patterns with objects and with shapes.

Number – addition and subtraction

Statutory requirements

Pupils should be taught to:

- read, write and interpret mathematical statements involving addition (+), subtraction (−) and equals (=) signs

- represent and use number bonds and related subtraction facts within 20

- add and subtract one-digit and two-digit numbers to 20, including zero

- solve one-step problems that involve addition and subtraction, using concrete objects and pictorial representations, and missing number problems such as $7 = \square - 9$.

Notes and guidance (non-statutory)

Pupils memorise and reason with number bonds to 10 and 20 in several forms (for example, $9 + 7 = 16$; $16 - 7 = 9$; $7 = 16 - 9$). They should realise the effect of adding or subtracting zero. This establishes addition and subtraction as related operations.

Pupils combine and increase numbers, counting forwards and backwards.

They discuss and solve problems in familiar practical contexts, including using quantities. Problems should include the terms: put together, add, altogether, total, take away, distance between, difference between, more than and less than, so that pupils develop the concept of addition and subtraction and are enabled to use these operations flexibly.

Number – multiplication and division

Statutory requirements

Pupils should be taught to:

- solve one-step problems involving multiplication and division, by calculating the answer using concrete objects, pictorial representations and arrays with the support of the teacher.

Notes and guidance (non-statutory)

Through grouping and sharing small quantities, pupils begin to understand: multiplication and division; doubling numbers and quantities; and finding simple fractions of objects, numbers and quantities.

They make connections between arrays, number patterns, and counting in twos, fives and tens.

Number – fractions

Statutory requirements

Pupils should be taught to:

- recognise, find and name a half as one of two equal parts of an object, shape or quantity

- recognise, find and name a quarter as one of four equal parts of an object, shape or quantity.

Notes and guidance (non-statutory)

Pupils are taught half and quarter as 'fractions of' discrete and continuous quantities by solving problems using shapes, objects and quantities. For example, they could recognise and find half a length, quantity, set of objects or shape. Pupils connect halves and quarters to the equal sharing and grouping of sets of objects and to measures, as well as recognising and combining halves and quarters as parts of a whole.

Measurement

Statutory requirements

Pupils should be taught to:

- compare, describe and solve practical problems for:
  - lengths and heights [for example, long/short, longer/shorter, tall/short, double/half]
  - mass/weight [for example, heavy/light, heavier than, lighter than]
  - capacity and volume [for example, full/empty, more than, less than, half, half full, quarter]
  - time [for example, quicker, slower, earlier, later]
- measure and begin to record the following:
  - lengths and heights
  - mass/weight
  - capacity and volume
  - time (hours, minutes, seconds)
- recognise and know the value of different denominations of coins and notes
- sequence events in chronological order using language [for example, before and after, next, first, today, yesterday, tomorrow, morning, afternoon and evening]
- recognise and use language relating to dates, including days of the week, weeks, months and years
- tell the time to the hour and half past the hour and draw the hands on a clock face to show these times.

Notes and guidance (non-statutory)

The pairs of terms: mass and weight, volume and capacity, are used interchangeably at this stage.

Pupils move from using and comparing different types of quantities and measures using non-standard units, including discrete (for example, counting) and continuous (for example, liquid) measurement, to using manageable common standard units.

In order to become familiar with standard measures, pupils begin to use measuring tools such as a ruler, weighing scales and containers.

Pupils use the language of time, including telling the time throughout the day, first using o'clock and then half past.

Geometry – properties of shapes

Statutory requirements

Pupils should be taught to:

- recognise and name common 2-D and 3-D shapes, including:
    - 2-D shapes [for example, rectangles (including squares), circles and triangles]
    - 3-D shapes [for example, cuboids (including cubes), pyramids and spheres].

Notes and guidance (non-statutory)

Pupils handle common 2-D and 3-D shapes, naming these and related everyday objects fluently. They recognise these shapes in different orientations and sizes, and know that rectangles, triangles, cuboids and pyramids are not always similar to each other.

Geometry – position and direction

Statutory requirements

Pupils should be taught to:

- describe position, direction and movement, including whole, half, quarter and three-quarter turns.

Notes and guidance (non-statutory)

Pupils use the language of position, direction and motion, including: left and right, top, middle and bottom, on top of, in front of, above, between, around, near, close and far, up and down, forwards and backwards, inside and outside.

Pupils make whole, half, quarter and three-quarter turns in both directions and connect turning clockwise with movement on a clock face.

Year 2 programme of study

Number – number and place value

Statutory requirements

Pupils should be taught to:

- count in steps of 2, 3, and 5 from 0, and in tens from any number, forward and backward

- recognise the place value of each digit in a two-digit number (tens, ones)

- identify, represent and estimate numbers using different representations, including the number line

- compare and order numbers from 0 up to 100; use <, > and = signs

- read and write numbers to at least 100 in numerals and in words

- use place value and number facts to solve problems.

Notes and guidance (non-statutory)

Using materials and a range of representations, pupils practise counting, reading, writing and comparing numbers to at least 100 and solving a variety of related problems to develop fluency. They count in multiples of three to support their later understanding of a third.

As they become more confident with numbers up to 100, pupils are introduced to larger numbers to develop further their recognition of patterns within the number system and represent them in different ways, including spatial representations.

Pupils should partition numbers in different ways (for example, 23 = 20 + 3 and 23 = 10 + 13) to support subtraction. They become fluent and apply their knowledge of numbers to reason with, discuss and solve problems that emphasise the value of each digit in two-digit numbers. They begin to understand zero as a place holder.

Number – addition and subtraction

Statutory requirements

Pupils should be taught to:

- solve problems with addition and subtraction:
  - using concrete objects and pictorial representations, including those involving numbers, quantities and measures
  - applying their increasing knowledge of mental and written methods
- recall and use addition and subtraction facts to 20 fluently, and derive and use related facts up to 100
- add and subtract numbers using concrete objects, pictorial representations, and mentally, including:
  - a two-digit number and ones
  - a two-digit number and tens
  - two two-digit numbers
  - adding three one-digit numbers
- show that addition of two numbers can be done in any order (commutative) and subtraction of one number from another cannot
- recognise and use the inverse relationship between addition and subtraction and use this to check calculations and solve missing number problems.

Notes and guidance (non-statutory)

Pupils extend their understanding of the language of addition and subtraction to include sum and difference.

Pupils practise addition and subtraction to 20 to become increasingly fluent in deriving facts such as using $3 + 7 = 10$; $10 - 7 = 3$ and $7 = 10 - 3$ to calculate $30 + 70 = 100$; $100 - 70 = 30$ and $70 = 100 - 30$. They check their calculations, including by adding to check subtraction and adding numbers in a different order to check addition (for example, $5 + 2 + 1 = 1 + 5 + 2 = 1 + 2 + 5$). This establishes commutativity and associativity of addition.

Recording addition and subtraction in columns supports place value and prepares for formal written methods with larger numbers.

Number – multiplication and division

Statutory requirements

Pupils should be taught to:

- recall and use multiplication and division facts for the 2, 5 and 10 multiplication tables, including recognising odd and even numbers

- calculate mathematical statements for multiplication and division within the multiplication tables and write them using the multiplication (×), division (÷) and equals (=) signs

- show that multiplication of two numbers can be done in any order (commutative) and division of one number by another cannot

- solve problems involving multiplication and division, using materials, arrays, repeated addition, mental methods, and multiplication and division facts, including problems in contexts.

Notes and guidance (non-statutory)

Pupils use a variety of language to describe multiplication and division.

Pupils are introduced to the multiplication tables. They practise to become fluent in the 2, 5 and 10 multiplication tables and connect them to each other. They connect the 10 multiplication table to place value, and the 5 multiplication table to the divisions on the clock face. They begin to use other multiplication tables and recall multiplication facts, including using related division facts to perform written and mental calculations.

Pupils work with a range of materials and contexts in which multiplication and division relate to grouping and sharing discrete and continuous quantities, to arrays and to repeated addition. They begin to relate these to fractions and measures (for example, 40 ÷ 2 = 20, 20 is a half of 40). They use commutativity and inverse relations to develop multiplicative reasoning (for example, 4 × 5 = 20 and 20 ÷ 5 = 4).

Number – fractions

Statutory requirements

Pupils should be taught to:

- recognise, find, name and write fractions $\frac{1}{3}$, $\frac{1}{4}$, $\frac{2}{4}$ and $\frac{3}{4}$ of a length, shape, set of objects or quantity

- write simple fractions for example, $\frac{1}{2}$ of 6 = 3 and recognise the equivalence of $\frac{2}{4}$ and $\frac{1}{2}$.

Notes and guidance (non-statutory)

Pupils use fractions as 'fractions of' discrete and continuous quantities by solving problems using shapes, objects and quantities. They connect unit fractions to equal sharing and grouping, to numbers when they can be calculated, and to measures, finding fractions of lengths, quantities, sets of objects or shapes. They meet $\frac{3}{4}$ as the first example of a non-unit fraction.

Pupils should count in fractions up to 10, starting from any number and using the $\frac{1}{2}$ and $\frac{2}{4}$ equivalence on the number line (for example, $1\frac{1}{4}$, $1\frac{2}{4}$ (or $1\frac{1}{2}$), $1\frac{3}{4}$, 2). This reinforces the concept of fractions as numbers and that they can add up to more than one.

Measurement

Statutory requirements

Pupils should be taught to:

- choose and use appropriate standard units to estimate and measure length/height in any direction (m/cm); mass (kg/g); temperature (°C); capacity (litres/ml) to the nearest appropriate unit, using rulers, scales, thermometers and measuring vessels

- compare and order lengths, mass, volume/capacity and record the results using >, < and =

- recognise and use symbols for pounds (£) and pence (p); combine amounts to make a particular value

- find different combinations of coins that equal the same amounts of money

- solve simple problems in a practical context involving addition and subtraction of money of the same unit, including giving change

- compare and sequence intervals of time

- tell and write the time to five minutes, including quarter past/to the hour and draw the hands on a clock face to show these times

- know the number of minutes in an hour and the number of hours in a day.

Notes and guidance (non-statutory)

Pupils use standard units of measurement with increasing accuracy, using their knowledge of the number system. They use the appropriate language and record using standard abbreviations.

Comparing measures includes simple multiples such as 'half as high'; 'twice as wide'.

They become fluent in telling the time on analogue clocks and recording it.

Pupils become fluent in counting and recognising coins. They read and say amounts of money confidently and use the symbols £ and p accurately, recording pounds and pence separately.

Geometry – properties of shapes

Statutory requirements

Pupils should be taught to:

- identify and describe the properties of 2-D shapes, including the number of sides and line symmetry in a vertical line
- identify and describe the properties of 3-D shapes, including the number of edges, vertices and faces
- identify 2-D shapes on the surface of 3-D shapes, [for example, a circle on a cylinder and a triangle on a pyramid]
- compare and sort common 2-D and 3-D shapes and everyday objects.

Notes and guidance (non-statutory)

Pupils handle and name a wide variety of common 2-D and 3-D shapes including: quadrilaterals and polygons, and cuboids, prisms and cones, and identify the properties of each shape (for example, number of sides, number of faces). Pupils identify, compare and sort shapes on the basis of their properties and use vocabulary precisely, such as sides, edges, vertices and faces.

Pupils read and write names for shapes that are appropriate for their word reading and spelling.

Pupils draw lines and shapes using a straight edge.

Geometry – position and direction

Statutory requirements

Pupils should be taught to:

- order and arrange combinations of mathematical objects in patterns and sequences

- use mathematical vocabulary to describe position, direction and movement, including movement in a straight line and distinguishing between rotation as a turn and in terms of right angles for quarter, half and three-quarter turns (clockwise and anti-clockwise).

Notes and guidance (non-statutory)

Pupils should work with patterns of shapes, including those in different orientations.

Pupils use the concept and language of angles to describe 'turn' by applying rotations, including in practical contexts (for example, pupils themselves moving in turns, giving instructions to other pupils to do so, and programming robots using instructions given in right angles).

Statistics

Statutory requirements

Pupils should be taught to:

- interpret and construct simple pictograms, tally charts, block diagrams and simple tables

- ask and answer simple questions by counting the number of objects in each category and sorting the categories by quantity

- ask and answer questions about totalling and comparing categorical data.

Notes and guidance (non-statutory)

Pupils record, interpret, collate, organise and compare information (for example, using many-to-one correspondence in pictograms with simple ratios 2, 5, 10).

Lower key stage 2 – years 3 and 4

The principal focus of mathematics teaching in lower key stage 2 is to ensure that pupils become increasingly fluent with whole numbers and the four operations, including number facts and the concept of place value. This should ensure that pupils develop efficient written and mental methods and perform calculations accurately with increasingly large whole numbers.

At this stage, pupils should develop their ability to solve a range of problems, including with simple fractions and decimal place value. Teaching should also ensure that pupils draw with increasing accuracy and develop mathematical reasoning so they can analyse shapes and their properties, and confidently describe the relationships between them. It should ensure that they can use measuring instruments with accuracy and make connections between measure and number.

By the end of year 4, pupils should have memorised their multiplication tables up to and including the 12 multiplication table and show precision and fluency in their work.

Pupils should read and spell mathematical vocabulary correctly and confidently, using their growing word reading knowledge and their knowledge of spelling.

Year 3 programme of study

Number – number and place value

Statutory requirements

Pupils should be taught to:

- count from 0 in multiples of 4, 8, 50 and 100; find 10 or 100 more or less than a given number
- recognise the place value of each digit in a three-digit number (hundreds, tens, ones)
- compare and order numbers up to 1000
- identify, represent and estimate numbers using different representations
- read and write numbers up to 1000 in numerals and in words
- solve number problems and practical problems involving these ideas.

Notes and guidance (non-statutory)

Pupils now use multiples of 2, 3, 4, 5, 8, 10, 50 and 100.

They use larger numbers to at least 1000, applying partitioning related to place value using varied and increasingly complex problems, building on work in year 2 (for example, 146 = 100 + 40 and 6, 146 = 130 + 16).

Using a variety of representations, including those related to measure, pupils continue to count in ones, tens and hundreds, so that they become fluent in the order and place value of numbers to 1000.

Number – addition and subtraction

Statutory requirements

Pupils should be taught to:

- add and subtract numbers mentally, including:
  - a three-digit number and ones
  - a three-digit number and tens
  - a three-digit number and hundreds
- add and subtract numbers with up to three digits, using formal written methods of columnar addition and subtraction
- estimate the answer to a calculation and use inverse operations to check answers
- solve problems, including missing number problems, using number facts, place value, and more complex addition and subtraction.

Notes and guidance (non-statutory)

Pupils practise solving varied addition and subtraction questions. For mental calculations with two-digit numbers, the answers could exceed 100.

Pupils use their understanding of place value and partitioning, and practise using columnar addition and subtraction with increasingly large numbers up to three digits to become fluent (see Mathematics Appendix 1).

Number – multiplication and division

Statutory requirements

Pupils should be taught to:

- recall and use multiplication and division facts for the 3, 4 and 8 multiplication tables
- write and calculate mathematical statements for multiplication and division using the multiplication tables that they know, including for two-digit numbers times one-digit numbers, using mental and progressing to formal written methods
- solve problems, including missing number problems, involving multiplication and division, including positive integer scaling problems and correspondence problems in which n objects are connected to m objects.

Notes and guidance (non-statutory)

Pupils continue to practise their mental recall of multiplication tables when they are calculating mathematical statements in order to improve fluency. Through doubling, they connect the 2, 4 and 8 multiplication tables.

Pupils develop efficient mental methods, for example, using commutativity and associativity (for example, $4 \times 12 \times 5 = 4 \times 5 \times 12 = 20 \times 12 = 240$) and multiplication and division facts (for example, using $3 \times 2 = 6$, $6 \div 3 = 2$ and $2 = 6 \div 3$) to derive related facts (for example, $30 \times 2 = 60$, $60 \div 3 = 20$ and $20 = 60 \div 3$).

Pupils develop reliable written methods for multiplication and division, starting with calculations of two-digit numbers by one-digit numbers and progressing to the formal written methods of short multiplication and division.

Pupils solve simple problems in contexts, deciding which of the four operations to use and why. These include measuring and scaling contexts, (for example, four times as high, eight times as long etc.) and correspondence problems in which m objects are connected to n objects (for example, 3 hats and 4 coats, how many different outfits?; 12 sweets shared equally between 4 children; 4 cakes shared equally between 8 children).

Number – fractions

Statutory requirements

Pupils should be taught to:

- count up and down in tenths; recognise that tenths arise from dividing an object into 10 equal parts and in dividing one-digit numbers or quantities by 10

- recognise, find and write fractions of a discrete set of objects: unit fractions and non-unit fractions with small denominators

- recognise and use fractions as numbers: unit fractions and non-unit fractions with small denominators

- recognise and show, using diagrams, equivalent fractions with small denominators

- add and subtract fractions with the same denominator within one whole [for example, $\frac{5}{7} + \frac{1}{7} = \frac{6}{7}$]

- compare and order unit fractions, and fractions with the same denominators

- solve problems that involve all of the above.

Notes and guidance (non-statutory)

Pupils connect tenths to place value, decimal measures and to division by 10.

They begin to understand unit and non-unit fractions as numbers on the number line, and deduce relations between them, such as size and equivalence. They should go beyond the [0, 1] interval, including relating this to measure.

Pupils understand the relation between unit fractions as operators (fractions of), and division by integers.

They continue to recognise fractions in the context of parts of a whole, numbers, measurements, a shape, and unit fractions as a division of a quantity.

Pupils practise adding and subtracting fractions with the same denominator through a variety of increasingly complex problems to improve fluency.

Measurement

Statutory requirements

Pupils should be taught to:

- measure, compare, add and subtract: lengths (m/cm/mm); mass (kg/g); volume/capacity (l/ml)

- measure the perimeter of simple 2-D shapes

- add and subtract amounts of money to give change, using both £ and p in practical contexts

- tell and write the time from an analogue clock, including using Roman numerals from I to XII, and 12-hour and 24-hour clocks

- estimate and read time with increasing accuracy to the nearest minute; record and compare time in terms of seconds, minutes and hours; use vocabulary such as o'clock, a.m./p.m., morning, afternoon, noon and midnight

- know the number of seconds in a minute and the number of days in each month, year and leap year

- compare durations of events [for example to calculate the time taken by particular events or tasks].

Notes and guidance (non-statutory)

Pupils continue to measure using the appropriate tools and units, progressing to using a wider range of measures, including comparing and using mixed units (for example, 1 kg and 200g) and simple equivalents of mixed units (for example, 5m = 500cm).

The comparison of measures includes simple scaling by integers (for example, a given quantity or measure is twice as long or five times as high) and this connects to multiplication.

Pupils continue to become fluent in recognising the value of coins, by adding and subtracting amounts, including mixed units, and giving change using manageable amounts. They record £ and p separately. The decimal recording of money is introduced formally in year 4.

Pupils use both analogue and digital 12-hour clocks and record their times. In this way they become fluent in and prepared for using digital 24-hour clocks in year 4.

Geometry – properties of shapes

Statutory requirements

Pupils should be taught to:

- draw 2-D shapes and make 3-D shapes using modelling materials; recognise 3-D shapes in different orientations and describe them

- recognise angles as a property of shape or a description of a turn

- identify right angles, recognise that two right angles make a half-turn, three make three quarters of a turn and four a complete turn; identify whether angles are greater than or less than a right angle

- identify horizontal and vertical lines and pairs of perpendicular and parallel lines.

Notes and guidance (non-statutory)

Pupils' knowledge of the properties of shapes is extended at this stage to symmetrical and non-symmetrical polygons and polyhedra. Pupils extend their use of the properties of shapes. They should be able to describe the properties of 2-D and 3-D shapes using accurate language, including lengths of lines and acute and obtuse for angles greater or lesser than a right angle.

Pupils connect decimals and rounding to drawing and measuring straight lines in centimetres, in a variety of contexts.

Statistics

Statutory requirements

Pupils should be taught to:

- interpret and present data using bar charts, pictograms and tables

- solve one-step and two-step questions [for example, 'How many more?' and 'How many fewer?'] using information presented in scaled bar charts and pictograms and tables.

Notes and guidance (non-statutory)

Pupils understand and use simple scales (for example, 2, 5, 10 units per cm) in pictograms and bar charts with increasing accuracy.

They continue to interpret data presented in many contexts.

Year 4 programme of study

Number – number and place value

Statutory requirements

Pupils should be taught to

- count in multiples of 6, 7, 9, 25 and 1000

- find 1000 more or less than a given number

- count backwards through zero to include negative numbers

- recognise the place value of each digit in a four-digit number (thousands, hundreds, tens, and ones)

- order and compare numbers beyond 1000

- identify, represent and estimate numbers using different representations

- round any number to the nearest 10, 100 or 1000

- solve number and practical problems that involve all of the above and with increasingly large positive numbers

- read Roman numerals to 100 (I to C) and know that over time, the numeral system changed to include the concept of zero and place value.

Notes and guidance (non-statutory)

Using a variety of representations, including measures, pupils become fluent in the order and place value of numbers beyond 1000, including counting in tens and hundreds, and maintaining fluency in other multiples through varied and frequent practice.

They begin to extend their knowledge of the number system to include the decimal numbers and fractions that they have met so far.

They connect estimation and rounding numbers to the use of measuring instruments.

Roman numerals should be put in their historical context so pupils understand that there have been different ways to write whole numbers and that the important concepts of zero and place value were introduced over a period of time.

Number – addition and subtraction

Statutory requirements

Pupils should be taught to:

- add and subtract numbers with up to 4 digits using the formal written methods of columnar addition and subtraction where appropriate

- estimate and use inverse operations to check answers to a calculation

- solve addition and subtraction two-step problems in contexts, deciding which operations and methods to use and why.

Notes and guidance (non-statutory)

Pupils continue to practise both mental methods and columnar addition and subtraction with increasingly large numbers to aid fluency (see Mathematics Appendix 1).

Number – multiplication and division

Statutory requirements

Pupils should be taught to:

- recall multiplication and division facts for multiplication tables up to 12 × 12

- use place value, known and derived facts to multiply and divide mentally, including: multiplying by 0 and 1; dividing by 1; multiplying together three numbers

- recognise and use factor pairs and commutativity in mental calculations

- multiply two-digit and three-digit numbers by a one-digit number using formal written layout

- solve problems involving multiplying and adding, including using the distributive law to multiply two digit numbers by one digit, integer scaling problems and harder correspondence problems such as n objects are connected to m objects.

Notes and guidance (non-statutory)

Pupils continue to practise recalling and using multiplication tables and related division facts to aid fluency.

Pupils practise mental methods and extend this to three-digit numbers to derive facts, (for example 600 ÷ 3 = 200 can be derived from 2 x 3 = 6).

Notes and guidance (non-statutory)

Pupils practise to become fluent in the formal written method of short multiplication and short division with exact answers (see Mathematics Appendix 1).

Pupils write statements about the equality of expressions (for example, use the distributive law 39 × 7 = 30 × 7 + 9 × 7 and associative law (2 × 3) × 4 = 2 × (3 × 4)). They combine their knowledge of number facts and rules of arithmetic to solve mental and written calculations for example, 2 x 6 x 5 = 10 x 6 = 60.

Pupils solve two-step problems in contexts, choosing the appropriate operation, working with increasingly harder numbers. This should include correspondence questions such as the numbers of choices of a meal on a menu, or three cakes shared equally between 10 children.

Number – fractions (including decimals)

Statutory requirements

Pupils should be taught to:

- recognise and show, using diagrams, families of common equivalent fractions

- count up and down in hundredths; recognise that hundredths arise when dividing an object by one hundred and dividing tenths by ten.

- solve problems involving increasingly harder fractions to calculate quantities, and fractions to divide quantities, including non-unit fractions where the answer is a whole number

- add and subtract fractions with the same denominator

- recognise and write decimal equivalents of any number of tenths or hundredths

- recognise and write decimal equivalents to $\frac{1}{4}$, $\frac{1}{2}$, $\frac{3}{4}$

- find the effect of dividing a one- or two-digit number by 10 and 100, identifying the value of the digits in the answer as ones, tenths and hundredths

- round decimals with one decimal place to the nearest whole number

- compare numbers with the same number of decimal places up to two decimal places

- solve simple measure and money problems involving fractions and decimals to two decimal places.

Notes and guidance (non-statutory)

Pupils should connect hundredths to tenths and place value and decimal measure.

They extend the use of the number line to connect fractions, numbers and measures.

Pupils understand the relation between non-unit fractions and multiplication and division of quantities, with particular emphasis on tenths and hundredths.

Pupils make connections between fractions of a length, of a shape and as a representation of one whole or set of quantities. Pupils use factors and multiples to recognise equivalent fractions and simplify where appropriate (for example, $\frac{6}{9} = \frac{2}{3}$ or $\frac{1}{4} = \frac{2}{8}$).

Pupils continue to practise adding and subtracting fractions with the same denominator, to become fluent through a variety of increasingly complex problems beyond one whole.

Pupils are taught throughout that decimals and fractions are different ways of expressing numbers and proportions.

Pupils' understanding of the number system and decimal place value is extended at this stage to tenths and then hundredths. This includes relating the decimal notation to division of whole number by 10 and later 100.

They practise counting using simple fractions and decimals, both forwards and backwards.

Pupils learn decimal notation and the language associated with it, including in the context of measurements. They make comparisons and order decimal amounts and quantities that are expressed to the same number of decimal places. They should be able to represent numbers with one or two decimal places in several ways, such as on number lines.

Measurement

Statutory requirements

Pupils should be taught to:

- Convert between different units of measure [for example, kilometre to metre; hour to minute]
- measure and calculate the perimeter of a rectilinear figure (including squares) in centimetres and metres
- find the area of rectilinear shapes by counting squares
- estimate, compare and calculate different measures, including money in pounds and pence

Statutory requirements

- read, write and convert time between analogue and digital 12- and 24-hour clocks
- solve problems involving converting from hours to minutes; minutes to seconds; years to months; weeks to days.

Notes and guidance (non-statutory)

Pupils build on their understanding of place value and decimal notation to record metric measures, including money.

They use multiplication to convert from larger to smaller units.

Perimeter can be expressed algebraically as $2(a + b)$ where a and b are the dimensions in the same unit.

They relate area to arrays and multiplication.

Geometry – properties of shapes

Statutory requirements

Pupils should be taught to:

- compare and classify geometric shapes, including quadrilaterals and triangles, based on their properties and sizes
- identify acute and obtuse angles and compare and order angles up to two right angles by size
- identify lines of symmetry in 2-D shapes presented in different orientations
- complete a simple symmetric figure with respect to a specific line of symmetry.

Notes and guidance (non-statutory)

Pupils continue to classify shapes using geometrical properties, extending to classifying different triangles (for example, isosceles, equilateral, scalene) and quadrilaterals (for example, parallelogram, rhombus, trapezium).

Pupils compare and order angles in preparation for using a protractor and compare lengths and angles to decide if a polygon is regular or irregular.

Pupils draw symmetric patterns using a variety of media to become familiar with different orientations of lines of symmetry; and recognise line symmetry in a variety of diagrams, including where the line of symmetry does not dissect the original shape.

Geometry – position and direction

Statutory requirements

Pupils should be taught to:

- describe positions on a 2-D grid as coordinates in the first quadrant
- describe movements between positions as translations of a given unit to the left/right and up/down
- plot specified points and draw sides to complete a given polygon.

Notes and guidance (non-statutory)

Pupils draw a pair of axes in one quadrant, with equal scales and integer labels. They read, write and use pairs of coordinates, for example (2, 5), including using coordinate-plotting ICT tools.

Statistics

Statutory requirements

Pupils should be taught to:

- interpret and present discrete and continuous data using appropriate graphical methods, including bar charts and time graphs.
- solve comparison, sum and difference problems using information presented in bar charts, pictograms, tables and other graphs.

Notes and guidance (non-statutory)

Pupils understand and use a greater range of scales in their representations.

Pupils begin to relate the graphical representation of data to recording change over time.

Upper key stage 2 – years 5 and 6

The principal focus of mathematics teaching in upper key stage 2 is to ensure that pupils extend their understanding of the number system and place value to include larger integers. This should develop the connections that pupils make between multiplication and division with fractions, decimals, percentages and ratio.

At this stage, pupils should develop their ability to solve a wider range of problems, including increasingly complex properties of numbers and arithmetic, and problems demanding efficient written and mental methods of calculation. With this foundation in arithmetic, pupils are introduced to the language of algebra as a means for solving a variety of problems. Teaching in geometry and measures should consolidate and extend knowledge developed in number. Teaching should also ensure that pupils classify shapes with increasingly complex geometric properties and that they learn the vocabulary they need to describe them.

By the end of year 6, pupils should be fluent in written methods for all four operations, including long multiplication and division, and in working with fractions, decimals and percentages.

Pupils should read, spell and pronounce mathematical vocabulary correctly.

Year 5 programme of study

Number – number and place value

Statutory requirements

Pupils should be taught to:

- read, write, order and compare numbers to at least 1 000 000 and determine the value of each digit

- count forwards or backwards in steps of powers of 10 for any given number up to 1 000 000

- interpret negative numbers in context, count forwards and backwards with positive and negative whole numbers, including through zero

- round any number up to 1 000 000 to the nearest 10, 100, 1000, 10 000 and 100 000

- solve number problems and practical problems that involve all of the above

- read Roman numerals to 1000 (M) and recognise years written in Roman numerals.

Notes and guidance (non-statutory)

Pupils identify the place value in large whole numbers.

They continue to use number in context, including measurement. Pupils extend and apply their understanding of the number system to the decimal numbers and fractions that they have met so far.

They should recognise and describe linear number sequences, including those involving fractions and decimals, and find the term-to-term rule.

They should recognise and describe linear number sequences (for example, 3, $3\frac{1}{2}$, 4, $4\frac{1}{2}$...), including those involving fractions and decimals, and find the term-to-term rule in words (for example, add $\frac{1}{2}$).

Number – addition and subtraction

Statutory requirements

Pupils should be taught to:

- add and subtract whole numbers with more than 4 digits, including using formal written methods (columnar addition and subtraction)

- add and subtract numbers mentally with increasingly large numbers

- use rounding to check answers to calculations and determine, in the context of a problem, levels of accuracy

- solve addition and subtraction multi-step problems in contexts, deciding which operations and methods to use and why.

Notes and guidance (non-statutory)

Pupils practise using the formal written methods of columnar addition and subtraction with increasingly large numbers to aid fluency (see Mathematics Appendix 1).

They practise mental calculations with increasingly large numbers to aid fluency (for example, 12 462 – 2300 = 10 162).

Number – multiplication and division

Statutory requirements

Pupils should be taught to:

- identify multiples and factors, including finding all factor pairs of a number, and common factors of two numbers

- know and use the vocabulary of prime numbers, prime factors and composite (non-prime) numbers

- establish whether a number up to 100 is prime and recall prime numbers up to 19

- multiply numbers up to 4 digits by a one- or two-digit number using a formal written method, including long multiplication for two-digit numbers

- multiply and divide numbers mentally drawing upon known facts

- divide numbers up to 4 digits by a one-digit number using the formal written method of short division and interpret remainders appropriately for the context

- multiply and divide whole numbers and those involving decimals by 10, 100 and 1000

Statutory requirements

- recognise and use square numbers and cube numbers, and the notation for squared (^{2}) and cubed (^{3})
- solve problems involving multiplication and division including using their knowledge of factors and multiples, squares and cubes
- solve problems involving addition, subtraction, multiplication and division and a combination of these, including understanding the meaning of the equals sign
- solve problems involving multiplication and division, including scaling by simple fractions and problems involving simple rates.

Notes and guidance (non-statutory)

Pupils practise and extend their use of the formal written methods of short multiplication and short division (see Mathematics Appendix 1). They apply all the multiplication tables and related division facts frequently, commit them to memory and use them confidently to make larger calculations.

They use and understand the terms factor, multiple and prime, square and cube numbers.

Pupils interpret non-integer answers to division by expressing results in different ways according to the context, including with remainders, as fractions, as decimals or by rounding (for example, $98 \div 4 = \frac{98}{4} = 24$ r $2 = 24\frac{1}{2} = 24.5 \approx 25$).

Pupils use multiplication and division as inverses to support the introduction of ratio in year 6, for example, by multiplying and dividing by powers of 10 in scale drawings or by multiplying and dividing by powers of a 1000 in converting between units such as kilometres and metres.

Distributivity can be expressed as $a(b + c) = ab + ac$.

They understand the terms factor, multiple and prime, square and cube numbers and use them to construct equivalence statements (for example, $4 \times 35 = 2 \times 2 \times 35$; $3 \times 270 = 3 \times 3 \times 9 \times 10 = 9^2 \times 10$).

Pupils use and explain the equals sign to indicate equivalence, including in missing number problems (for example, $13 + 24 = 12 + 25$; $33 = 5 \times \square$).

Number – fractions (including decimals and percentages)

Statutory requirements

Pupils should be taught to:

- compare and order fractions whose denominators are all multiples of the same number

- identify, name and write equivalent fractions of a given fraction, represented visually, including tenths and hundredths

- recognise mixed numbers and improper fractions and convert from one form to the other and write mathematical statements > 1 as a mixed number [for example, $\frac{2}{5} + \frac{4}{5} = \frac{6}{5} = 1\frac{1}{5}$]

- add and subtract fractions with the same denominator and denominators that are multiples of the same number

- multiply proper fractions and mixed numbers by whole numbers, supported by materials and diagrams

- read and write decimal numbers as fractions [for example, $0.71 = \frac{71}{100}$]

- recognise and use thousandths and relate them to tenths, hundredths and decimal equivalents

- round decimals with two decimal places to the nearest whole number and to one decimal place

- read, write, order and compare numbers with up to three decimal places

- solve problems involving number up to three decimal places

- recognise the per cent symbol (%) and understand that per cent relates to 'number of parts per hundred', and write percentages as a fraction with denominator 100, and as a decimal

- solve problems which require knowing percentage and decimal equivalents of $\frac{1}{2}$, $\frac{1}{4}$, $\frac{1}{5}$, $\frac{2}{5}$, $\frac{4}{5}$ and those fractions with a denominator of a multiple of 10 or 25.

Notes and guidance (non-statutory)

Pupils should be taught throughout that percentages, decimals and fractions are different ways of expressing proportions.

They extend their knowledge of fractions to thousandths and connect to decimals and measures.

Notes and guidance (non-statutory)

Pupils connect equivalent fractions > 1 that simplify to integers with division and other fractions > 1 to division with remainders, using the number line and other models, and hence move from these to improper and mixed fractions.

Pupils connect multiplication by a fraction to using fractions as operators (fractions of), and to division, building on work from previous years. This relates to scaling by simple fractions, including fractions > 1.

Pupils practise adding and subtracting fractions to become fluent through a variety of increasingly complex problems. They extend their understanding of adding and subtracting fractions to calculations that exceed 1 as a mixed number.

Pupils continue to practise counting forwards and backwards in simple fractions.

Pupils continue to develop their understanding of fractions as numbers, measures and operators by finding fractions of numbers and quantities.

Pupils extend counting from year 4, using decimals and fractions including bridging zero, for example on a number line.

Pupils say, read and write decimal fractions and related tenths, hundredths and thousandths accurately and are confident in checking the reasonableness of their answers to problems.

They mentally add and subtract tenths, and one-digit whole numbers and tenths.

They practise adding and subtracting decimals, including a mix of whole numbers and decimals, decimals with different numbers of decimal places, and complements of 1 (for example, 0.83 + 0.17 = 1).

Pupils should go beyond the measurement and money models of decimals, for example, by solving puzzles involving decimals.

Pupils should make connections between percentages, fractions and decimals (for example, 100% represents a whole quantity and 1% is $\frac{1}{100}$, 50% is $\frac{50}{100}$, 25% is $\frac{25}{100}$) and relate this to finding 'fractions of'.

Measurement

Statutory requirements

Pupils should be taught to:

- convert between different units of metric measure (for example, kilometre and metre; centimetre and metre; centimetre and millimetre; gram and kilogram; litre and millilitre)

- understand and use approximate equivalences between metric units and common imperial units such as inches, pounds and pints

- measure and calculate the perimeter of composite rectilinear shapes in centimetres and metres

- calculate and compare the area of rectangles (including squares), and including using standard units, square centimetres (cm^2) and square metres (m^2) and estimate the area of irregular shapes

- estimate volume [for example, using 1 cm^3 blocks to build cuboids (including cubes)] and capacity [for example, using water]

- solve problems involving converting between units of time

- use all four operations to solve problems involving measure [for example, length, mass, volume, money] using decimal notation, including scaling.

Notes and guidance (non-statutory)

Pupils use their knowledge of place value and multiplication and division to convert between standard units.

Pupils calculate the perimeter of rectangles and related composite shapes, including using the relations of perimeter or area to find unknown lengths. Missing measures questions such as these can be expressed algebraically, for example $4 + 2b = 20$ for a rectangle of sides 2 cm and b cm and perimeter of 20cm.

Pupils calculate the area from scale drawings using given measurements.

Pupils use all four operations in problems involving time and money, including conversions (for example, days to weeks, expressing the answer as weeks and days).

Geometry – properties of shapes

Statutory requirements

Pupils should be taught to:

- identify 3-D shapes, including cubes and other cuboids, from 2-D representations

- know angles are measured in degrees: estimate and compare acute, obtuse and reflex angles

- draw given angles, and measure them in degrees ($^{\circ}$)

- identify:

    - angles at a point and one whole turn (total 360°)

    - angles at a point on a straight line and $\frac{1}{2}$ a turn (total 180°)

    - other multiples of 90°

- use the properties of rectangles to deduce related facts and find missing lengths and angles

- distinguish between regular and irregular polygons based on reasoning about equal sides and angles.

Notes and guidance (non-statutory)

Pupils become accurate in drawing lines with a ruler to the nearest millimetre, and measuring with a protractor. They use conventional markings for parallel lines and right angles.

Pupils use the term diagonal and make conjectures about the angles formed between sides, and between diagonals and parallel sides, and other properties of quadrilaterals, for example using dynamic geometry ICT tools.

Pupils use angle sum facts and other properties to make deductions about missing angles and relate these to missing number problems.

Geometry – position and direction

Statutory requirements

Pupils should be taught to:

- identify, describe and represent the position of a shape following a reflection or translation, using the appropriate language, and know that the shape has not changed.

Notes and guidance (non-statutory)

Pupils recognise and use reflection and translation in a variety of diagrams, including continuing to use a 2-D grid and coordinates in the first quadrant. Reflection should be in lines that are parallel to the axes.

Statistics

Statutory requirements

Pupils should be taught to:

- solve comparison, sum and difference problems using information presented in a line graph

- complete, read and interpret information in tables, including timetables.

Notes and guidance (non-statutory)

Pupils connect their work on coordinates and scales to their interpretation of time graphs.

They begin to decide which representations of data are most appropriate and why.

Year 6 programme of study

Number – number and place value

Statutory requirements

Pupils should be taught to:

- read, write, order and compare numbers up to 10 000 000 and determine the value of each digit

- round any whole number to a required degree of accuracy

- use negative numbers in context, and calculate intervals across zero

- solve number and practical problems that involve all of the above.

Notes and guidance (non-statutory)
Pupils use the whole number system, including saying, reading and writing numbers accurately.

Number – addition, subtraction, multiplication and division

Statutory requirements

Pupils should be taught to:

- multiply multi-digit numbers up to 4 digits by a two-digit whole number using the formal written method of long multiplication

- divide numbers up to 4 digits by a two-digit whole number using the formal written method of long division, and interpret remainders as whole number remainders, fractions, or by rounding, as appropriate for the context

- divide numbers up to 4 digits by a two-digit number using the formal written method of short division where appropriate, interpreting remainders according to the context

- perform mental calculations, including with mixed operations and large numbers

- identify common factors, common multiples and prime numbers

- use their knowledge of the order of operations to carry out calculations involving the four operations

- solve addition and subtraction multi-step problems in contexts, deciding which operations and methods to use and why

Statutory requirements

- solve problems involving addition, subtraction, multiplication and division

- use estimation to check answers to calculations and determine, in the context of a problem, an appropriate degree of accuracy.

Notes and guidance (non-statutory)

Pupils practise addition, subtraction, multiplication and division for larger numbers, using the formal written methods of columnar addition and subtraction, short and long multiplication, and short and long division (see Mathematics Appendix 1).

They undertake mental calculations with increasingly large numbers and more complex calculations.

Pupils continue to use all the multiplication tables to calculate mathematical statements in order to maintain their fluency.

Pupils round answers to a specified degree of accuracy, for example, to the nearest 10, 20, 50 etc., but not to a specified number of significant figures.

Pupils explore the order of operations using brackets; for example, 2 + 1 x 3 = 5 and (2 + 1) x 3 = 9.

Common factors can be related to finding equivalent fractions.

Number – fractions (including decimals and percentages)

Statutory requirements

Pupils should be taught to:

- use common factors to simplify fractions; use common multiples to express fractions in the same denomination

- compare and order fractions, including fractions > 1

- add and subtract fractions with different denominators and mixed numbers, using the concept of equivalent fractions

- multiply simple pairs of proper fractions, writing the answer in its simplest form [for example, $\frac{1}{4} \times \frac{1}{2} = \frac{1}{8}$]

- divide proper fractions by whole numbers [for example, $\frac{1}{3} \div 2 = \frac{1}{6}$]

- associate a fraction with division and calculate decimal fraction equivalents [for example, 0.375] for a simple fraction [for example, $\frac{3}{8}$]

- identify the value of each digit in numbers given to three decimal places and multiply and divide numbers by 10, 100 and 1000 giving answers up to three decimal places

Statutory requirements

- multiply one-digit numbers with up to two decimal places by whole numbers
- use written division methods in cases where the answer has up to two decimal places
- solve problems which require answers to be rounded to specified degrees of accuracy
- recall and use equivalences between simple fractions, decimals and percentages, including in different contexts.

Notes and guidance (non-statutory)

Pupils should practise, use and understand the addition and subtraction of fractions with different denominators by identifying equivalent fractions with the same denominator. They should start with fractions where the denominator of one fraction is a multiple of the other (for example, $\frac{1}{2} + \frac{1}{8} = \frac{5}{8}$) and progress to varied and increasingly complex problems.

Pupils should use a variety of images to support their understanding of multiplication with fractions. This follows earlier work about fractions as operators (fractions of), as numbers, and as equal parts of objects, for example as parts of a rectangle.

Pupils use their understanding of the relationship between unit fractions and division to work backwards by multiplying a quantity that represents a unit fraction to find the whole quantity (for example, if $\frac{1}{4}$ of a length is 36cm, then the whole length is 36 × 4 = 144cm).

They practise calculations with simple fractions and decimal fraction equivalents to aid fluency, including listing equivalent fractions to identify fractions with common denominators.

Pupils can explore and make conjectures about converting a simple fraction to a decimal fraction (for example, 3 ÷ 8 = 0.375). For simple fractions with recurring decimal equivalents, pupils learn about rounding the decimal to three decimal places, or other appropriate approximations depending on the context. Pupils multiply and divide numbers with up to two decimal places by one-digit and two-digit whole numbers. Pupils multiply decimals by whole numbers, starting with the simplest cases, such as 0.4 × 2 = 0.8, and in practical contexts, such as measures and money.

Pupils are introduced to the division of decimal numbers by one-digit whole number, initially, in practical contexts involving measures and money. They recognise division calculations as the inverse of multiplication.

Pupils also develop their skills of rounding and estimating as a means of predicting and checking the order of magnitude of their answers to decimal calculations. This includes rounding answers to a specified degree of accuracy and checking the reasonableness of their answers.

Ratio and proportion

Statutory requirements

Pupils should be taught to:

- solve problems involving the relative sizes of two quantities where missing values can be found by using integer multiplication and division facts

- solve problems involving the calculation of percentages [for example, of measures, and such as 15% of 360] and the use of percentages for comparison

- solve problems involving similar shapes where the scale factor is known or can be found

- solve problems involving unequal sharing and grouping using knowledge of fractions and multiples.

Notes and guidance (non-statutory)

Pupils recognise proportionality in contexts when the relations between quantities are in the same ratio (for example, similar shapes and recipes).

Pupils link percentages or 360° to calculating angles of pie charts.

Pupils should consolidate their understanding of ratio when comparing quantities, sizes and scale drawings by solving a variety of problems. They might use the notation $a:b$ to record their work.

Pupils solve problems involving unequal quantities, for example, 'for every egg you need three spoonfuls of flour', '$\frac{3}{5}$ of the class are boys'. These problems are the foundation for later formal approaches to ratio and proportion.

Algebra

Statutory requirements

Pupils should be taught to:

- use simple formulae
- generate and describe linear number sequences
- express missing number problems algebraically
- find pairs of numbers that satisfy an equation with two unknowns
- enumerate possibilities of combinations of two variables.

Notes and guidance (non-statutory)

Pupils should be introduced to the use of symbols and letters to represent variables and unknowns in mathematical situations that they already understand, such as:

- missing numbers, lengths, coordinates and angles
- formulae in mathematics and science
- equivalent expressions (for example, $a + b = b + a$)
- generalisations of number patterns
- number puzzles (for example, what two numbers can add up to).

Measurement

Statutory requirements

Pupils should be taught to:

- solve problems involving the calculation and conversion of units of measure, using decimal notation up to three decimal places where appropriate
- use, read, write and convert between standard units, converting measurements of length, mass, volume and time from a smaller unit of measure to a larger unit, and vice versa, using decimal notation to up to three decimal places
- convert between miles and kilometres
- recognise that shapes with the same areas can have different perimeters and vice versa
- recognise when it is possible to use formulae for area and volume of shapes
- calculate the area of parallelograms and triangles
- calculate, estimate and compare volume of cubes and cuboids using standard units, including cubic centimetres (cm^3) and cubic metres (m^3), and extending to other units [for example, mm^3 and km^3].

Notes and guidance (non-statutory)

Pupils connect conversion (for example, from kilometres to miles) to a graphical representation as preparation for understanding linear/proportional graphs.

They know approximate conversions and are able to tell if an answer is sensible.

Using the number line, pupils use, add and subtract positive and negative integers for measures such as temperature.

Notes and guidance (non-statutory)

They relate the area of rectangles to parallelograms and triangles, for example, by dissection, and calculate their areas, understanding and using the formulae (in words or symbols) to do this.

Pupils could be introduced to compound units for speed, such as miles per hour, and apply their knowledge in science or other subjects as appropriate.

Geometry – properties of shapes

Statutory requirements

Pupils should be taught to:

- draw 2-D shapes using given dimensions and angles

- recognise, describe and build simple 3-D shapes, including making nets

- compare and classify geometric shapes based on their properties and sizes and find unknown angles in any triangles, quadrilaterals, and regular polygons

- illustrate and name parts of circles, including radius, diameter and circumference and know that the diameter is twice the radius

- recognise angles where they meet at a point, are on a straight line, or are vertically opposite, and find missing angles.

Notes and guidance (non-statutory)

Pupils draw shapes and nets accurately, using measuring tools and conventional markings and labels for lines and angles.

Pupils describe the properties of shapes and explain how unknown angles and lengths can be derived from known measurements.

These relationships might be expressed algebraically for example, $d = 2 \times r$, $a = 180 - (b + c)$.

Geometry – position and direction

Statutory requirements

Pupils should be taught to:

- describe positions on the full coordinate grid (all four quadrants)
- draw and translate simple shapes on the coordinate plane, and reflect them in the axes.

Notes and guidance (non-statutory)

Pupils draw and label a pair of axes in all four quadrants with equal scaling. This extends their knowledge of one quadrant to all four quadrants, including the use of negative numbers.

Pupils draw and label rectangles (including squares), parallelograms and rhombuses, specified by coordinates in the four quadrants, predicting missing coordinates using the properties of shapes. These might be expressed algebraically for example, translating vertex (a, b) to $(a – 2, b + 3)$; (a, b) and $(a + d, b + d)$ being opposite vertices of a square of side d.

Statistics

Statutory requirements

Pupils should be taught to:

- interpret and construct pie charts and line graphs and use these to solve problems
- calculate and interpret the mean as an average.

Notes and guidance (non-statutory)

Pupils connect their work on angles, fractions and percentages to the interpretation of pie charts.

Pupils both encounter and draw graphs relating two variables, arising from their own enquiry and in other subjects.

They should connect conversion from kilometres to miles in measurement to its graphical representation.

Pupils know when it is appropriate to find the mean of a data set.

Mathematics Appendix 1: Examples of formal written methods for addition, subtraction, multiplication and division

This appendix sets out some examples of formal written methods for all four operations to illustrate the range of methods that could be taught. It is not intended to be an exhaustive list, nor is it intended to show progression in formal written methods. For example, the exact position of intermediate calculations (superscript and subscript digits) will vary depending on the method and format used.

For multiplication, some pupils may include an addition symbol when adding partial products. For division, some pupils may include a subtraction symbol when subtracting multiples of the divisor.

Addition and subtraction

789 + 642 becomes	874 – 523 becomes	932 – 457 becomes	932 – 457 becomes
$$\begin{array}{r} 789 \\ +\ 642 \\ \hline 1431 \\ \scriptstyle 1\ \ 1 \end{array}$$	$$\begin{array}{r} 874 \\ -\ 523 \\ \hline 351 \end{array}$$	$$\begin{array}{r} {}^{8}\,{}^{12}\,{}^{1}\\ \cancel{9}\ \cancel{3}\ 2 \\ -\ 4\ 5\ 7 \\ \hline 4\ 7\ 5 \end{array}$$	$$\begin{array}{r} {}^{1}\quad{}^{1}\\ 9\ 3\ 2 \\ -\ \cancel{4}\ \cancel{5}\ 7 \\ \scriptstyle 5\ \ 6\\ \hline 4\ 7\ 5 \end{array}$$
Answer: 1431	Answer: 351	Answer: 475	Answer: 475

Short multiplication

24 × 6 becomes	342 × 7 becomes	2741 × 6 becomes
$$\begin{array}{r} 24 \\ \times\ \ 6 \\ \hline 144 \\ \scriptstyle 2 \end{array}$$	$$\begin{array}{r} 342 \\ \times\quad 7 \\ \hline 2394 \\ \scriptstyle 2\ \ 1 \end{array}$$	$$\begin{array}{r} 2741 \\ \times\qquad 6 \\ \hline 16446 \\ \scriptstyle 4\ \ 2 \end{array}$$
Answer: 144	Answer: 2394	Answer: 16 446

Long multiplication

24 × 16 becomes

```
      2
    2  4
×   1  6
─────────
    2  4  0
    1  4  4
─────────
    3  8  4
```

Answer: 384

124 × 26 becomes

```
    1  2
    1  2  4
×      2  6
─────────
    2  4  8  0
       7  4  4
─────────
    3  2  2  4
       1  1
```

Answer: 3224

124 × 26 becomes

```
    1  2
    1  2  4
×      2  6
─────────
       7  4  4
    2  4  8  0
─────────
    3  2  2  4
       1  1
```

Answer: 3224

Short division

98 ÷ 7 becomes

```
      1  4
    ───────
  7 │ 9  ²8
```

Answer: 14

432 ÷ 5 becomes

```
      8  6  r 2
    ─────────
  5 │ 4  ³3  2
```

Answer: 86 remainder 2

496 ÷ 11 becomes

```
       4  5  r 1
     ─────────
1  1 │ 4  9  ⁵6
```

Answer: 45 $\frac{1}{11}$

Long division

432 ÷ 15 becomes

```
        2  8  r 12
      ───────────
1  5 │ 4  3  2
       3  0  0
      ───────
       1  3  2
       1  2  0
      ───────
       1  2
```

Answer: 28 remainder 12

432 ÷ 15 becomes

```
        2  8
      ───────────
1  5 │ 4  3  2
       3  0  0     15×20
      ───────
       1  3  2
       1  2  0     15×8
      ───────
       1  2
```

$$\frac{12}{15} = \frac{4}{5}$$

Answer: 28 $\frac{4}{5}$

432 ÷ 15 becomes

```
        2  8 · 8
      ───────────
1  5 │ 4  3  2 · 0
       3  0  ↓
      ───────
       1  3  2
       1  2  0   ↓
      ─────────
       1  2  0
       1  2  0
      ─────────
             0
```

Answer: 28·8

© Crown copyright 2013

You may re-use this information (excluding logos) free of charge in any format or medium, under the terms of the Open Government Licence.
Reference: DFE-00180-2013

Index